W9-CFK-625

LONDON:
THE UNIQUE CITY

LONDON:
THE UNIQUE CITY

by Steen Eiler Rasmussen

Revised Edition

THE MIT PRESS

Cambridge, Massachusetts
London, England

Printed and bound in the United States of America

Library of Congress Cataloging in Publication Data

Rasmussen, Steen Eiler, 1898–
  London, the unique city.

  Translation of: London.
  Includes index.
  1. London (England)—History. 2. London
  (England)—City Planning. 3. City planning—
  England. 4. Architecture—England—London.
  I. Title.
DA677.R273 1982   942.1'2   82-132
ISBN 0-262-68027-0 (pbk.)   AACR2

CONTENTS

CONTENTS

6

CONTENTS

7

CONTENTS

INTRODUCTION

THIS book gives, I think, what students of London have long sought for, and what the average sentient Londoner more and more wants to know. Steen Eiler Rasmussen of Copenhagen, architect, town planner, social student and author, who has given many years of his life to the study of London, found that there was information on all possible details in the many books on London, but not one complete picture of the development of the town. He discerned during the whole of its history a tendency towards a particular type of city, quite different from the great cities of the Continent. This he calls the 'scattered city' as distinguishable from the 'concentrated city' of which Paris and Vienna were the prototypes in the European town planning of the nineteenth century. To trace and elucidate this tendency is the aim of his book. From the long history of London he has taken that part which can help us to understand more clearly the city of the present day. Why does London now differ so organically from the great Continental cities, and what are the factors by which this Spirit of London has worked through the centuries to produce our unique city? For to Mr. Rasmussen London has always been essentially different, different from the city-states of the Middle Ages and from the great cities of the Renaissance, the capital of all capitals that has resisted absolutism and maintained the rights of the citizen within the state, and developed itself consistently, despite all interruption, after its own fashion. To the Continental traders of the Middle Ages London was like what Shanghai was to us: a centre for semi-international trade, and a point of access to a large market in an unknown country; to-day, although shorn of Free Trade — Mr. Rasmussen thinks the day on which England gave up Free Trade was as fatal as the outbreak of the War in 1914 — it has 'the civilization that the Continent admires and imitates as best it can'. Or does he still think so of our surrender of Free Trade? In his Postscript to this edition Rasmussen ponders over London's situation after its terrible losses under the German fury and the new problems

9

that have been thrust upon our diminished material and man-power. One hint to safety he offers us: 'rather individual life in standardised houses than standardised life in individual houses'; and he warns us against our proverbial patience. But he has not lost faith. He is looking forward somehow in English version the house that will be typical of our century!

The object of his book, which was first published in Copenhagen in 1934, was to show his compatriots how much they had to learn from the form of civilization in which London had taken the lead. But he warned them that all conditions of life in English towns which awaken admiration on the Continent to-day belong to a special English world that is entirely different from the Continental and forms an indivisible unity. Having written the book, he came to the conclusion that it was of even greater importance to tell the English themselves something about their own civilization. He did not find us very well informed about that. I think this informed, highly-trained, clear-minded, humane and witty observer has much to tell us that is fresh, and much to which he gives a new significance by his gift for relating together facts that had seemed without connection. Before the War he had come regularly to London, year after year, usually for a month's visit, examining London, district by district (as the photographs in the book, which are—apart from the air views—nearly all his own, so clearly indicate), studying its history at the British Museum, and at architectural libraries and in discussions with his many architect friends, whom the intimacy of his knowledge constantly surprises — and at times intimidates. No foreigner, I think, has ever studied London so thoroughly as Rasmussen. Back in Copenhagen, one presumes, the author then brooded over what he had amassed, and considered it in the light of his knowledge of the growth and organization of the great Continental cities to which he has also given years of study. Since the War he has thrice returned to London and has seen the dire toll the Unique City had to pay to the bombs and flying bombs and incendiaries of the enemy, and how much of what he had so happily and understandingly described existed no more. His writing and photographs will tell much to Londoners of the future about unconsidered buildings and forgotten quarters whose virtues he discerned and estimated. He was, as it turned out, writing their epitaphs.

In his writing one seems to see a rare combination of intimacy and a far perspective. One has heard of a famous artist whose drawings had a quality different from all other drawings, which baffled the critics and led to much discussion and fine writing. It really arose from a difference in the artist's eyes, one being long-sighted, by which he could see the distance better than other artists, and the other near-sighted, by which he could draw with lapidary minuteness. Our author by his combination of the near and the far produces something of the same rare effect in his picture of London. To appreciate the greatness of the mountain and its relation to the hills one has to be at a distance. This Danish observer beholds the mountain of London from afar, but he knows it, too, like a geologist who has penetrated its strata and pondered over its crystallization and formation through the ages.

The mastering influences that wrought London into its particular form and character he identifies as these: always a commercial city, London has steadily been facing in Westminster a Royal City with all that that means in influence and development: it began as a small walled city, and while other great cities burst and enlarged their circumvallation, London simply scattered itself outside its walls. The passion of the average Englishman for his single-family house and plot of garden could be satisfied under this loose, unregulated development, and other factors, his insistence on spaces for his games and diversions — exemplified by the author in a hundred instances, but especially in the detailed account of the battle between the law students and speculative builders for the preservation of Lincoln's Inn Fields — and the sharing of this instinct even by the ducal landlords who laid out the great squares with gardens for the tenants in the middle, all these factors combined to produce London, the unique city. Contrary to the prevailing custom in other countries, the traffic in and out of London was allowed to develop quite independent of all municipal boundaries. There was no question of preventing removal from one part to another as in other countries, because of the technicalities of taxation. Aided by the looseness of its extensions and their freedom from harassing boundaries and regulations, London has developed organically, like the body of English law, out of the life of the people. To Rasmussen there is more true town-planning in the unrestricted growth of London than in the contemporary Continental towns that developed according to plans. For that reason he sees in the rejection of Wren's plan for the rebuilding of London after the Fire a triumph for the *daemon* of London. To him, indeed, Wren's best contribution to London is the houses in the Temple, not St. Paul's or Greenwich Hospital. St. Paul's and the City Churches, the Port of London, the bridges, the ancient street markets (of which some eighty still survive in London streets and enclosures) are outside his purview. But the parks and the English garden ideas that live in them are thoroughly examined and appraised, while the underground railway system is, for the first time in a London book, appreciated at its proper value as one of the modern Seven Wonders of the World.

He sees the one-family homestead developing through the ages from the medieval city passing outside its walls to provide them, on to the laying out of the Bloomsbury squares and the Regent's Park quarter and to Bedford Park — one of London's most significant developments that most London writers do not know — and to the Garden Suburb, and so to London's satellite garden cities of Letchworth and Welwyn.

And through our national characteristics, too, it seems even our slums are not so bad as those of other nations, for they are low and flimsy houses compared with the tall heavy tenements that have been built for, or become, slums in other lands; so to clear ours always costs much less money. Even our idle upper class of Georgian and Victorian times, he will have it, paid their way in cultivating something; 'in English culture', he suggests, 'idleness has been the root of all good'. Foreign architects have wondered how it is possible to construct sash windows — which the Londoners will use — so that they fit. The answer is, Rasmussen, explains, that they do not fit. That is why they are used. The Englishman considers it absolutely necessary that his living-rooms be constantly ventilated, so he uses open fireplaces and non-fitting windows — when abroad he will long for his lightly constructed houses where the damp winter air whistles through the roof accompanied by the rattle of the doors and windows!

He wears his expertism lightly. What could be a better way of describing Nash's porch of All Souls, Langham Place, in the plan of Upper Regent Street and Portland Place, than 'like the knee of a jointed doll'! Of Hampstead Heath he says that London made the choice between a park made for plants, and a park made for people, and there in the middle of the great city they have an instance of the right preservation of nature — human nature! Sport, he says, is the music of the Englishman. He notes the English concern for regular clothes in social and sporting life, but not in work. He has noticed that our bricklayers in shabby suits and old patent leather shoes are not nearly as practically dressed as sportsmen. The English way of life seems to him very conventional, but in many respects less ceremonial than the Danish or German way.

His studies of the English have left him wondering about the change that came over our character and morals and even physique, no longer ago than the nineteenth century. All the games for which the race is known all over the world were only organized in their present form in Victoria's reign. Tolerance and dispassion about religious questions only arrived then. 'The balanced and self-controlled Englishman, who only through exquisite courtesy shows his interest in the fair sex, is a direct descendant of the plethoric and passionate individual whom we know so well from English history.' The modern slender type of Englishman trained to sport is not a bit like the stout John Bull, rather a Dutch merchant type, that we still use without complaint in our national symbolism.

Rasmussen holds that our national characteristics are not of a special race, but for special educational ideals. He is with those who see Arnold of Rugby as the maker of the modern Englishman. He has a quaint fancy, too, about the change in our women. Alice in Carroll's fable is a sound little human being that can play merrily with all the old English pedantry and sentimentality, who becomes at the end of the nineteenth century grown up and developed into the Shavian Candida who knows how to manage an English parson as

Alice managed the creatures in Wonderland; and into Lady Cicely in *Captain Brassbound's Conversion* taking their nonsense and fury with the cheerful literalness with which Alice took the Red King or the Mad Hatter; and finally The Maid is canonized as St. Joan. Many cannot follow him there, but Shaw, like Carroll, shows us that a world where pure logic reigns is no place for human beings. So the English have produced their own moderately happy world without too much logic.

The villain of London — and since this book was written he has grown taller and bigger — is the tenement and the block of flats. Our author ends his book with a reasoned warning that is a serious contribution to what is more and more a dividing question of our time — is London to become a city of flats like the cities of the Continent? Passionately, Rasmussen implores us to pause and think this out. He marshals all the disadvantages of the tenement from the long experience of Continental usage and holds that the only reason for the existence of the tenement is that the landlord gets higher interest on his property. Le Corbusier is a modernist in his artistic form but a conservative in his planning of a city. When he plans to rebuild Paris with rows of sky-scrapers he is merely keeping up the old tradition from the reigns of the Bourbons and the Bonapartes. 'In England slums largely develop in houses that have been given up by their middle-class owners. On the Continent we construct slums.' His hope seems to be satellite town development. The monumental city of antiquity, Peking, he points out, is ruined by the intrusion of houses of European type which destroy all the harmony of its plan. London, the capital of English civilization, he fears, has caught the infection of Continental experiments which are at variance with its whole character and tendency. On that disturbing note he leaves us. Is London selling its birthright, the cottage, for a mess of permanent slums? That is how Rasmussen sees it.

An essential part of the book are the illustrations which the author has selected not as applied decorations, but as part of its very fabric. Though an amateur of London for thirty years, I must admit that many of them disclose new things to me. If the translation at any point seems a little hard to follow, some share of that must be attributed to my theory that the gentle reader should not be allowed to forget that it is a foreigner who is giving his ideas about London to Englishmen; and it is easy to forget that with Mr. Rasmussen. In modern times many foreigners have written well on London: Taine, with his amazing postulation of London types, so dryly complete that no one could quite believe in them; Hawthorne, whose ingrained New England suspicion of Old England, always rubbing the wrong way, produced by sheer friction sparks and glows of beauty that illuminated corners of London down to our day; Henry James, whose London Essay remains a masterpiece of delicate irony and love; and the many brilliant Continentals: Czechoslovaks — Karel Capek's 'Letters from England', so fantastic and so penetrating — Dutchmen, Italians, Frenchmen and Germans, who have in recent years thought London worth attention. Mr. Rasmussen, however, seems to me to stand by himself by the alert thoroughness of his exploration, and the thoughtfulness of his conclusions. Once upon a time London feared and suffered from the Danes. They had their settlement where the Strand runs to-day; their name lingers in the name of the parish in which our Law Courts stand. Perhaps some ancestor of Mr. Rasmussen was of them, for he seems to feel London in his bones.

JAMES BONE

To

the memory of

SIR RAYMOND UNWIN

and

DR. VERNER HEGEMANN

*whose work has inspired me in the writing
of this book*

LONDON:
THE UNIQUE CITY

LONDON, THE SCATTERED CITY

Two chief types are distinguishable among large cities: the concentrated and the scattered. The former is the more common on the Continent and is clearly represented in the big government seats of Paris and Vienna, which were the prototypes of European town-planning at the end of the last century. The second type is represented by the English town, which now seems to many of us the ideal.

Land values in the concentrated town are comparatively high, not only in its centre but in the outskirts. Consequently the houses are usually built with as many stories as are allowed by the existing building laws. Most of the people live in flats and as they may be obliged to move out of them at short notice, they take no very keen interest in the houses and do not, therefore, demand much of them. The area of the flats is relatively high-priced, and a large number of the inhabitants with small means are obliged to live in over-crowded flats. Conditions are rendered still more unfavourable when, again on account of the high rents, the open spaces for sport and recreation offered by the town to its citizens are few and far between.

The scattered type of town has lower ground rents, the houses have generally few stories and the buildings are spread over a greater area. The usual type of dwelling is the house for one family. Here, people are more closely attached to their homes and demand more space than in the compact town, and, owing to the lower ground rents, there are much larger open spaces, partly private gardens and partly public parks.

Long ago it became apparent on the Continent that concentration was an evil, but it was believed to be the natural consequence of the growth of a large city. It was supposed that the important interests tied to a particular site in a great city must naturally force the rent up so much that it could only be made to pay by building houses with many stories close together, just as it was thought that the general use of the one family house would create too great distances between home and work and cause insuperable traffic difficulties. On this theory, therefore, the English example is amazing, for their great industrial cities, in which each family has its own house, have been created without any difficulty — and London, the largest city in the world, is the very type of the scattered city.

Many think the difference in the way in which English and continental towns have developed is due to one single cause. Some say: Paris is a fortified city whose space was restricted by its fortifications, while London is an open city, which enabled it to spread freely in all directions. Others seek the explanation in the fact that the London building sites were often leased for a long period (99 or even 999 years!) which checked speculation. It is, however, not due to one single and particular reason that London has become the type of the spreading city. It is due to the co-operation of many circumstances. During the whole of its history there appears to have been a steady — though unconscious — tendency towards that particular type. To trace this tendency is the aim of this book. Modern towns which have arisen little by little can only be understood by the study of their history, and this is more exact of the capital of the English, to whom tradition is so dear, than of any other. To us, the history of London is not the end but the means, and only that part of it which can help us to understand the city of the present day more clearly is of any interest to us.

An exceedingly large number of books have been written on the history of London. But what we seek cannot be found in one single book. It seems as if the English cannot, as a rule, see the peculiarities of their own town in the same way as foreigners see them. There is information on all possible details to be found in the many books on London but not one complete picture of the development of the town.

So we must draw from many and various sources and always keep our aim in view; that is, to form for ourselves a general picture of how people live in London, to get a clear understanding why the city, in this particular respect, has become as it is, different from the capitals of the Continent.

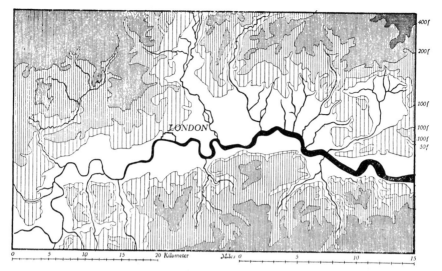

WHEN AND HOW LONDON CAME INTO EXISTENCE IS UNCERTAIN. Some authors maintain that there was already some kind of a settlement, on the site of the present town, in the early centuries of our era, before the Romans occupied the country. That, however, does not seem probable, and it was, in any case, of so little importance that its possible existence is of no interest to us. There are, on the other hand, many traces of a Roman city fortified with strong walls. The plan of it is unknown. It might perhaps be possible to reconstruct it with the help of discoveries and reports, and that again might be of some archaeological interest, but for us who only seek to understand the present town better, it would be irrelevant to try to deduce the form of ancient city from that of modern London, as has been attempted again and again. Apart from the walls, there is nothing in the plan of later London which might not have arisen without necessarily originating from a Roman city. That which the Romans created, and which was of vital importance for the history of London, is the *great centre of communication,* and it was that which determined the site of the city, for the importance of London — then as always — was primarily due to its position as the great centre of commercial policy. The city was not the seat of the government. There were five towns which could be thus designated, *but London was not one of them.*

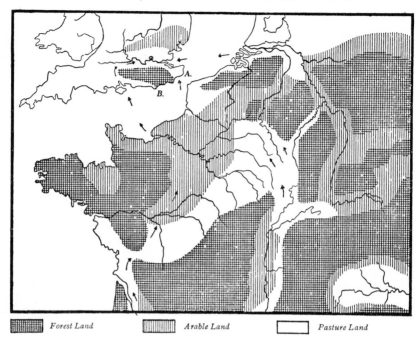

| | Forest Land | | Arable Land | | Pasture Land |

The nearest was Verulamium, where St. Albans now lies, about 20 miles north of the Thames. Possibly London originally was merely its port.

From the map it is easy to distinguish the importance of the position of London. The Thames runs into the North Sea through a broad clay valley bordered on each side by hills. The one to the south, called the Weald, which was covered with impenetrable primeval forest, stretches down to the coast and is continued on the Continent in Artois and Picardy. It is cut through by the Channel, which it meets with steep cliffs, from Dover (A) onwards to Beachy Head (B). South of this point are the lowlands again and unprotected stretches of coast which are easy to navigate. These lie near the mouth of the Seine and this territory was inhabited from early times. The Thames corresponds to the mouth of the Rhine and received with open arms the tribes which were moving northwards along the great waterways.

The British Isles had considerable attraction for the various peoples of the Continent. In spite of its northerly situation, the country had a surprisingly mild climate. Large areas

26

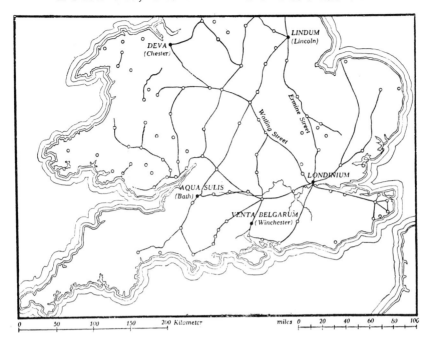

were easy to cultivate and the damp mild weather was favourable for primitive agriculture. Under such conditions, the site of London became, so to speak, the key to this land of promise. The site was not only determined by the natural geographical conditions, it was strengthened by the system of Roman roads. The Romans had succeeded in dominating the country completely and turning it into safe and peaceful territory. Many Romans were living out in the country in unprotected villas with no fear of attack. This safety, which was not attained again until centuries later, was a result of the strict Roman rule. The ruling power was strongly centralized; armies were always mobilized — and the fleet too at one time — as a guarantee of peace. The most disciplined and best equipped of armies would however have availed nothing in the impenetrable tracts of forest which lay there when the Romans came. So they intersected it with broad and excellently constructed roads whose most important points were protected by forts, so that an armed force could be sent out with comparative speed wherever there was need of it. One of the most

27

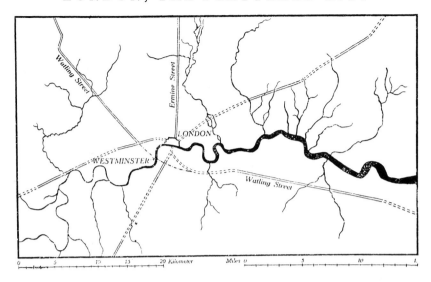

important fortified points was *London*. The town was not only
the junction of a series of main roads but it protected them
as they crossed the broad river Thames. Its possibilities as a
commercial centre were unique. It was at the same time a
great seaport and the main junction of all the roads of the
interior.

There were in fact two places of great importance quite
close together, those which later on were called London and
Westminster. It cannot be said with certainty which was at
the beginning the chief of the two. A road, later named
Watling Street, led up to this junction from somewhere near
Dover; it continued north of the Thames in a north-westerly
direction up to Verulamium, then one of the principal towns,
and further on to the north-west. It must be pictured as
crossing the Thames in a fairly unbroken line and passing
the north bank by the projecting peninsula of Westminster;
there is some probability that the first crossing was here, even
if there was no fixed connection, merely a ferry or a pontoon
bridge. The other main road, Stane Street, which came from
a port to the south-west, protected by the Isle of Wight,
continues in a northerly direction in the road that was later
called Ermine Street. This line was carried over the Thames
by a permanent bridge, London Bridge, which continued to
be the only crossing until 1729. At the northern end of this

bridge the town of London was situated. The strategic importance of the bridge was manifest and it was necessary to protect it. This was done by means of walls round the town. Another road was running along the north bank of the Thames. It ran from the north-east to the south-east of England, traversed London from east to west, and connected Ermine Street with Watling Street. Thus the features of decisive importance for the town were — the Thames, the roads, the City walls, and the townships of London and Westminster.

During the decline of the Roman Empire the safety of the country was on the wane. It was felt in the fourth century when the government had need of the Legions elsewhere and in the fifth century they departed, and left the unprotected country to its fate. The Celtic population which had been subject to the Roman rule had not assimilated their methods of civilization so far that they could in any way carry on or uphold what had been gained. As soon as the Romans left the country, it fell back into about the same condition in which it had been before their arrival.

The British Isles became an easy prey for new immigrants belonging to Teutonic tribes. The Anglo-Saxon inundated the country in great waves from east to west. They appear to have tried to destroy every trace of Roman civilization which they found on their arrival. They advanced plundering and laying waste as they came, and instead of living in the sumptuous and uninhabited villas, they burnt them and pulled them down and then built their primitive wooden huts close by. Several towns show traces of complete destruction, and in many cases the new settlements came to lie at some distance from them. There is no proof that the history of London continues uninterrupted from the time of the Romans. Possibly the town lay for nearly a century as a conglomeration of uninhabited ruins.

Almost all trade must have come to a standstill. After the Romans had left England, the population lived on the land, and, in the main, looked after themselves. Every household was, somehow, able to produce enough for its own needs, food, clothing, and the very few luxuries; only spices, certain articles of luxury and metal work had to come from abroad.

As soon as the big landowners grew wealthy and greater demands were made than the home production could satisfy, favourable conditions arose again for the founding of a city where Roman London had lain — the point from which wares from over the seas could be received and sent further on along the big roads which still stretched out on all sides through the impenetrable country. From the sixth century there is evidence that London was in existence as a living city. Bede mentions it as 'a mart town of many nations which repaired thither by sea and land'. What it was like otherwise, no one knows. In a country which was continually being inundated by immigrating and devastating tribes, it was of great importance to the traders to find a port where they not only could land but also find protection. Whether they were protected by some great man, by some big lord, or whether the merchants founded a militia of their own, we do not know. It is probable, however, that the population did not consist exclusively of traders. Commerce alone could hardly yield so much that it could support a town of any consequence. (About 1800, Reykjavik, the principal town of Iceland, with a cathedral, a school and officials, had only about 300 inhabitants and it was the commercial centre in a highly civilized country whose population demanded more of the necessaries of life than the English of the early Middle Ages.) If, however, there were great lords living under the walls of London, who with their large retinues and great resources created big demands for the supplies of the merchants, then of course far greater possibilities would be present for the existence of a town. The so-called *Port-Reeve* of London is mentioned in early times, originally the Vicgerêfa — that is Lord of the Vic. But mention is also made in very early times of the independence of London. In any case the town appears to have been fairly independent of the minor Saxon kings on either side of the Thames. Sir Laurence Gomme held that the town had continued its existence as a relic of Roman times and an independent Roman community. There is perhaps equally good reason to suppose that the general insecurity of the country strengthened the bond of union among the population within its walls. When Pope Gregory the Great sent missionaries to England (597) London showed so much independent spirit and so much ill-will that the Pope chose Canterbury as the ecclesiastical capital of the country instead of London, as was originally intended.

Alfred the Great saw clearly the strategic importance of London. In order to protect the south of England against the Danes, he fixed the boundaries of their territory so that it went right up to London without including it. The fortified town which protected the passage over the Thames came to be the great gate of his kingdom. It was not yet the seat of the government, but he saw to it that the Roman walls were restored and enlarged, and from this time London was a fortified garrison town which served the interests of the King by maintaining its own independence. Alfred used the tactics of the Northmen against themselves by concentrating his strength in fortified cities. London became, as it is called in the Icelandic Sagas, *Lundunaborg*. The sense of the word 'Borg' is earth-wall or fort, but for the Northmen this was so closely connected with the idea of a town, that the suffix finally came to mean a city. And, seen merely from the outside, it was the walls which gave the city its character. The Danish monk, Saxo Grammaticus (thirteenth century), in his *History of Frode* speaks of London as the town which was so strong that it could only be taken by a ruse. The Icelandic historian, Snorre Sturlason, also always refers to London as the 'Borg', and it was a real fortress, the conquest of which was repeatedly attempted. Already at that time there was a settlement on the south side of London Bridge as well — Snorre calls it *Sudvirki* — and it was the southern fortification. This suburb, the Southwark of the present day, had probably no stone walls but earthworks or bulwarks which have completely disappeared and have not, even as in other cities, left a reminiscence in the form of a 'boulevard' — the French word derived from the Nordic bulwark.

To picture to oneself the importance of London in the early Middle Ages, one must think of England as a half civilized country, far from the centres of the great world. Merchants came right up to the North from the wealthy commercial cities of the South and founded trading-centres, which corresponded to modern commercial intercourse with the ports of the Far East. London was to the Italians and French, and later also to the German merchants, approximately the same as Shanghai now is to England: a centre for semi-international trade, and the point of access to a large market in an unknown country. During the incessant invasions of foreign peoples in England and the continuous struggles for supremacy, London kept its leading position, not as the capital of England, for that it never was, but as its chief commercial centre. When at last the Church gained access to London, it was on an unlimited scale. Innumerable churches were built and as there was no room for the convents inside the walls, they gradually extended far out into the country. The importance of the fortified independent town is easy to understand, especially before the country came under the rule of the powerful Norman kings. Without strong government, which could ensure peace by means of regular armies and a system of roads and fortified towns as the Romans had done, the impenetrable country was at the mercy of the great landowners who divided the kingdom among themselves as its feudal lords and who, even when they acknowledged a king, were merely a band of independent robbers. In the midst of this confusion stood the 'Borg' of London with its strong walls, as a firm central point, whence civilization was spreading, connected with the culture of the South by the many threads originating in Commerce and the Church. It is hardly possible now to realize the significance of the Church at that time. It was an international organization, representing the civilization of the time in its highest form. It was governed by men of the widest views, as they were not bound to any one town or country but were removed from one place to another all over the civilized world, and who brought with them culture and education, based upon the great literature of an international language, and were in constant communication with learned men in far cities. Many tasks now devolving upon the State were then undertaken by the Church. It had to care for the sick and suffering and among these we must certainly count those who had to travel along the execrable roads of the Middle Ages. The Church undertook, as a deed of mercy, not only to look after those who fell among thieves, but also to mend the roads.

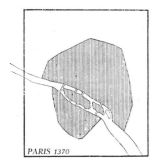 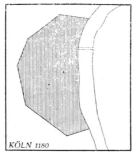 

The Roman walls formed a narrow barrier round the town. One usually imagines the cities of the Middle Ages as very crowded and narrow. This was by no means always the case. The fortifications were frequently advanced so far outwards that space was left inside them for gardens and open fields, a fact of importance during a siege. London *was*, however, closely packed. Comparing it with Paris and Cologne one can see how small the area was. And yet the walls were never moved. These huge old walls were so costly and of such great value, that no one ever thought of the possibility of moving them. Besides the inner districts — the *Wards within*, there were stretches of land outside — the *Wards without* — but beyond these the *City of London* never extended. Other towns have developed by adding ring to ring around the original nucleus. London City petrified its form, but not because it was falling into decay. The wealthy city, centre of gravity for the commerce of the whole country, attracted not only merchants, who found specially favourable conditions here for disposing of their goods, but gradually all the different sections of the government were moved here. They did not, however, settle inside the walls, but found new centres at some distance from the City.

And so, paradoxical as it appears, just because London's boundaries were so narrow, the town developed early by means of new settlements outside the walls and became a *scattered city*, while for instance Cologne, which had so much space within its walls that they were not moved until 1882, gradually became so congested that it became the type of a concentrated city. Instead of a concentrated capital a group of townships arose, each with its own important function inside the realm. That dispersion, so characteristic of Greater London, has its origin far back in the conditions of the Middle Ages. Kings sometimes lived in London for a short time but never had a fixed residence there. We shall see, later, how the City was regarded as being almost independent of the Crown. To this day the curious tradition still exists, that the King comes to the boundary of the City as to a foreign country, whose Head, the Lord Mayor, bids the King welcome, bringing and handing over to him the Sword of the City. Westminster became the seat of government. Sir Laurence Gomme presents an interesting hypothesis, that there was once a place of assize here on the so-called Thorn Island, lying high above the Thames, where the King publicly dispensed justice, seated among his men in the open air. Therefore the place is of special significance for the nation. It was preserved as the spot where one could seek redress from the King. The stone upon which he sat was later built into Westminster Hall and covered with cushions. It was called the King's Bench, a name which was later used to designate a particular court of justice. But whether this be the case or not, the kings felt themselves closely associated with Westminster from the earliest times. Edward the Confessor built churches and convents there and lived there himself. William the Conqueror, who wished to be acknowledged as rightful King of England, had himself crowned there. Gradually all the most important functions of the government were removed to Westminster — the Royal Treasury, the Supreme Court, and finally the Parliament.

Just outside the walls, the Knights Templars had built the Temple in 1185. They had Temples of the kind in many towns, but the one in London was the most important of them all. They became so wealthy, however, that the King grew envious of them and found occasion to drive them out and seize their treasure. From the thirteenth century the Temple acquired a fresh significance: it became 'the homestead of English law'. Trevelyan in his *History of England* says:

And as the English universities developed colleges, so the English lawyers built their Inns of Court. During the reigns of the first three Edwards they grouped their halls, libraries and dwelling places in and around the deserted groves of the

34

Templars. Their place of public performance lay two miles further westward, in the shadow of the royal residence, where they were royally accommodated in Westminster Hall, the magnificent excrescence which William Rufus had added to the Confessor's Palace, as it were in rivalry to the Abbey. But the lawyers slept, dined and studied in their own Inns of Court, half way between the commercial capital at London and the political capital at Westminster, a geographic position that helped the English lawyer to discover his true political function as mediator between Crown and people.

In very early times we find other settlements close to the walls of London. Southwark was a kind of second-class London. It was not finally incorporated until 1554, but was closely associated with the town long before then. Various irregularities can incidentally be noted here. It sheltered the dregs of the City and was also visited by people of other classes in search of diversion. In Elizabeth's time, theatrical performances and bear-fights, the two favourite forms of amusement, took place in Southwark.

The land lying between London and Westminster became gradually built over. Sir Laurence Gomme is of the opinion that the Danes, who did not enter London itself, had already a colony outside its walls at about the place where St. Clement Danes now stands. (Saint Clement was the patron saint of Danish sailors, as one sees in St. Clement's church in Aarhus in Denmark.) Henry III's favourites, the uncles of his French queen, received extensive lands in England. One of them, Peter of Savoy, built the Savoy Palace in the Strand in the thirteenth century (the name of which was preserved in the 'Savoy' Hotel). This was soon followed by a row of stately buildings with splendid gardens down to the river. The Strand became the faubourg of the aristocracy and was much admired by its contemporaries.

Thus we already find in the Middle Ages a colony of townships grouped round the two chief — and very dissimilar — cities of London and Westminster. The danger of war was diminished so that one could build outside the walls without risk. The free extension of the town was, however, brought to a standstill by the circle of convents and their properties which surrounded the town.

35

The entire county of Middlesex was under the supremacy of the City of London. But most of the ground had been given as a fief to the Church and therefore there were few buildings of any consequence. A number of villages sprang up as the land became cultivated. After the abolition of the convents by Henry VIII there were no further hindrances for the growing city, and yet no formal extension of the City took place, and its medieval boundaries exist to this very day. Around every little village the buildings crystallized into a borough and that development of which we have seen the beginning was to continue, so that London became a greater and still greater accumulation of towns, an immense colony of dwellings where the people still live in their own houses in small communities, with local governments, just as they had done in the Middle Ages.

CHAPTER ONE

BOOKS OF REFERENCE

Among the many books on London, one only treats the subject from the point of view chosen here, i.e. *Werner Hegemann: Der Städtebau nach den Ergebnissen der allgemeinen Städtebau - Ausstellung II. Berlin 1913*, in which (pp. 272 to 306) there is a brief but thoroughly well executed picture of the development of London. The author is much indebted to this inspiring book. *John Stow's Survey of London*, 1598, of which many editions have been published, is basic for the study of the history of London. More recent books, like *W. J. Loftie: A History of London I—II*, 1884 and *Walter Besant: London* with their numerous details, prove most entertaining reading, but are of little interest from this particular point of view. A series of books by *Sir Laurence Gomme* are more important as they treat the history of London from a clearly defined point of view: *London, 1914, The Governance of London*, 1907, *Making of London*, 1912. The geography of London is excellently treated in *London on the Thames* by *Hilda Ormsby. Robert Sinclair Metropolitan Man: The future of the English*, 1937, should not be missed by anybody interested in the development of London.

CHAPTER TWO

THE INDEPENDENCE OF LONDON

LONDON DEVELOPED MORE FREELY THAN OTHER CAPITALS. That is primarily due to the fact that the town had always enjoyed a remarkably independent position inside the kingdom. It was perhaps never as independent as the German Free City, nor did it need to be, for conditions in England developed in such different ways from those on the Continent — and it never became as dependent as Paris, Vienna, or other Continental seats of government.

It was fortunate that the commercial town and the seat of the government were not one city but came to lie side by side as did London and Westminster. The City of London never became a seat of government, and the fact of its having surpassed all other English towns in wealth and size from the earliest Middle Ages is primarily due to its importance as a commercial city. If we go back to the time before the Conquest in 1066, we see that if we can speak of a capital at all, in this rather disjointed country, it must be Winchester. It was the chief town of the minor Kingdom of Wessex, and when the King of Wessex subdued the whole of England, he made it a kind of political capital. This tradition continued during the dominion of the Danes. The government of Canute the Great had its seat there and the kings were buried in its cathedral. At the same time London enjoyed complete independence with a local government. Its position was not defined in any document and was certainly not due to any special favour shown by the kings. During the many and constant wars it lay unassailed within its walls and in this way its independence became, so to speak, a traditional right. It was not necessary to confirm this independence as no one ever thought of violating it.

When William the Conqueror came to England he found there two cities of particular importance, the royal City of Winchester, and the commercial City of London. Winchester, which lay near Southampton, one of the principal ports for the Continent, went over to him at once and he soon won London as well. He was skilfully cautious and did not use arms against the City, merely announcing his arrival by burning Southwark, just opposite London. After that he withdrew and gave the Londoners time to think matters over while he outflanked the city. As we know, there were many foreign citizens, and among them not a few Normans, and it was probably easy for them to turn the tide in William's favour. A deputation was sent to his camp at Berkhampstead in the North to inform him that London had chosen him for their King. Shortly afterwards he was crowned in Westminster.

The decision of London settled the choice of the King. It was not the King which made London, it was London which made the King. Theoretically the kingdom was hereditary, but this has been disregarded when convenient and so, according to an unwritten law, London had the right to elect a king. Later, they made use of their right when Stephen was elected in 1135 and it never fell completely into abeyance. Freeman in his *Norman Conquest of England* says:

That right did not wholly die out, the tradition of it lived on to appear in after times, twice in tumultuous, once in a more regular form. Edward the Fourth and Richard the Third were called to the Crown, no less than Stephen, by the voice of the citizens of London. And in the Assembly which called on William of Orange to take on himself the provisional government of the kingdom, along with the Lords and the members of the former Parliaments, the citizens of London had their places as of old.

After the hasty conquest of England followed the steady organization of the kingdom. William worked continuously to acquire greater power for the Crown than it possessed in other feudal countries. He laid there the foundation of that rule which was to become so very different from the systems of the Continent. We must look into it more closely as the English Constitution is the basis of the development of London. The way in which the Norman kings treated the City throws a strong light on the peculiar position of London.

William had conquered the country with the help of an army

of Norman nobles — according to modern ideas astoundingly small — who had joined him in his enterprise in the hope of ample booty. They were not disappointed. During the years following he divided the country into a number of fiefs which he gave to his trusty men. English revolts had to be suppressed now and then and in each case he put a Norman noble in the place of an English one, until practically the whole of England was granted to the Normans. He took great care, however, not to let them get too much power. The country had formerly been divided into a few great earldoms which might easily have become a menace to the unity of the kingdom, as did the minor German principalities. Now he divided it into smaller parts, and owing to the hereditary succession, many Barons acquired fiefs consisting of estates widely distant from each other. In order to ensure the supremacy of the Crown, he placed — and this was a great innovation — Royal officers, Sheriffs, and others, by the side of the Barons or even above them, to see to it that taxes were duly paid. With this institution, which was in force all over the country, he introduced a form of development which was to be continued by his successors and was gradually to give to the government of the kingdom a unity and firmness which was unknown elsewhere in Europe. The Domesday Book, a detailed survey of all landed property in England with a specification of the acreage, persons, cattle and everything which was of account in the collecting of the revenue, stands as a grand monument of his bureaucracy. It is significant that London and Winchester were both exempted from this national stocktaking!

In London he did not follow the same policy as in the rest of England. He did not try to subdue the town by forcing new masters on it. On the contrary he immediately granted privileges to the city in a charter which completely confirms its established rights. William saw that it was best to be on good terms with the merchants, but intended to be the stronger in case of trouble. He granted them in their charter all the freedom they could wish, but at the same time he began building the Tower on the very boundary of the town as the impregnable and threatening fortress of the Crown. His successors continued the building of it at the same time as they assured the town, in charter after charter, of their amiable intentions. London got the revenues of the whole of Middlesex and was allowed to elect its own Sheriff so that it could maintain an authority which in all other parts of the country was exercised by the Crown.

It was surprising that the King showed so much favour to the City, but he certainly had good reasons for doing so. When William landed in England with an army of about 12,000, a town with strong walls and a population of say 20,000 was of no little importance. Coming centuries showed that the population of London did not consist of weakling shopkeepers, but of enterprising men who were trained to arms, and who played a part of no little consequence in the Crusades and in the Hundred Years War. It could not actually be said that London had an army but in time of war the town supported the King with considerable armed forces. And it had one advantage above all others: London had money. That was of the greatest importance, greater than the power of arms. The want of banking institutions and the scarcity of ready money rendered in the Middle Ages all undertakings very difficult which demanded large sums and this was particularly felt by the Crown. Added to this, there was little elasticity in the social order of the time and the government had no resources whatever from which to draw in an unforeseen crisis. In theory the system was most carefully and well constructed. Every man in the kingdom had a lord above him and everyone had binding obligations in return for certain advantages. The feudal lord got his great fief from the King in return for which he had to fight for him, cultivate the land, see to it that justice was administered in his domain, and pay taxes. To enable him to fulfil these obligations he again had to distribute his land among those below him, who in turn contributed labour and taxes, and so on down to the serf, who enjoyed the safety under his master and gave him labour in return. The land was cultivated and peace secured by means of this system. But the possibilities of new enterprises were few. If for instance war broke out or big buildings, churches or fortresses were to be built, the King had to undertake it. But he had to do it as a private individual in spite of its being on behalf of the State.

There was no organization which could distribute the responsibility among the many and procure the necessary means, so he had to take upon himself many of the tasks which now devolve upon the State, and virtually at his own risk and at his own expense. Consequently, he was always in need of money, and kept a greedy eye on all places where money accumulated. The towns were the chief sufferers and one of the means the King employed to get money was to grant charters.

When William the Conqueror confirmed the independence of London in *his* charter, he intimated therewith that nothing could now, as formerly, be taken as a matter of course, for then the charter would be superfluous. No, just as he could grant independence formally to the citizens, so, formally, he could deprive them of it again when he pleased. In reality the power of the City within the State was so great that it need not have put up with this. When its vital interests were attacked, it could successfully resist the King but it was averse to doing so. War is always injurious to trade, so the City usually made the best of it. William's successors kept up the fiction that the towns owed their independence to the Crown and granted one charter after the other. The rights and the freedom which London had acquired long ago were granted over and over again, and the King levied large sums for those imaginary favours. When he was in particular need of money, he granted very special rights to the City which it was difficult for him later to withdraw. And so it happened that the most ambitious kings gave London the most extensive freedom. As time went on, the Crown invented many new methods of getting a share in the wealth of the City. Not only ordinary privileges but also a series of special rights could be granted and withdrawn by the kings and these were used as a means of extorting money from the citizens. In exactly the same way as he could grant a piece of land which involved military or other obligations he could also grant staple right or the franchise to hold a market, but these rights were valuable and could not be granted for nothing. Moreover, he could grant special favours to foreign merchants for which he was, of course, careful to exact payment either in ready money or as an advantageous loan.

The position of the Jews in the country was characteristic of this strange state of things. Beside being supreme lord of all feudal lands and of all privileges the King possessed, as King, certain property. There were the Royal domains and there were the forests, but the most valuable of all were — the Jews. They were not considered as a part of the social system at all but as chattels belonging to the Crown. They had no right to demand justice and the King could, in fact, do exactly as he pleased with them. While the ordinary Christian citizen could be brought before an ecclesiastical court for usury, the Jews, who were beyond the pale of the Church, could not be interfered with as regards their investments, so they became the money-lenders of the country and drew large sums from the population. They lived in special quarters in well-built stone houses and the King protected them as a rule. For it was of the greatest consequence for him to have a place where he could at any time obtain large sums of ready money. The position of the Jews was by no means enviable. Royal protection was all very well against the King's own subjects, but was not always sufficient. They were often subjected to terrible persecution. But the worst was when the King himself was in need of money and ill-treated them, and even though they were the property of the King legally, his treatment of them was incredible. No peasant would ever treat his milch-cow in such a manner. If they did not pay, a tooth would be pulled out every day, for instance, until they gave in. It was not an uncommon thing for them to have an eye put out. It was particularly bad in the twelfth and thirteenth centuries. One year the King seized a fourth of all their personal property and another year he seized a third of all they possessed. We read that he demanded 66,000 marks one year, and Henry III, after having squeezed large sums of money out of them, ended by pawning all the Jews in a body to an earl as if they had been cattle, as security for a large loan. Although Jews played an important part in the economy of the nation on account of the want of banking institutions, they were intensely hated. The end of it was that Edward I, pressed by his subjects, determined in 1290 that all the Jews who would not conform to Christianity must leave the country. It was by no means because he was not in need of money that he did this 'noble deed' — as it was considered at the time — but because he had found a substitute for the Jews in the Italian money-lenders who were immigrating into the country. John Stow, relates how the King in 1283, went to the Temple whose strongly constructed buildings were used by many as a storing place for their valuables. The King called for the keeper of the treasure-house as if he had come to see his mother's jewels which were kept there, and was let into the Treasure House. Here he opened the coffers belonging to other people and stole money to the value of £1000 — an astounding instance of a king's desperate need of money. The need possibly arose through a king sometimes being obliged to pawn the Crown and the Crown jewels. They were used more often in those days than they are now and when the monarch on various occasions had to show himself in all his glory, it can be easily imagined how distressing it must have been when they were in pawn in Flanders and had to be sent for in a great hurry. These instances show of what great importance a large commercial city could be for obtaining money. London was of about the same use to the King as the Jews were. It absorbed the money of the country like a sponge and the King made a point of trying to squeeze it dry.

All these attempts to obtain money by irregular means appeared to the people as a despotic encroachment on their rights. In reality it was a sign of a weakness in the social system. Seen from the point of view of the monarch, regular means were wanting to procure money for all extraordinary enterprises and therefore he was obliged to have recourse to more or less honourable transactions. For those who were the sufferers it was all equally wrong. The Crown procured the money it needed, not by lawful and regular taxation but by a series of special measures which weighed as heavily as the direct taxes, and were apparently much more unjust. Besides this, the King could carry out his plans almost as he chose, both as regards the greatness of the sums he took and the use he made of the money. Some alteration was an absolute necessity if it were to be possible for the State to carry out new and great tasks. It was conceivable that the conflict might lead to the strengthening of the Royal power by more intense centralization which would increase the active power of the State. A very energetic attempt in that direction was made during the reign of Henry II at the end of the twelfth century, But it was also conceivable that the effect would be just the opposite so that the barons, indignant at the King's usurpation of power, would take the government into their own hands. This actually happened under John, when they forced him, in 1215, to sign the Magna Charta. But the final solution of the conflict was not to be brought about in either way. This was only attained little by little by means of an entirely new form of government, by the development of the English Parliamentary system, which did not allow either the King or the great nobles to gain the supremacy but solved the problems by negotiations in which the Commons were consulted.

The Commons had already played an important part in the thirteenth century and thus the foundation was laid for the new constitution. Amongst the nobility the eldest son inherited the whole of the possessions. Estates were protected against partition and diminution and wealthy upper classes had a permanent existence. Their luxurious and early developed habits were of great importance for the town whose existence in the Middle Ages was largely based on trade in articles of luxury, for every household produced a sufficient supply of necessaries for its daily needs. The younger sons who had inherited little or no property formed an active link between the nobles and the lower classes. They gave proofs of much energy and became landed proprietors, merchants, lawyers, or clergymen and were the backbone of that class which later on was called the Commons in Parliament.

As we have seen the feudal system was nicely constructed, like a pyramid. The King was the top and the serfs the basis, and each man between these two had one above him and many under him. But the mortar was wanting in the building. There was nothing which could keep it upright in its place. This deficiency had to be remedied by means of a number of institutions which were not included in the system. Commerce and the Church connected the various parts of the country. The Crown had done its best to re-unite the scattered people with the help of its system of officials; and the Common Law and Justice, which was now the same for the whole of the country as was not the case in former times. In England special assemblies of civilians were called together to take part in the law-suits; originally they were a kind of meeting of witnesses, but it changed character as time went on, until it developed into the modern jury. The citizens were united together in many other ways, some by the universities, others by the numerous orders of monks, and a number of organizations arose in the towns. Every man who did not belong to the ruling classes was obliged to be a member of some organization or other if he were to hold his own, and traders, companies and artisans' guilds were formed, with strict and detailed regulations for the admission and behaviour of their members. In these assemblies and their numerous meetings and sessions, people grew used to settling questions by means of discussion and the foundation of the activities of Parliament was laid.

The London guilds acquired a special significance through their struggles with the great landowners of the City. According to its privileges and regulations London was a free community, but in reality the town was governed in a fairly autocratic fashion by the aldermen, whose position practically corresponded to that of the barons in the rest of the kingdom. Each of them owned his own part of the town and the other citizens lived there as their tenants. They did not actually earn their money as merchants but as great exploiters of land. Many of them held remunerative offices under the Crown as chamberlains, collectors of the revenue, privileged vintners, officials, master of the Mint, etc. In this way they could lead the agreeable lives of the members of the aristocracy and unite power with wealth. Sometimes, however, they got into trouble, for if a man grew too rich the King soon found a pretext to confiscate his property.

The rule of the aldermen was very arbitrary. One of their chief aims was to shift all heavy responsibility on to the shoulders of the rest of the population so that they themselves were free. The result was that as a powerful middle class gradually arose beside them, it sought to defy them and therefore these numerous organizations arose. In the beginning, the guilds were the losers. They were prosecuted and forced to pay considerable fines. But they could not be kept under for long, for it was not a struggle between a wealthy upper class and a poor lower one, but between two different parties of the upper class, which may be described as the landed proprietors and the merchants. What then was going on in London was in reality the same as was happening all over the kingdom: the development of an enterprising middle class. But in the concentrated life of the City, we see the development as focused in a concave mirror.

It was, however, not sufficient that the foundation of the Parliamentary system be thus laid, an incentive from outside was necessary so that a new form of government could arise, and this was, of course, the fact that one of the kings spent too much money. That excellent historian, George Macaulay Trevelyan, calls attention in a footnote in his *History of England* to the strange fact that every one of the medieval kings of England who had been, so to speak, a 'political failure' had left a memorial in something particularly fine in stone. He mentions William Rufus who built Westminster Hall, Richard I who gave it its present character by moving the pillars, and finally Henry III who built Westminster Abbey. It is not, however, so strange as it sounds; for it was very expensive to build, and as we have seen, the kings had to resort to doubtful methods to procure the money, so they became, as Trevelyan puts it: 'political failures'. It was they who came to carry out the alterations in the form of government, and it was that worst of all political failures, Henry III, who was to be the cause of the most epoch-making novelty — the representative Parliament. He was magnificently extravagant. Not content with building the large church, he allowed himself all kinds of luxury; he was surrounded by a brilliant court; he made favourites of the French nobles related to his Queen and gave them high offices in the realm; he claimed hereditary rights in France for himself and in Sicily for his son (which was of no practical use at all from an English point of view and cost enormous sums of money); he assisted poets and artists and — kept a French jester. In short, he had all possible extravagant tastes, which, in his opinion, increased the glory of the Crown, but were of no practical value to the kingdom. Consequently, he was always in need of money and was obliged to borrow wherever it was possible to do so. It was not until no one else would lend him more, that he summoned a council of the barons to grant him money. The first time he was successful but the second time they demanded to have some influence on the appointment of the officials under the Crown — and to that he would not agree on any account. So the barons were sent home and he raised money by selling his silver plate to the wealthy citizens of London. London was altogether most useful to the Kings, just as the Jews were. Henry III however abused them both. It was he who ended by pawning the Jews and he gradually spoilt all his chances with London. As many of the aldermen held offices under the Crown, they were, as will readily be understood, extremely loyal, but his treatment of the town was too much even for them. Again and again he took, as it was called, 'the town in his hand', that is to say, he appointed the Lord Mayor and other public officers himself, which was contrary to the privileges he had granted, and — worst of all — he seized the revenues of the City! Neither did it increase his popularity when — evidently in order to procure money for the building of Westminster Abbey — he granted to its Abbot the most valuable privilege of holding a weekly market in Westminster and a fortnight's fair once a year. During that time no trade might be carried on elsewhere, so one can imagine the fury of the citizens of London. They were quite ready to turn against the King on the first occasion.

That occasion soon arose. During a famine in 1256 it was believed that the King had seized and sold large supplies of corn which had been sent from Germany by his brother, Richard of Cornwall, to allay the distress. The result was that the barons took over the leadership and decided how the country was to be governed so that such abuses could not take place again. Three times a year a council was to be convened, a Parliament, and it was already settled at that time that the Commons were to have a seat in it. It became evident, during the first sessions, however, that the barons were only considering their own interests. They agreed to appoint the French King, 'Saint Louis', to judge their differences and agreed to submit to his decision. As might easily have been predicted, this referee was entirely on the side of his less saintly colleague, the English King, and stood by him in everything. According to his judgment all arrangements and agreements which had been concluded between the King and the barons were abolished again.

Simon de Montfort, however, that man of genius, who had been the soul of the opposition against the King, would not give up the struggle. He was one of the most powerful of the nobles — and brother-in-law to the King. He realized that the time had come for the Commons to be consulted concerning the government. He did not meet with much encouragement from the rest of the nobility, but his views met with approval in London. At the same time as he had been working for the rights of the Commons in the kingdom, the City had at last got a Lord Mayor, Thomas Fitz-Thomas, who was working for the same ideals in London. He was an opponent of the aldermen and strongly supported the new trend of ideas by acknowledging several fresh guilds and granting them privileges. He appealed to the people in all matters of civic policy.

Simon de Montfort was in Southwark, deserted by the nobles who should have been his allies. The aristocratic elements in London prevented the gates being opened to him, but when the report spread that the King had attempted to seize him, the people gained the upper hand, broke open the gates at London Bridge and admitted him to the City. These must have been troublous days in London. The King was in France and the Queen in the impregnable fortress of the Tower. She tried to get away from there to join the King and was sailing the Thames towards Windsor. *Sundry Londoners got them together to the bridge, under the which she was to pass, and not only cried out upon her with reproachful words, but also threw mire and stone at her, by which she was restrained to return for the time* (Stow). The bells of St. Paul's called the people to arms. Simon de Montfort collected his army and London joined with a force that was put at 15,000 men. He encountered the King at Lewes, defeated him and took him prisoner. The London army's part in the victory, however, was not fortunate, as it was put to flight and pursued for four miles, losing some 3000 men, but so many of the enemy troops were engaged in this, that it played a decisive part in the battle all the same. The King was taken as a prisoner to St. Paul's and the fate of the kingdom was then in the hands of London and of Simon de Montfort. The result was the first Parliament in which the Commons were officially represented — by two men from each town in England.

During the years which followed, all that had been gained appeared to have been lost again. Simon was killed the year after, and the Lord Mayor, Fitz-Thomas, was imprisoned at Windsor and all the privileges which he had granted to the guilds were declared null and void. But the new forms of governance which had been created were not forgotten. Successive kings saw what an advantage it was to get the necessary money for governing the kingdom granted by a representative council instead of struggling on as they best could, and the Commons were again convened to Parliament. To begin with, they probably played a very modest part. It is supposed that they were allowed to express their opinion through their leader (when it was asked for) at the same time as the barons. In order to enable the leader to answer for all of them, they used to hold meetings beforehand, and come to an agreement on the situation. These private meetings were probably the origin of the debates of the House of Commons. At first, it was not considered a privilege to be permitted to have a seat in Parliament. It was considered troublesome and was a great expense, necessitating long and trying journeys and staying in strange towns. So when Parliament was convened, not many members were present. When, however, matters had so far progressed that money could only be granted by Parliament, interest increased. The clergy abstained from taking part, however, for which later they had to pay dearly. For one fine day, King Henry VIII was able to sweep them aside: they had themselves abstained from taking a part in the government of the kingdom. The towns, however, became more and more eager to take part, and their representatives travelled, at the expense of the corporations, to Parliament which sat in various towns until it got its final seat assigned in Westminster under Elizabeth.

In London the ancient form of governance did not last very long. The aldermen were now each elected as representatives for a particular district, or ward, of which there were twenty-four. From 1346, the City had an advisory council, consisting of men who were elected by the wards, who sent, eight, six or four according to their size. Gradually, however, the guilds and companies grew more and more powerful and from 1375 the members of the Council were no longer elected by the wards but by the trading guilds. They decided who were to be made what was called the 'Freemen' of London. (He who was not a freeman was not even allowed a vote at the elections of the aldermen.) They ruled the town with great severity and it was still the wealthier classes who were in power. Now, however, enterprising merchants and artisans came on to the Council, elected by their guilds. London kept its powerful position in the kingdom on account of its wealth. Trevelyan characterizes the relations of the King and the City in the following words: *'Edward IV lived on intimate terms with the great London citizens, not only because he liked their wives but because he borrowed their money.'* The relations between the City and the Crown were already indicated by the revolutionary Lord-Mayor Fitz-Thomas when he renewed his oath of fealty to the King, in the following plain words: *My Lord, so long as unto us you will be a good lord and king, we will be faithful and duteous unto you.* These words caused great indignation at the time among the more conservative citizens, but in reality no declaration has ever given a more true and clear statement of the relations as they were and as they were to remain for the future.

We have gone thoroughly into the events attendant on the development of the British Constitution because this chapter of history shows us clearly the importance of the City of London. It is also important for us, because this special English form of government was in time to exercise decisive influence on the growth and development of the City. The fact that the power was divided among three parties, the King, Lords, and Commons, was a guarantee against despotism from any one of the sides. At the same time, the arrangement was so elastic that it could be altered by degrees to suit the exigencies of the changing times.

CHAPTER THREE

THE CENTRE OF WORLD COMMERCE

THE SIXTEENTH CENTURY WAS A TURNING-POINT FOR LONDON. Until then, it had been a town on the outer edge of the large net of European trade, now it became the centre of the still larger one which was to spread over continents. Great discoveries had created new openings for trade and London was more successful than any other city in turning the new state of things to account. The explanation of this lies in the reciprocality between the City on one side and the country and its government on the other. At the same time as the English merchants' most dangerous rivals, the French and Flemish seafarers, were hampered by the religious persecution of their own governments, profitable intercourse was continued in England between London and Westminster — between the trading city and the government. The two cities became more and more dependent on one another without, however, merging into each other. The wealthier families in England rallied round the government and the Court, and much of what was earned in various parts of the realm was consumed in the quarters to the west of the City. The great consumers just outside the City increased the possibilities of trade, and consequently its wealth, to an extraordinary degree. Nor could Westminster do without London. The government had no army, while the City could call their trained bands to arms when necessary for the security of the country; and the ships of London's merchant service were an important and necessary supplement to the navy founded by Henry VIII. It may have been the nobility who brought great wealth to the place, but it certainly was the City which accumulated it, and it was the trading centre which had to be consulted when large sums of money were required. A government whose policy was common with that of London was certain of military and financial aid and this could not be obtained in England by any other means. Thus the commercial interests of London in the long run decided the politics of the country. Any other course could only be followed for a short time. This was clearly seen in the seventeenth century, when the efforts of the Crown to escape from the influence of Parliament and of London were unsuccessful; with no army and no money there could be no absolutism. Henry VIII and Elizabeth, however, who encouraged trade in London, relied upon the City and so kept a firm seat on the throne.

Venice of the Middle Ages might be regarded as a kind of preliminary study for the London of later days. In far distant times when the Huns advanced through Italy ravaging as they went, numerous wealthy merchants from the richest towns of Northern Italy fled to the islands of the Lagoon to bring their property into safety: the migratory tribes, who were for ever on the march, had no ships. When the worst of the danger was over, the merchants were able to return to their own cities. They were so often obliged to flee, however, as time went on, that they finally at the end of the sixth century settled on these sheltered islands, when they drove out the original inhabitants. In this way Venice arose, as a perfectly independent city, which soon became the trading centre of the Mediterranean. From distant Asia, from China even, as we know from the Journeys of Marco Polo, convoys of valuable merchandise were sent to the wealthy city whose numerous ships cruised all over the Mediterranean. Once a year Venice equipped the so-called Flemish fleet, which sailed along the coast, through the Straits of Gibraltar and right up to the Netherlands and England. It carried a sumptuous cargo of luxurious articles which could not be produced in northern lands; precious stones, silk, brocade and other costly stuffs, camphor and all kinds of spices which could only be obtained in the East. It was a most profitable business undertaking. The Venetians could make several hundreds per cent by bringing the goods to the market themselves, as the usual method of transit trade, through so many hands, caused the prices to rise enormously before the wares reached London. In this manner the English merchants could get the goods delivered at their doors without needing to trouble about sea journeys or other risky adventures. From the sixteenth century, however, we see a different picture. Venice stagnated and London grew as a commercial city. As long as rivers were the chief means of commercial intercourse, the cities of the Continent, the Hansa towns particularly, had the advantage of the others. But when sea-trade developed, it was London's turn. The resemblance between London and Venice is most striking. Both lay isolated from the Continent and thus protected from war and disturbances which were so destructive to commerce. But the essential difference was this — London was the centre of a trading district and Venice was not. Or to put it more correctly, England provided London with an article which world commerce could not do without — cloth. The merchants of Venice and the Hansa towns retailed it. They sailed to far distant countries which had little or no communication with the great net of commerce and made money by transporting the goods from one place to another. But they did not produce anything themselves, and so others could take their places without any detriment to trade. London made its supremacy sure with the help of the trade in English cloth, which was so highly developed from the end of the sixteenth century, and an article of such importance that it could not be dispensed with anywhere. It was even used as a means of currency. When London merchants imported goods from foreign parts they were exchanged for cloth, and London was the centre of all the English cloth trade and had thus secured a position unique in universal commerce.

The basis of this monopoly was wool. Climatic conditions in England were specially favourable for sheep-breeding and the export of wool was important from early times. After the Cistercian monks had settled in the country in the twelfth century, sheepbreeding made great headway and the wool-trade with the Continent became a considerable source of income. Sheep were kept all over the country and the raw wool was exported in large quantities to the Continent where it was manufactured. As early as the thirteenth century the production of English wool was greater than that of any other country. In continental countries which were continually devastated by wars, it was difficult to breed such large flocks and let them run loose, as in England, which lay more or less in peace surrounded by the sea. At first only small quantities of woollen goods were manufactured in England, chiefly of coarser material which could be used for sacking or for the sails of the windmills. All fine cloth was manufactured outside the country. Nine-tenths of its wool was sent to Ghent and Bruges and the English bought it back again in the shape of finely woven and beautifully dyed stuffs. The English realized early, however, of what great consequence it would be for the country to have its own wool industry. The kings were keenly interested in everything connected with wool, its export was the chief source of income, and consequently the best object for taxation. When the kings had to borrow money, the duties on wool and the wool tax were their most valuable assets. When Edward III had to raise money for his Continental wars, he did not always ask a grant of Parliament, but often acted slyly behind Parliament's back and negotiated directly with the wool-merchants. His entire policy, which apparently was merely a short-sighted attempt to get as much money as possible from the wool trade for the Crown, proved in the end to be of the greatest benefit to the wool and cloth trade. Among others he encouraged the Flemish weavers to come to England. That was in the fourteenth century. But a long time was to elapse before England could compete with the Continent. It was now not only the raw wool which was exported but often coarse stuffs, not prepared in any way, which were to be milled and dyed abroad. The towns of the Netherlands were the best customers. This was certainly of great consequence when England joined in the Hundred Years War. At the outset it was merely from the love of conquest. Later on, however, it was manifest of what great importance it was, from the point of view of commercial policy, to protect communication with Calais, and prevent the Flemish towns, which bought the English wool, from becoming French. London was particularly interested in the enterprise. The famous Lord Mayor of London, Dick Whittington, was one of those who helped to finance the wars of Henry IV and Henry V.

When English cloth began to be a dangerous rival in the fifteenth century, the Netherlands prohibited its import. But it was impossible to carry it through, as England was the stronger in commercial struggles. It was impossible to manufacture Flemish cloth without English wool and so the threat of stopping all trade was sufficient to open the market again for English cloth at Antwerp. At the end of the fifteenth century both Brabant and Flanders had to give way and permit the sale of English textile wares.

At the same time as they made sure of the market abroad, the cloth industry was built up at home, where it steadily improved. After getting the better of the cloth industry of the Netherlands, the home industry no longer had dangerous rivals. About 1500, the export of English cloth was about seventeen to eighteen times as big as it had been 150 years earlier. In Henry VIII's reign, the export of cloth amounted to about 70 per cent of the entire exports of the country, while the export of raw wool was only about 8 per cent. At the end of the sixteenth century, the export of raw wool had practically ceased.

While all this was going on, considerable capital had been amassed in England. Formerly, the Kings borrowed from abroad, first from the Italians (exiled Lombards — Lombard Street in London still reminds one of the money-changers) and later from Antwerp. But from the middle of the sixteenth century, money appears to have been plentiful among English merchants. Capital which had been saved up was not used for lending money as the Lombards had done, but was invested in enterprises which would increase the trade in English goods. Before then, foreign merchants came to England with finer foreign products and exchanged them for raw wool. Now it was England which produced a fine ware for export, its cloth; and imported in return raw goods from distant countries. In 1532 Venice sent the Flemish fleet to London for the last time.

A series of events occurred simultaneously, all in favour of English trade. The English were now first in the cloth trade and transferred the principal market from Antwerp to London. Great discoveries created new centres for overseas trade. London merchants had sufficient capital to equip expeditions and England had active and able seamen to carry them out, seamen who could not be beaten by those of any other nation. They were backed up both directly and indirectly by the government, and indirectly by the policy of the Church. Every right-minded Englishman considered it his bounden duty to capture as much as possible from the Spanish papists. The Hansa towns and the Italian commercial cities had neither fleets nor seamen to sail over the ocean. The worst rivals were the Flemish and French towns (La Rochelle) and their bold sailors were as able and daring as the English. The Roman Catholics, however, saw to it that as much harm was done to them as possible. The best of the Huguenots were murdered in France. In England 'the noble pirate', to use the expression of the time, Francis Drake, became a national hero.

London had been most lucky. Formerly the City had produced a fair amount of cloth and the Flemish weavers who had settled there in the reign of Edward III had been of the greatest benefit to the City. From the end of the fourteenth century, all cloth was brought to London, for it was only permitted to sell it to the exporters from the City. As time went on and the cloth trade became of greater and greater importance, it became more and more concentrated in London. The many companies which were formed, especially in the reign of Elizabeth, to promote trade with distant towns, had their chief seats in London. Such companies were not new, but in old days they had existed under another form. They had been associations of merchants in foreign cities. English merchants had their companies in the towns of the Continent just as the Hanseatic towns had them in London. Under Elizabeth, however, conditions were altered and now companies were founded in their native cities to support merchants abroad, and the enormous expansion of trade was organized from London. Under Henry VII London had contributed about 50 per cent of the entire revenues for the Customs, in Henry VIII's time it had risen to about 66, but in 1581-1582 it was over 86. The cloth trade was in the hands of the London merchants and thus they possessed the means to dominate world commerce.

From the sixteenth century one can distinctly see the difference between Continental and English policy. The government of the Tudors has been called tyrannical, and Henry VIII is usually considered a great despot. He *was* a tyrant, but chiefly a domestic tyrant, for his power was restricted. His body-guard consisted of fewer men than the trained bands of a single one of London's wards. But as long as he was on good terms with London he needed no soldiers. In 1539, when he feared that the Pope and various Princes intended to attack England, he had the forts and seaports put into a state of defence and got the City to muster the men who were fit for service. They were informed that the King himself would inspect them. On May 8th, 1539, a great parade of the citizens was held on the eastern boundary of the City. According to Stow, they were all in shining armour, with jerkins of white silk or cloth and gold chains, divided into three big battalions of about 15,000 (?). They marched through London and on to Westminster, marched past the King in St. James's Park — and a fine day they must have had. Elizabeth, who knew how to keep on good terms with the merchants, never called on the City in vain in time of need. When Spain threatened England in 1588, the Queen called upon London to equip fifteen ships and 5000 men. Instead of that, it sent thirty ships and 30,000 seamen, while the militia of the City, the so-called trained bands, to the number of about 10,000, held a parade every evening on a drill-ground outside the City.

It will be readily understood that neither Henry VIII nor Elizabeth felt any desire to become absolute monarchs, such as began to appear everywhere on the Continent. The English had already become a nation with strong concentration and an accumulation of capital in their chief city. The country had its frontiers clearly defined, and the power of the nobility had been checked during the struggles of the Wars of the Roses. Of the families of the original feudal nobility descending from the followers of William the Conqueror, only twenty-nine were left. The Crown could create new nobles and it made extensive use of its prerogative. They were recruited from among the London merchants. Much of the capital which flowed so plentifully towards the City in the following centuries was accumulated by the new nobility from their ground-rents. The Dukes of Bedford and Westminster and many others, who owned large estates outside the walls, could steadily increase their incomes, not by selling their land but by leasing it, according to ancient custom, as the town increased and spread. Henry VIII's policy, like that of Elizabeth, was conducted in the main in accordance with the exigencies of commerce. His Protestantism, for instance, suited the country exceedingly well. The yoke of Rome was cast off, and the result, from a purely economical point of view, was that much money which would otherwise have gone out of the country could be used for national purposes. The Wars of Religion broke out — and they proved beneficial as they were continuously waged against the worst rivals, the Spaniards, first, and then the French. After Antwerp had suffered terribly from the Spanish invasions and had been plundered in 1567 and again in 1585, the wise Sir Thomas Gresham got the Queen to invite the ruined and persecuted weavers to come to London, where they were promised a good reception. There was a good deal of opposition from the privileged guild but the government did not allow its efforts to be checked. In the reign of Elizabeth there was continuous immigration of Flemish weavers and little by little the finer cloth-weaving was introduced into England.

The Tudors, who judged the temper of the English correctly, reigned with a firm hand as rulers by the Grace of the People. The next dynasty, the Stuarts, were strangers to England, and remained so. They wanted to reign as the monarchs of the Continent did, as Kings by the Grace of God! This speedily led to dissensions between Westminster and London. James I became unpopular chiefly because of his attempts to raise money for purposes in which the City took no interest whatever. His son, Charles I, fared still worse; he imagined that one could reign in England against the Parliament and against London. The situation is clearly illustrated in that little episode when the King, in direct opposition to the Constitution, attempted to arrest five members of the House of Commons. It is well known how they left Westminster, where they felt themselves to be in danger, and took shelter in London. The King drove to the Guildhall in person. He made a speech to the assembled City council and demanded that they should give up the five members. He was received with the formal courtesy due to the King but received no answer, and the members were not given up. The King had to return to Westminster without having achieved his aim while the five members went about freely in London, fearing no danger. As long as the King tried to obtain money by irregular means the City opposed him with all its might. It was not desirable that the Crown should have an army at its disposal — as in other countries — which might paralyse the independence of the town. But when open war broke out, London was parsimonious no longer, but supplied both soldiers and considerable sums of money to carry on the struggle against the King. It was the City indeed which turned the scales, and it was again made evident that the party which had London on its side would win. Charles I lost his life because he never understood this. It was London who paved the way for Cromwell's rule. He kept the power because his policy was favourable to the commerce of London. Again, it was London who made Charles II King, and it was with the help of London that William of Orange came to the throne.

The difference between English and Continental politics is perhaps best shown in the way they conducted their wars. After the Hundred Years War England no longer dreamed of conquests on the Continent. No sacrifices were to be made to enforce claims to territory which was of no interest to the country, which as far as the Continent is concerned, now lives in 'splendid isolation'. Wars of succession, as in France, were unknown, and wars of religion only in so far as they were of decisive importance for trade. This does not imply that the English outlook is narrower than that of Continental nations. On the contrary, their world is much wider and they are bound to it by their lines of commerce across the seas. It can be said with all truth that the sun never sets on their Empire. But it is not an empire in the ancient sense of the word, founded on the rights of succession of their monarchs, but a country which has been conquered by the enterprise of venturesome merchants and pirates. Backed by the wealth of London, they opened markets in distant countries by means of private expeditions. In some cases, they robbed other peoples of them, and in others penetrated into territory which had never been opened to European trade before. It was not executed according to some pre-concerted plan and these continuous conquests were not the work of the government. But enterprising private individuals knew that the government would back them up — if they were successful. The Crown was often financially interested in these trading expeditions.

Under an absolute monarchy, where everything was carried out according to system, attempts were made to succour trade by means of special government measures. Customs duties and prohibition of imports were resorted to, and was granted to State industries, roads and canals were constructed and all mercantile means were tried. Everything was to be regulated from above, but at the same time so much harm could be done by aimless wars and the persecution of heretics, that even a Colbert himself could not put things right again. The English Government was less absolute and the rule less arbitrary. The course to be followed was not determined by a governmental office but by an association of merchants. London was behind it and London did not endeavour to display its power, like an absolute monarch without any particular object, but continually strove to attain entirely concrete and, as a rule, commercial advantages. The government was not carried on according to a political system, but was entirely sensitive to fluctuation, like the Exchange, and that again influenced Westminster.

Even if there was seldom any interference in Continental disputes, there was one thing which would always arouse England. As soon as some Great Power attempted the conquest of an important seaport, which might become a rival to London through being the mouth of a trading district, *then* England was always ready to take measures to prevent it. Wars of this kind were often conducted as wars of religion, and by the Grace of the English God, they always yielded considerable secular profits. In Tudor times, Catholic Spain was the enemy. England joined Protestant Holland against Papist Spain in order to capture the Spanish markets in America and seize the Spanish ships. When that peril was past, Holland, with its towns at the mouth of the Rhine and its excellent fleet, was the greatest danger for London. It was no matter now that the Dutch were fighting for the true faith — almost! Cromwell, good protestant as he was, declared war on them, and Charles II continued in his footsteps. He, Charles II, did not, however, understand the particular English turn of mind well enough. When the French king proposed that they should divide Holland, which had just fought against England, between them, he did not realize that this was not exactly the thing to do. Parliament opposed it. Holland, against which England had recently been fighting, was now to be supported. It did look rather strange, but it was, of course, sensible enough. For if France were to take possession of the Rhine Delta — and France was already a great power — it would not be a very promising outlook for English naval supremacy. England was altogether very much on her guard against France. When there was a question of her being invited, with Spain, in the War of Spanish Succession, 1702—1713, England at once went against it. The prospect of the French seaports, with their excellent sailors, being able to utilize the many possibilities offered by the Spanish colonies, was sinister indeed. When this danger, too, was past, there were again signs of renewed prosperity in the Flemish cities. The Austrian Emperor, Charles VI, joined Spain and agreed that Ostend should be permitted to trade with the Spanish colonies. Together with Holland, England had undertaken to see to it beforehand, that Antwerp had no communication with the sea. Now England joined Prussia and got Ostend cut off from the sea by the Treaty of Vienna in 1731. When France again, towards the close of the century, stretched its hand out after Belgium (and showed signs of attempting to annex it) and the great Napoleon saw the significance of the Dutch commercial cities as ports for his new empire, why — then France became automatically the enemy again! And so on until Germany marched into Belgium in 1914 and it was evident that Antwerp would be annexed in case Germany was victorious, then there was no wavering or hesitation — Germany was now the enemy!

In the policy of William of Orange, there is an instance of how the King became the ally of London. By founding the Bank of England he increased facilities for borrowing money from the City for his warlike enterprises. In this manner he became dependent on the City. But at the same time he made sure of the loyalty of London by turning himself into a limited company, so to speak. For everyone knew perfectly well that if the Jacobites came into power again they would never acknowledge William's debts.

The continual interaction between the commercial city and the government proved to be of the greatest benefit to the trade of the country and it is easy to understand that England became of necessity the place where the maxims of Free Trade found expression. The commercial city, London, became the antithesis of Paris, the city of absolutism.

CHAPTER THREE

BOOKS OF REFERENCE

THE economical history of England is related in the works of *William Cunningham*. *The Growth of English Industry and Commerce during the Early and Middle Ages* is important. *Finance and Trade under Edward III* gives in a series of treatises, edited by *George Unwin*, a very full account of an interesting period, from a point of view which differs considerably from that of Cunningham.

CHAPTER FOUR

ATTEMPTS TO CHECK THE GROWTH OF LONDON

Towards 1600 the growth of London became alarming. During the course of the previous century the number of inhabitants had increased considerably and large quarters had sprung up outside its walls. The increase of commerce brought many people to the capital. In 1598 John Stow in his description of one of the wards of London quotes the following account which he says is written 'not many years ago': '*In Billingsgate Ward were one and fifty households of strangers, whereof thirty of these households inhabited in the parish of St. Botolph, in the chief and principal houses, where they give twenty pounds the year for a house lately letten for four marks; the nearer they dwell to the water-side the more they give for houses, and within thirty years before there was not in the whole ward above three Netherlanders; at which time there was within the said parish levied, for the help of the poor, seven and twenty pounds by the year; but since they came so plentifully thither, there cannot be gathered above eleven pounds, for the strangers will not contribute to such charges as other citizens do.*' This passage gives a true picture of (1) the large invasion which took place; (2) of the prompt increase in ground value; and (3) of the Londoners' unfriendly feeling towards the newcomers. London inside the walls was — as we have already seen — very crowded, and the immense increase in the population therefore caused the growth of the quarters 'without'. In 1583 there were 5141 foreigners, of whom 1604 lived outside the city. The weavers in London were almost all of foreign extraction. Of seventy masters who signed an agreement in 1456 thirty-three lived within the walls and the rest of them outside. They were wool weavers. Another wave of immigrants, who introduced silk weaving in the sixteenth century, settled in the villages of Shoreditch and Spitalfields. A colony of French hatters, who introduced felt hats, settled in Southwark, together with the Flemings, who introduced the brewing of beer from hops. Printers from the Netherlands settled in Westminster, in Clerkenwell, and elsewhere. Most of them moved to these suburbs because they felt safer there, the crowded town being very unfriendly towards aliens. Until the middle of the sixteenth century several persecutions of aliens took place. But even after the anti-alien demonstrations had ceased it was no easy life to be a foreigner in the City, whose inhabitants were strongly organized in guilds and companies.

Simultaneously with the invasion of craftsmen from abroad to the quarters without, there was also a considerable *emigration to these quarters from the City itself*. This was mostly due to economic changes. Formerly the producer (the craftsman) had sold directly to the consumer, but now the traders appeared, dealers who did not produce anything themselves but only bought and sold the goods. This development caused great indignation; measures were taken to hinder it, but with no success. A contemporary writer describes circumstances as follows: '*Before May Day poor handicraft people which were wont to keep shops and servants and had labour and living by making pins, points, girdles, gloves, and all such other things . . . had thereof sale and profit daily, until thirty years ago a sort began to occupy to buy and sell such handicraft wares called haberdashers . . . whereby many rich men is risen upon the destruction of the poor people, which poor people perceived themselves having no living and were bound prentices in London not able to keep no houses nor shops, but in alleys sitting in a poor chamber working all the week to make their ware, on the Saturday brought in to the haberdashers to sell . . . which would not give them so much winning for their wares to find them meat and drink saying they had no need thereof; their shops lay stored full of (wares from) beyond the sea.*' It became more and more common for wealthy traders to make the most out of small masters. The traders purchased the raw material, mostly from abroad, and took over again the selling of finished goods from the craftsmen. Competition from other cities and other countries enabled them to reduce the prices. This *differentiating of the trades* led also to a *differentiating of the quarters of London.* The new merchants wanted to get the best sites for their warehouses and shops. The sites in the centre therefore increased in value and the impoverished craftsmen, who gradually had stopped selling to the consumer, neither needed nor could afford to live inside *the City* of London, but had to move outside. The City changed into a mere business and residential quarter while the hamlets outside the town became the industrial quarters. In centuries to come a further differentiating was to take place: the *residential houses* of the merchants were also moved outside the walls, leaving the City to shops and offices only. And finally in our days the shops have a tendency to leave the City.

As for the manufacturing of cloth purely capitalistic methods were soon adopted. People who had earned some money bought large quantities of wool and distributed it among artisans who worked at home; some carded and spun it, some weaved it, others dyed it, and still others fulled it. They all depended upon the one person who was the financier and who finally got the finished product to sell. The different guilds of course objected strongly to all these new enterprises which through their efficient economic methods were dangerous competitors. They fought for their chartered right to monopolize their trade inside the town and also pointed out how ruinous it would be to the trade when the guild lost control of it. When newcomers wanted to take up the trade they therefore had to settle somewhere outside London or in other cities. Encouraged by the success of the cloth trade a series of new enterprises came into existence, and towns sprung up where there had formerly been only small villages. When the companies in those days had new charters granted by the King they always saw to it that their sphere of action was made as wide as possible. The cabinet-makers of London got a charter in 1571, which was good for two miles in circuit, the blacksmiths got one the same year for four miles outside the City and its suburbs; for the charters which followed the sphere of action had an average of four to five miles. This indicates clearly the growth of London.

At the same time many of the more inferior craftsmen thus lost their position and became mere labourers. Crowds of people came in from the country, attracted by the numerous new possibilities for work in the town, for in the country also great changes had taken place. In the Middle Ages the peasants had been villeins. The squires could make use of their labour as compensation for the right to live in a house and enjoy the fruits of the land which was *his* property. Their work therefore was not paid in cash and they were not permitted to move to another place, even if they thought they could live better there. When, however, the Great Plague in the middle of the fourteenth century had seriously reduced the population of England — probably by 50 per cent — labour became valuable and many lords were willing to pay for it — and pay well — if only they could keep up the cultivation of their land. The peasants, who for centuries had toiled at the bottom of the ladder, became conscious of their value. The outcome of this was the peasant revolts and in the course of time this led to a complete revolution of the organization of labour. Villeinage was abolished. Some peasants simply evaded their old obligations, but many bought themselves free and became copyholders. At the beginning of the six- teenth century about 1 per cent only of the population consisted of bondmen. At the end of the century even those had virtually disappeared. Now the peasants were indepen- dent and could as freemen go wherever they wanted. But at the same time the lords had also become more independent. They had no longer permanent villeins of whom they were bound to take care. Of course, they could not evict their copyholders whenever they wanted — some were absolutely immovable, possessing copyholds of inheritance — for the greater part the leaseholds were valid 'for three lives' (as it was called), and for some the grants were for a term of years. As it proved more advantageous to manage larger parts of the estates as an aggregate a great many of the copyholds were enclosed. In this case, too, it was the development of the woollen trade which became decisive. High prices were paid for the wool and the extension of sheep-farming demanded less labour in laying out the land as pastures than in cultivating it. The object of agriculture in former days had been to provide the inhabitants of the farm with the products they needed in their daily life; the new economy was more efficient: it produced the articles which paid best.

Consequently crowds of labourers were wandering about in a hopeless search for work. They went to the cities and through the great supply of labour the wages naturally fell, and matters became still worse on account of the difficult state of the money market. Throughout the century the value of money decreased considerably because of the influx of gold. Nobody could tell the cause, but everybody saw with consternation how the cost of living increased. There had not been for centuries such an enormous rise in prices. It was considered a great disaster and one which it was necessary to remedy. One remedy was an attempt to fix prices and especially the price of labour. It helped but little and was hard on the wage-earning classes. At the time of Queen Elizabeth workmen were not paid more than at the end of the fifteenth century. But during the same period the price of food had been nearly tripled! The result was a greater poverty than ever in the cities and especially in London. Moreover the monasteries had all been dissolved during the reign of Henry VIII, and the friars, who formerly had relieved the poor, now added to their numbers themselves. In this way London had been endowed with *a large proletariat* which had to find abodes as best it could. Contrary to what had formerly been the case there were now a *great number of lodgers. Many people moved to the suburbs* to miserable cottages. The old guilds and companies watched this development with great dissatisfaction. More and more work escaped them and was executed as trade speculation by untrained workers or by aliens living outside the walls of the City, and at the same time the City itself was invaded by beggars and vagabonds as never before.

This state of things inspires a proclamation issued by Queen Elizabeth in 1580. It is said therein: that '*The Queen's Majestie perceiving the state of the city of London (being anciently termed her chamber) and the suburbs and confines thereof to increase daily, by access of people to inhabit the same, in such ample sort, as thereby many inconveniences are seen already, but many greater of necessity like to follow, being such as her majesty cannot neglect to remedy, having the principal care, under Almighty God, to foresee aforehand, to have her people in such a city and confines not only well governed by ordinary justice, to serve God and obey her majesty (which by reason of such multitudes lately increased can hardly be done without devise of more new jurisdictions and officers for that purpose), but to be also provided of sustentation of victual, food, and other like necessaries for man's life, upon reasonable prices, without no city can long continue. — And finally, to the preservation of her people in health which may seem impossible to continue, though presently, by God's goodness, the same is perceived to be in better estate universally than hath been in man's memory; yet where there are such great multitudes of people brought to inhabit in small rooms, whereof a great part are seen very poor, yea, such as must live of begging, or by worse means, and they heaped up together, and in a sort smothered with many families of children and servants in one house or small tenement; it must needs follow, if any plague or popular sickness should, by God's permission, enter amongst those multitudes, that the same would not only spread itself, and invade the whole city and confines, but that a great mortality would ensue the same, where her maj.' personal presence is many times required: besides (by) the great confluence of people from all parts of the realm, by reason of the ordinary terms of justice there holden, the infection would be also dispersed through all other parts of the realm, to the manifest danger of the whole body thereof. . . .'*

After this drastic description of the bad housing conditions it is declared, that: *'her maj., by good and deliberate advice of her council, and being also thereto moved by the considerate opinions of the lord mayor, aldermen, and other the grave wise men in and about the city, doth charge and strictly command all manner of persons, of what quality soever they be, to desist and forbear from any new buildings of any house or tenement within three miles from any of the gates of the said city of London, to serve for habitation or lodging for any person, where no former house hath been known to have been in the memory of such as are now living; and also to forbear from letting or setting, or suffering any more families than one only to be placed, or to inhabit from henceforth in any house that heretofore hath been inhabited.'* And further, the Lord Mayor and Aldermen are enjoined to see to it, that these regulations are complied with; upon due notice workmen who have violated these regulations will be imprisoned or fined. Confiscated material accrues to the city. Breaches of the regulations about one family in each house involves penalty of imprisonment. Also *'the offences in this part of increase of many indwellers, or, as they be commonly termed, inmates or undersitters, which have been suffered within 7 years, contrary to the good ancient laws and customs of the city, or of the boroughs and parishes within the aforesaid limit of three miles aforementioned'* will be punished and *'such undersitters or inmates may provide themselves other places abroad in the realm, where many houses rest uninhabited, to the decay of divers ancient boroughs and towns . . .'* Werner Hegemann in his account of the development of London[1] has attributed considerable importance to this remarkable proclamation. To him it is the result of very far-seeing town-planning politics at a time when these questions were absolutely ignored in other countries. He considers it as an introduction to that future spreading of the town which was to be of such great advantage to London. This result he attains by interpreting the interdiction to build within three miles from the gates as an attempt to create a broad agricultural belt round the town and at the same time as an encouragement for developing new quarters outside this open space. Read in this way the proclamation would certainly be in advance of its age, anticipating the garden city ideas of late years. But it proves impossible to uphold his interpretation. The different parts of the proclamation — especially when compared with other legislative measures of the period — show quite different aims.

This proclamation, transformed into an Act of Parliament in 1592, was but a single link in a chain of laws which tried to remedy the numerous evils caused by the economic change. It was thought that governmental regulations might impede natural development. It is characteristic of these Elizabethan enactments that, although passed for public weal, they are always most profitable to the upper classes, especially to the wealthy merchants and master-craftsmen of London. This is probably due to the fact that the government of the Realm was economically dependent on London, and London meant to Elizabeth the government of the City, that is to say the rich masters who governed as Lord Mayor and Aldermen, and from the proclamation we see that it is upon *their* advice it has been issued. They have evidently been well aware of their responsibility towards the people and have therefore filled the proclamation with comments on the benevolence of the new regulations. Seen from their point of view the town was overwhelmed by a wave of proletarians, an influx from the country. This disastrous state might be

[1] Werner Hegemann, *Der Städtebau nach den Ergebnissen der allgemeinen Städtebauausstellung*, II, p. 280 ff.

used by unscrupulous traders with great damage to the old crafts. It was furthermore hard for the poor devils themselves who had to live under such horrible conditions. Something had to be done. The mob should be sent back from whence it came, to the towns with empty houses, instead of 'pestering the houses' in London. That they should move out — and take up competition at a distance of three miles from the town was certainly never intended. If that had been their aim, why not say so instead of telling them to go to other towns.

In his account of the development of Paris, Hegemann mentions a proclamation issued by Henry II, 1548, about thirty years before that of Elizabeth. In its motives it also — according to Hegemann — emphasizes the horrors and vices of the big cities and how dangerous their growth and the ensuing desertion of the country are. It decidedly takes the side of the Parisian master-craftsmen, whose apprentices emigrated to the rapidly increasing suburbs in order to open workshops without having finished their apprenticeship and without being subject to the control which the master exercised in the city. In consequence of these arguments, both social and economic, the proclamation expressly prohibits the construction of any building outside the walls of Paris. Such efforts to restrain apprentices are also well known from regulations in London. Conditions in the two cities are so much alike, that the interdictions against building new houses, issued at about the same date in the two cities, may fairly be attributed to the same causes.

The English proclamation has, however, got a mark of its own, namely its obvious interest in housing hygiene. Certainly, after describing the evils caused by the living of several families in one house, it is not very logical to prohibit the building of new houses! The remedy is wrong, but the end — *each family its own house* — is right, and it is astonishing to see it so clearly pronounced already in the sixteenth century. As late as the nineteenth century the importance of this question had not yet dawned upon people on the Continent. When Industrialism, after the invention of the steam-engine, had attracted crowds of people to the big towns of the Continent, they found dwellings as best they could. The result was — exactly as in the London of Elizabeth — a terrible congestion of people ensued, only to a much greater extent. But nobody understood how fatal it was. On the contrary, although the flat-system had only by chance come into existence as a bad makeshift against the immigration for which no one was prepared, it became general and through building regulations was consecrated as the normal dwelling.

In England the strong and healthy reaction against overcrowding must have been deeply rooted in the population, otherwise it would hardly have appeared in the proclamation as it did. Elizabethan proclamations and enactments have a note of their own. They are not orders of an absolute monarch, but rather the thoughtful advice and admonitions of a judicious and prudent householder. They are always very full of reasoning and common sense, written for the common people, to make them understand that it is to their advantage that the acts have been passed. Even if the actual *regulations* in which they result are generally an expression of the wishes of certain of the upper classes, the *explanations* which accompany them are generally destined for the people. The comments of the proclamation on housing may therefore be read as the true expression of the current ideas of those days. The average Englishman who is conservative in his views has always objected to living differently from what was usual in the good old days, and he has therefore continued to live in one-family houses from the Middle Ages up to the present day. And that is what makes the proclamation interesting to us: from its wording we can see that already at the time of Queen Elizabeth the English had a clear understanding that the one-family house was preferable.

It was of course a hopeless task to try to stop the growth of the City and we must give up trying to see any social benefit in that. *What saves the town is first of all the aversion of the citizens against overcrowding and their conservative clinging to the medieval form of housing.* This proved a better basis for a sound development of the town than such detailed building regulations and other enactments which during the latest centuries have determined the housing conditions in the big towns of the Continent. Among other instances of the legislation of those days the *Law against Building and Entertainment of houses* from 1588 is worth noticing. It does not apply to the so-called incorporated towns, and therefore not to London either, — but it applies to the environs of the town. It is said therein: '*For the avoydinge of the great Inconvenience whiche are founde by experience to growe by the erectinge and buyldinge of great nombers and multitude of Cotage which are daylie more and more increased in manye parte of this Realme: Be it enacted by the Quenes most excellent Majestie . . . (and Parliament) . . . That after thend of this Session of Parliament, noe person shall within this Realme of Englande make buylde or erect, or cause to be made buylded or erected, any manner of Cottage for habitacion or dwelling, nor convert or ordeyne anye Buyldinge or Howsinge made or hereafter to be made to be used as a Cottage for Habitacion or dwellinge, unlesse the same person doe assigne and laye to the same Cottage or Buyldinge fower acres of Grownde at the least, to be accompted accordinge to the Statute or Ordeynance De tris mensurandis, beinge his or her owne Freehold and Inheritance lienge nere to the saide Cottage, to be contynuablie occupied & manured therewith so longe as the same Cottage shalbe inhabited; upon payne . . .*' This act is apparently an attempt to prevent bad building and unhealthy houses. It is a temptation to point out this law as a model for housing regulations, a real law for Englishmen, who are anxious to preserve their independence. In other countries the building regulations have considered the congestion of people in the cities as inevitable and therefore only tried to remedy the worst evils by legislation on all sorts of technical details, but the English law of 1588 turns to the chief point: it simply prohibits the crowding and requires certain adjacent grounds for each house. That is the right thing to do. *For if all houses were surrounded by sufficient open space housing details would be of less importance hygienically. And on the other hand if there is no such open space even the most strict and detailed regulations will be of little use.* But a more close study of the law of 1588 shows all the same that it is less ideal than it looks at first sight. The piece of land demanded, which must be 'occupied and manured' as long as the house is inhabited, is fixed at four acres, an absolutely absurd size for small houses. As already mentioned, whole towns had sprung up for the people who worked in the rising woollen industry and who on account of the privileges granted to the guilds had to live outside the old cities. But these poor labourers had to live in small cottages and they neither needed nor could afford to cultivate four acres of land. If therefore it had been feasible to carry out the law of 1588 these settlements outside the old towns would have been impossible and that would have put a stop to the new, non-privileged enterprises. The object of the law was not to procure more healthy dwellings for the poor, but to limit the housing of the whole population — in order to avoid disagreeable competition. Only the more wealthy, who represented no danger to the privileged trades of the old towns, were allowed to settle where they chose. In order to make the law complete and difficult to elude it was added: '*Provided also and bee it enacted, That from and after the Feast of All Sainte next comynge there shall not be any Inmate or more Famylies or Householde then one, dwellinge or inhabitinge in anye one Cottage made or to be made or erected. . . .*'

It is difficult to follow in detail how the proclamation of 1580 worked, but it is certain that it did not succeed in checking the growth of London. It is sure to have restrained the building of new houses to a certain extent, but we know from a letter sent from the Privy Council to the Lord Mayor of London in April 1583 that the proclamation had been indifferently carried out and that many new buildings had been erected. It is said therein that measures must be taken against the proprietors. There is an answer from the Lord Mayor of the same month saying that an investigation is being made as to which buildings are lawful. It has proved difficult to investigate the matter and see how things developed, but in 1592 — that is to say twelve years after the proclamation — the question was raised anew. This time it was subject to discussion in Parliament and a law against new buildings was passed. It was based on the same reasons as the proclamation and prefaced as follows: '*For the reformynge of the great Mischiefes and Inconveniences that daylie grow and increase by reason of the pestering of Houses with diverse Famylies, harboringe of inmates and convertinge of great Houses into several Tenements or Dwellings ovd erectynge of New Buildings within the Cities of London and Westminster and other Places nere thereunto adjoining, whereby great Infection of Sickness and dearth of Victuals and Fuel hath growen and ensued and many idle vagrant and wicked persons have harboured themselves there and divers remote places of the Realme have been disappointed of Workmen and dispeopled: Be it enacted by the authoritie of this present Parliament, That noe person or persons of what Estate Degree or Condition soever shall from hence-forth make and erect any newe Building or Buildings House or Houses for habitation or dwelling within either of the said cities* (of London and Westminster) *or within three miles of any of the gates. . . .*' This law was, however, as most others, directed especially against the lower classes. A rich person would of course always be allowed to build a house in or outside London, but in this case, as in so many others in those days, severe pro-hibitions were issued and thereafter dispensation given against suitable remuneration. (The Crown was always in need of money and it was simply part of Queen Elizabeth's policy to carry through restrictions which the companies desired and then afterwards to grant special Royal privileges for a liberal sum to people who were not members of the company.) The law further says: '*And further be it enacted, That noe person or persons, of what Estate Degree or Condicion soever, shall at any tyme hereafter converte or devide any Dwellinge House or other Buyldinge, nowe erected and builded or hereafter to be erected and builded within the Citties and Places aforesaid, or any of them, into diverse and severall Habitacions or Dwellinge for severall and diverse Famylies; excepte everie severall House soe devided shalbe fytt for the Habitacion or Dwellinge of suche a person as heretofore hathe bene assessed to or for the Subsidie to her Majestie at Fyve Poundes in Goodes or Thre Pounde in Landes . . .*' At the same time the regulations prohibiting the taking of lodgers is renewed in the following words: '*And be it further enacted by the aucthoritie aforesaide, That noe person or persons inhabitinge & dwelling within the Citties and Places aforesaid, shall after Twentie Daies next ensuynge this Session of Parliament, receyve or take into his or their House or Houses any Inmate or Undersitter or Inmates or Undersitters; upon payne . . .*' *This means that it was liable to punishment to take lodgers at the time of Queen Elizabeth!* The law further contains some regulations which are important from a hygienic point of view. They concern open spaces destined for recreation and sport, but they will be dealt with in another chapter.

The law is given for seven years, but was renewed later. Under Elizabeth and her successors, proclamations with similar contents are issued in 1602, 1603, 1604, 1607, and 1615, and they are frequently used by James I, who was continually in difficulties financially, and continually squeezing money out of his subjects. It was again significantly said that new buildings were not allowed unless they were erected on old foundations. When a house was built on a site where formerly, within living memory, there had been a building, then no objections could be made and the King could not get as much as a penalty out of the owner. Some buildings were ordered to be demolished, but there is at least one case where such an order was revoked, as the churchwardens declared that the house had been built upon ancient foundations. The English restrictions with regard to new buildings outside London remind us to begin with — as we have already seen — of the corresponding French restrictions for Paris. But in this point they are unlike. The absolute French king fixed a limit for the town; in England, on the contrary, the legislation allows the rebuilding of what already exists, but not more than that. The first conception rests upon an abstract idea as to the right form of a city, the other simply legalizes what has already taken place. It gives a true picture of the judicial ideas of the two countries. English law is always based upon precedent and practice and the laws therefore do not form a coherent, logical system but are organically developed out of the life of the people.

As late as under the Commonwealth Parliament passed a law with the express object of hindering the increase of buildings in and outside the suburbs of London within a distance of ten miles (!) from the City. They tried to stop the building of unnecessary houses by fining the owner the amount of one year's rent for each new house, out-house or other buildings, but only if built on a new foundation or with less adjacent ground than four acres.

ORIGIN OF RECREATION GROUNDS

THE WORD SPORT HAS BEEN ADOPTED IN MANY LANGUAGES. But the sense of it has changed slightly according to the spirit of the people. On the Continent the word 'sport' signifies particularly physical culture and the foreigner realizes with surprise that in England the idea is as much spiritual as physical. The difference is illustrated in a striking way in the newspapers: German advertisements tell you how to *grow strong*, the English ones how to *keep fit*. The old-fashioned man on the Continent wants an abnormally developed chest in order to make an impression on other people and bulky muscles in order to protect himself. He has not realized that what he gains in strength he may lose in activity, so that a clumsy Goliath can be beaten by an agile David who is 'a good sportsman'. In the beginning he will not understand that the word *Sport* in England may be used in connection not only with pastimes and games developing the body but also with Chess, Bridge and Poker. Afterwards, however, he will learn to see the wisdom of the English conception, and he will find that it explains many facts in history. It is symbolized, for instance in the moulding of their cities. The Continental model city would be a strongly fortified town, laid out according to a regular plan and very impressive to look at. It was just as strong and imposing as a warrior in armour — and just as cumbersome. The fortifications were like a stiff corselet that made the whole body unsound. While the Continental cities suffered in this way — and still suffer — from serious congestion the English capital developed in all directions without any artificial limitations (but also without any plan), not strong and not imposing but sound and healthy. The inhabitants were 'good sports', abundant in vivacity, always engaged in exciting adventure and enterprises. The name *Merchant Adventurers* associated with a certain company could be used as a general characterization of the citizens of London.

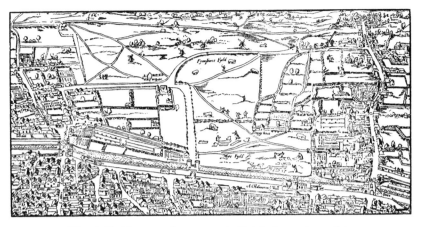

Moorfields 'the great fen or moor' (Ralph Agas, *circ.* 1580).

Sport has always been an important feature of London life, and the citizens considered facilities for sport a simple right of man of which one could not deprive them. History tells us over and over again how they defended this right. The result was remarkable, especially in the seventeenth century; in other countries common grounds were closed to the public in order to form stately Royal gardens; London, however, succeeded not only in preserving her old recreation grounds but also in making the King add to their area by opening Royal gardens and hunting fields and converting them into public pleasure grounds and sporting places.

As far back as the twelfth century we find a detailed chapter on 'Sports and Pastimes' in Fitz-Stephen's description of London. He begins with children's sports, 'seeing we all have been children'. Every year on Shrove Tuesday '*the school-boys do bring cocks of the game to their master, and all the forenoon they delight themselves in cock-fighting: after dinner all the youths go into the fields to play at the ball*'. '*The scholars of every school have their ball, or baton, in their hands; the ancient and wealthy men of the city come forth on horseback to see the sport of the young men, and to take part of the pleasure of beholding their agility. Every Friday in Lent a fresh company of young men comes into the field on horseback, and the best horseman conducteth the rest. Then march forth the citizens' sons, and other young men, with disarmed lances and shields, and there they practise feats of war. Many courtiers likewise, when the King lieth near, and attendants of noblemen do repair to these exercises; and while the hope of victory doth inflame their minds, do show good proof how serviceable they would be in martial affairs.'* Fitz-Stephen also tells us that *'in the holidays all the summer the youths are exercised in leaping, dancing, shooting, wrestling, casting the stone, and practising their shields'.* He tells us about winter sport: *'When the great fen, or moor, which watereth the walls of the city on the north side, is frozen, many young men play upon the ice; some, striding as wide as they may, do slide swiftly; others make themselves seats of ice, as great as millstones; one sits down, many hand in hand to draw him, and one slipping on a sudden all fall together; some tie bones to their feet and under their heels; and shoving themselves by a little picked staff, do slide as swiftly as a bird flieth in the air, or an arrow out of a cross-bow.'*

Wrestling was a favourite sport in the Middle Ages and even the King was not above patronizing the contests. On St. James's and St. Bartholomew's days special matches took place in St. Giles's Fields, whence they were afterwards transferred to Clerkenwell. The Lord Mayor and his Sheriffs were often present on these occasions. But gradually they got into bad repute. They often caused serious disturbances. As in our days, much local patriotism would be shown at such an event, and sometimes occasioned a regular battle between the spectators. The two parties represented, of course, Westminster and London. It is told, for instance, that at a wrestling match the men of Westminster treacherously armed themselves and attacked the citizens of London who being unarmed were obliged to take shelter within the protecting walls of the City. They revenged themselves afterwards by pulling down the house of the abbot. Such regrettable incidents might also occur on other occasions. In 1253 *'the youthfull citizens for an exercise of their activity, set forth a game to run at the quintain . . . Certain of the king's servants, because the court lay then at Westminster, came, as it were, in spite of the citizens to that game, and giving reproachful names to the Londoners, which for the dignity of the city, and ancient privileges which they ought to have enjoyed, were called barons, the said Londoners, not able to bear so to be misused, fell upon the king's servants, and beat them shrewdly.* They complained to the King. The King was Henry III, who—as we have seen—was always in need of money. He took the opportunity and fined the citizens a thousand marks.

Exercises of arms were usual in this city, whose aldermen were officers in times of war and whose citizens flocked to the standard when there was need of them. The kings did what they could to encourage them. It was in their interest to make good soldiers of them. Things went so far that Edward III sent the sheriffs of London a letter with the following contents:

'*The King to the Sheriffs of London, Greeting. Because the people of our Realm, as well of good Quality as mean, have commonly in their Sports, before these Times, exercised the Skil of Shooting Arrows, whence it is well known, that Honour and Profit have accrued to our whole Realm; and to us, by the Help of God, no small Assistance in our Warlike Acts. And now the said Skil being as it were wholly layed aside, the same People please themselves in hurling of Stones and Wood and Iron; and some in Hand-Ball, Foot-Ball, Bandy-Ball, and in Cambuck, and Cockfighting; and some also apply themselves to other dishonest Games, and less profitable or useful; whereby the said Realm is likely in a short Time to become destitute of Archers:*

'*We, willing to apply a reasonable remedy to this, command you that in places in the foresaid City, as well within the Liberties as without, where you shall see it expedient, you cause publick Proclamation to be made, that every one of the said City, strong in Body, at leisure times on Holydays, use, in their Recreations, Bows and Arrows, or Pellets or Bolts, and learn and exercise the Art of Shooting; forbidding all and singular on our behalf, that they do not after any manner apply themselves to the Throwing of Stones, Wood, Iron, Hand-Ball, Foot-Ball, Bandy-Ball, Cambuck or Cock-fighting or such other like vain Plays, which have no Profit in them; or concern themselves therein, under pain of Imprisonment.*' Even the King himself hardly succeeded in suppressing 'the vain plays' by these crass means. In any case Stow writes (at the end of the sixteenth century), '*The ball is used by noblemen and gentlemen in tennis courts, and by people of meaner sort in the open fields and streets.*' Otherwise he does not waste many words on that kind of sport but writes mostly about tournaments and boating.

The citizens of London, who — as we know — enjoyed a quantity of special privileges, had also the right of killing game in Middlesex, Hertfordshire, the whole of the Chilterns, and large districts of Kent. Here they went hunting with hawks and dogs. An old historian relates, that if they did not do it very frequently it was not from lack of inclination but because they could hardly find the time.

Those who took part in sport could be divided in three groups: courtiers from Westminster, students from Inns of Courts and young men from the City itself. Each of them had their own playgrounds which they guarded zealously, and they were all preserved for coming centuries as open spaces.

The youths of the City had of course to be content with the least advantageous place. Up to the Reformation London was quite encircled by the large properties of the many convents that had acquired land all round the city. The only open space the citizens could get for their sport was 'the great fen or moor' where Fitz-Stephen watched them skating. It was not very attractive. This 'Moorfields' was originally a swamp into which much of the City refuse was thrown. Little by little it was raised and attempts made to drain it, '*by these degrees was this fen or moor at length made main land and hard ground, which before being overgrown with flags, sedges and rushes served to no use*' (Stow, 1598).

In 1415 the City had easy access to Moorfields through the newly opened gate, *Moorgate*. '*This gate he* (Thomas Falconer, Lord Mayor) *made for ease of the citizens, that way to pass upon causeys into the field for their recreation: for the same field was at that time a parish.*' In spite of the great disadvantages of Moorfields it was much used for exercise in shooting of bows and arrows and all sorts of sport. The citizens acquired the right of prescription to the fields, although they were not by any means the property of the City. Over and over again we learn that the leaseholders (Moorfields, like most property near London, was leased on long leaseholds) fenced their fields to keep out trespassers, but had to abandon the fences. From 1478 there is an Ordnance '*for the removal of gardens, herbs, hedges, and rubbish in the Moor*', these being a serious obstacle to bowmen roving practice, and the fields were again '*made plain field for archers to shoot in*'. Hall's Chronicle (1542) tells us how the citizens in 1516 took the law into their own hands. He says: '*Before this time the inhabitants of the towns about London, as Iseldon, Hoxton, Shoreditch, and others, had so enclosed the common fields with hedges and ditches, that neither the young men of the city might shoot, nor the ancient persons walk for their pleasure in those fields, but that either their bows and arrows were taken away or broken, or the honest persons arrested or indicted; saying, "that no Londoner ought to go out of the city, but in the highways". This saying so grieved the Londoners, that suddenly this year a great number of the city assembled themselves in a morning, and a turner, in a fool's coat, came crying through the city, "Shovels and spades! Shovels and spades!" So many of the people followed, that it was a wonder to behold; and within a short space all the hedges about the city were cast down, and the ditches filled up, and everything made plain, such was the diligence of these workmen. The king's council hearing of this assembly, came to the Gray Friars, and sent for the mayor and council of the city to know the cause, which declared to them the injury and annoying done to the citizens and their liberties, which though they would not seek disorderly to redress, yet the commonalty and young persons could not be stayed thus to remedy the same. When the king's council had heard their answer, they dismissed the matter, and commanded the mayor to see that no other thing were attempted, but that they should forthwith call home the younger sort; who having speedily achieved their desire, returned home before the king's council, and the mayor departed without more harm: after which time,'* saith Hall, *'these fields were never hedged, but now we see the thing in worse case than ever, by means of enclosure for gardens, wherein are built many fair summer-houses; and, as in other places in the suburbs, some of them like Midsummer pageants, with towers, turrets, and chimney tops, not so much for use of profit as for show and pleasure, betraying the vanity of men's minds, much unlike to the disposition of the ancient citizens, who delighted in the building of hospitals and almshouses for the poor, and therein both employed their wits, and spent their wealths in preferment of the common commodity of this our city.'*

It is interesting to note how the government always protected the right of the citizens to recreation grounds. We have seen how the question of social hygiene was dealt with in an Act of Parliament of 1592 ('An Acte againste newe buyldings'). This same act has the following provisions: *'And Whereas div'se Comons Waste Groundes and Great Fieldes nere adjoyninge to the Citties aforesaid which have bene hereto fore used for trayninge and musteringe of Souldiors, and for recreacion comforte &*

health of the People inhabitinge the said Citties and Places, and for the use and exercise of Archerie, have of late yeres bene inclosed and converted into sev'alties and to other private uses: Be it enacted by the aucthoritie aforesaid, That it shall not be lawfull to any person or persons to inclose or take in any parte of the Commons or Waste Groundes scituate lienge or beinge within thre Myles of any of the Gates of the saide Cittie of London, nor to sever or to devide by any Hedge Ditche Pale or otherwise, anye of the saide Fieldes lying within three Myles of any of the Gates of the said Cittie of London as aforesaid, to the let or hindraunce of the traynyng or musteringe of Souldiors or of walkinge for recreacion comforte and healthe of her Maj. People, or of the laudable exercise of shotinge . . . Provided alwaies, that this Acte or any thinge ther in conteyned shall not extend to take awaye prejudice or impeache anye good Usage or Customes, heretofore used in the Citties of London and Westminster. . .'

The question was dealt with during the reign of the following kings. James I appointed a commission to defend the rights of archers, quoting a number of provisions, acts and proclamations from previous kings. The object of this commission was to stop a practice that had become usual, to enclose grounds formerly used for exercise with ditches and hedges in fields and enclosures where from time immemorial people used to shoot. During the reign of Charles I a similar proclamation was issued.

In 1605 the problem of Moorfields as public ground found its final solution. Two sisters, Mary and Cathrine Finnes or Fynnes, bequeathed *'the lower walks of Moorfields to the City for the use and enjoyment of the Citizens'*. In 1625 the Lord Mayor and the *Corporation* requested the King to lay out a road to Moorfields, calling attention to the fine 'walks' the City had made out there. Now at last the place had been properly drained and was laid out as a large pleasure ground.

From old maps we can tell how Moorfields was planned. It consisted of the three regular 'fields'. The one nearest the City was the one given by the Finnes sisters. That was again divided by walks into four smaller squares. The middle field had diagonal walks and the upper field was quite open, only surrounded by trees. This method of laying it out gave to the whole the character of a closed garden, and divided in this way, the comparatively small area appeared to be both

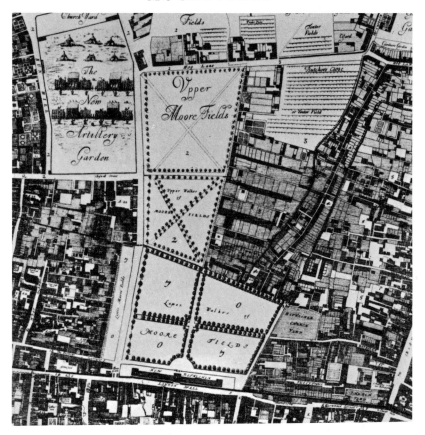

Moorfields, 1676, from John Ogilby's Map

larger and more varied. The new walks soon became a favourite promenade for London's beau-monde. On Sundays large crowds of citizens walked about under the trees in their best clothes. Pepys's *Diary*, June 28th, 1661, records: '*Went to Moorfields, and there walked and stood and saw the wrestling, which I never saw much of before, between the north and west country men.*' May 12th, 1667, records: '*Walked over the fields to Kingsland, and back again; a walk, I think, I have not taken these twenty years; but puts me in mind of my boy's time, when I boarded at Kingsland. . . .*'

There was also room for sports and games and on the upper fields they could practice archery as they did in ancient times. Finsbury Fields were neighbours to them and they were also kept open as a military ground. Laid out in this way Moorfields formed excellent public grounds, which might serve as a model even to-day. A minimum of maintenance was necessary to keep it in order. Within a very limited space recreation was provided for people of all ages. With the exception of the independent townships of Italy it will be difficult from that time onwards to find an example of the laying out of such public grounds.

People were so fond of the shady walks in Moorfields that they soon became the model for another pleasure ground outside London: the so-called Lincoln's Inn Fields west of the City. This garden was developed from the students' former sporting ground in the same way as Moorfields from that of the citizens. London was no university town. When the English students, during the continual wars with France in the Middle Ages, ceased to go to study in Paris, England got her own Universities, Oxford and Cambridge. There the students lived in small communities in the colleges and halls. To begin with the universities were also ecclesiastical institutions. Why they were not situated in London is not easy to say. But it conforms very well with the whole tendency to decentralization, which we have already perceived in the Middle Ages, and London, the commercial city, was never the principal seat of the English Church nor a centre of learning.

But when a regular training in English law for secular lawyers was established it had its seat in London, or to put it more exactly between London and Westminster. There the students resided in the Inns of Court, clustered together just outside the City wall, partly old ecclesiastical buildings. From an old document of about 1376 we learn that the field west of Lincoln's Inn was a common walking and sporting place for the clerks of the Chancery, apprentices, and students of the law, and citizens of London; and that *'upon a clamorous complaint made by them unto the King, that one Roger Leget, had privily laid and hid many iron engines called caltrappes, as well in the bottome as the top of a certaine trench in Fiket's Fields'* (adjoining Lincoln's Inn Fields) *'neere the Bishop of Chichester's house, where the said clerks, apprentices, and other men of the said city, had wont to have their common passage, in which place he knew that they daily exercised their common walks and disports, with a malicious and malevolent intent, that all who came upon the said trench should be*

84

maimed or else most grievously hurt; which engines were found by the foresaid clerkes, apprentices, and others passing that way, and brought before the King's councell, in the Chapter-house of the Friars, preachers of London, and there openly shewed; that hereupon the said Roger was brought before the said councell to answer the premises; and being there examined by the said councell, confessed his said fault and malice in manner aforesaid, and thereupon submitted himselfe to the King and his councell. Whereupon the said Roger was sent to the King's prison of the Fleete, there to expect the King's grace.' The petition concludes *'that any device to interrupt or deprive such clerks, and citizens, of their free common walking or disport there, is a nuisance and offence punishable by the King and his councell by fine and long imprisonment; and that the King and councell have ever been very careful of preserving the liberties and interests of the lawyers and citizens in these fields, for their cure and refreshment'.*

There were three fields which had originally belonged to St. John's and St. Giles's hospitals. They were leased to Inns in the Strand who used them for pasture, so as far as that goes no conflicts arose between the interests of the owners and those of the students. Later, as the city increased in size, the fields became valuable as building ground. After the confiscation of the property of these hospitals by Henry VIII they belonged to the Crown but were always leased at a very low rent. In 1613 one of the fields came into the hands of a man who, realizing what he could make of it, petitioned the King for a licence to build houses on it. The Society of Lincoln's Inn immediately sent in a protest to the Privy Council.

Not only was the licence refused, but the Privy Council, on August 31st, 1613, issued instructions to certain local justices which, after mentioning that complaint had been made *'by the students of Lincoln's Inn that some doe goe aboute to errect new buildinges in a field neere unto them called Lincoln's Inne Fields, with an intent to convert the whole feild into new buildings, contrary to His Ma^{tie's} Proclamation . . . and to the greate pestring and annoyance of that Society'*, required them *'to restrayne and forbid that building by such effectuall meanes as you shall thinke meet'.*

Early in 1617 gentlemen of the Inns of Court and Chancery and from the four parishes adjoining the Fields petitioned the

King that the fields might '*be converted into walkes after the same manner as Morefeildes are now to the greater pleasure and benefite of that Citty.*' This petition '*His Mag^{tie} did take in very gracious and acceptable parte and did highly commend and allowe of the same as a matter both of speciall benefitt and ornament to that parte of the Cittie*'. A subscription was started to meet the cost of '*so worthie and commendable a work*'. In 1618 a commission was granted which had to survey the fields and prepare plans for the walks. Inigo Jones, who was the surveyor general, was among the commissioners and he designed the Plan for the Square divided with avenues. Afterwards a certain William Newton acquired the lease of the fields. He presented a petition to the King (Charles I) pointing out that under the existing conditions the Crown only received an annual rent of £5 6s. 8d. in respect of the property and asked licence to build thirty-two houses on the field. The King could not resist the prospect of increased revenue from the property and even before the Society of Lincoln's Inn had presented their protest, a licence was granted to Newton to build the thirty-two houses. He considered it best to keep on good terms with the gentlemen from Lincoln's Inn and made the agreement with them, that the 'Walks' should remain an open Square. That was in 1639. In August 1641 all the houses on the south side and most of those on the western side had been built. Fearing new building enterprises the Society of Lincoln's Inn sent in a fresh petition. But this time they were wiser and instead of addressing it to the King they sent it to the House of Commons. It is characteristic of the period that the Commons took the part of the Society and ordered a stay to be '*made of any farther Building in Lincolnes-inn-fields (especially by Mr. Newton) till this House shall take farther Order therein*'. Newton was very energetic. He lodged a counter-petition against the Society at the same time doing his best to make friends with them again. He does not appear to have succeeded very well. At any rate a large pile of timber stored in the Fields for building purposes was set on fire. The next year he died without having got any further with the matter. The new owners communicated with Lincoln's Inn and a new arrangement was made regarding the final building scheme. It was decided that the new

Extract from Map by Hollar, 1658. On the right: Lincoln's Inn Fields

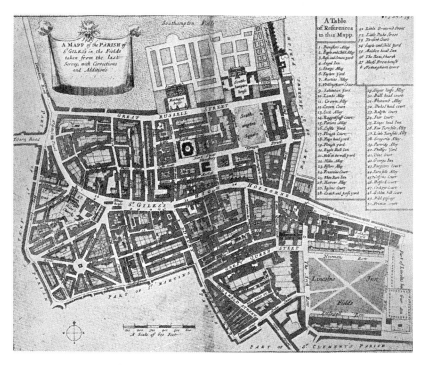

The parish of St. Giles in the Fields from Strype's London 1720

buildings on the north side should have the same proportions as to height and breadth as those already built on the south side so that the whole formed a regular square. During the Commonwealth the matter was still in abeyance. By a proclamation of 1656 Oliver Cromwell again stopped the building operations at the request of the Society of Lincoln's Inn. In the following year the unfinished state of the square was taken into consideration, and an agreement was accordingly entered into between Sir William Cowper, Robert Henley, and James Cowper, who had taken a lease of these and other fields for building purposes, and the Society of Lincoln's Inn. One of the clauses states *'that the said Society of Lincoln's Inn were interested in the benefit and advantage of the prospect and air of the said field, but were willing and content'* that the parties to whom the building was to be entrusted *'might proceed in their said design and undertaking ... with such caution and provision for the beautifying and adorning of the said intended building, and for levelling and plaining the said field, and casting the same into walks, and for prevention of any future building thereupon.'* And thus by their continued and energetic protest the students succeeded in preserving a large open square which is still lying there as public pleasure ground this very day. It was opened to the public in 1894.

Lincoln's Inn Fields. Tennis courts (August 1930)

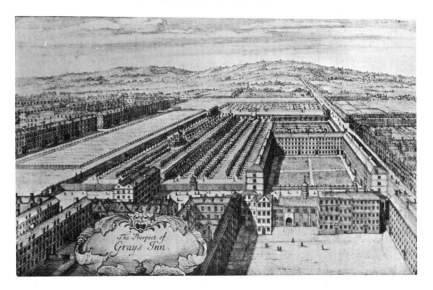

Gray's Inn. Engraving *circ.* 1755. Hampstead and Highgate in the distance

North of Lincoln's Inn lies Gray's Inn, which is also one of the old Inns of Court. From olden times the inhabitants used the Gray's Inn Fields as their ground for archery and open-air sport.

> Guarded with gunners, bill-men and a rout
> Of bow-men bold which at a cat do shoot.
> *(Cornacopia or Pasquil's Night-Cap, 1632)*

About 1600, when Bacon was treasurer for Gray's Inn, the grounds which were adjacent to Gray's Inn were laid out as a pleasure garden with walks just like the others we have seen. It was probably the model for Moorfields Walks. It soon became a favourite promenade, especially on Sundays. Pepys, May 4th, 1662, records: '*When Church was done, my wife and I walked to Gray's Inne, to observe fashions of the ladies, because of my wife's making some clothes.*' He also sometimes walked alone and '*was very well pleased with the sight of a fine Lady that I had often seen walk in Gray's Inn Walks*'. But it was not always 'fine ladies', and the walks gradually fell into disrepute. More interesting is the origin of a little playground in the vicinity, the 'Red Lion Square', west of Gray's Inn. In Narcissus Luttrell's *Diary*, June 10th, 1680, we read the

Gray's Inn from the Gardens (January 1930). Badly damaged

following account: '*Dr. Barebone, the great builder, having some-time since bought the Red Lyon Feilds, near Graies Inn walks, to build on, and having for that purpose employed several workmen to go on with the same, the gentlemen of Graies Inn took notice of it, and think-ing it an injury to them, went with a considerable body of one hundred persons; upon which the workmen assaulted the gentlemen, and flung bricks at them, and the gentlemen at them again; so a sharp engage-ment ensued, but the gentlemen routed them at the last, and brought away one or two of the workmen to Graies Inn; in this skirmish one or two of the gentlemen and servants of the house were hurt and*

Gray's Inn Walks (January 1930)

severall of the workmen.' The result was that Dr. Barebone, instead of building on the whole area as was his first intention spared an open square in the middle surrounded by houses. The Court itself wanted more space for its sport than the citizens and the students. The Norman knights that came into England with William the Conqueror were originally a warrior-cast, and in the beginning their sport was warlike exercises, tournaments and the like. But later, as this warrior-class found its occupation gone, hunting in the great forests became the pastime of the knights The country was sparsely peopled and vast districts were covered with woods and forests, with plenty of game and deer. The lord of the manor had few duties and could spend days and weeks in hunting. This 'fine' sport was of course also a favourite occupation of the Court. The vigorous Henry VIII, as we know, diverted himself with many kinds of sport; he was a powerful wrestler, an elegant tennis player, and was also a mighty hunter before the Lord. There is a proclamation from his time (1545) saying: *'As the King's most royal Majesty is desirous to have the games of hare, partridge, pheasant, and heron preserved in and about the honour of his palace of Westminster, for his own disport and pastime, no person, on the pain of imprisonment of their bodies, and further punishment at his Majesty's will and pleasure, is to presume to hunt or hawk, from the palace of Westminster to St. Giles-in-the-Fields, and from thence to Islington, to Our Lady of the Oak, to Highgate, to Hornsey Park, and to Hampstead Heath.'* The King did not only forbid people to hunt in these hunting grounds but he also fenced in large areas. The primary result of his efforts was that the citizens were excluded from places where they hitherto could walk as they pleased. But it meant that the countryside near London was protected for later times against building speculation and beautiful open spaces spared as pleasure grounds, which in England became parks at a very early period.

The most important of the popular parks was Hyde Park. It is impossible to trace the date at which it was opened to the public, but it must have been sometime between 1630 and 1640. It was still a Royal park, but we have accounts of both horse-racing and foot-racing. There was a regular racecourse called 'the Ring'. Although it was far from London at that time people flocked out there, particularly on Sundays. The King was often present at the races. Later, when the Puritans came into power, it was resolved that the park should be kept closed and no person should be allowed to go into it on the Lord's-day and fast-days. In 1649, after the King's fall, it was resolved in Parliament that Hyde Park, as well as Whitehall, Hampton Court, New Park at Richmond, Westminster Palace, Windsor House and Parks, and Greenwich Park and Castle should be kept for the use of the Commonwealth and be thrown open to the public. These

Sheep in Hyde Park (August 1931). Photo. Roloff Nielsen

glorious conditions were not to last long. Three years after the journals of the House of Commons contain this laconic entry: '*Resolved that Hyde Park be sold for ready money.*' That, however, did not interfere with its use as a public garden. John Evelyn writes in his diary, April 11th, 1653: '*I went to take the air in Hyde Park, where every coach was made to pay a shilling, and horse sixpence, by the sordid fellow who had purchased it of the State, as they called it.*' Although the Puritans were against all kinds of entertainments and particularly against the festivities of May-day — the first day of 'the month of Mary' — in which they saw a remnant of rank popery, Hyde Park was crowded with merry people *the first of May 1654*. A Puritan paper of the time tells us about '*hundreds of coaches, and gallants in attire, but most shameful powder'd-hair men, and painted and spotted women*', and as a comfort for the right-minded reader it adds: '*But his Highness the Lord Protector was not thither, nor any of the Lords of the Council, but were busy about the great affairs of the Commonwealth.*'

From other sources we know, however, that the Lord Protector *was* there that very day. He was on the whole 'a good sport', just the man to please English taste. Sir William

93

Dugdale refers in some Royalist propaganda to Oliver Cromwell as indulging in his youth in cricket and football and as acquiring 'the name of royster'. As Lord Protector he often took the air in Hyde Park among the ordinary people. By advice of his physicians he took as much exercise as he possibly could and his favourite sport was driving his own coach in the Ring. The Dutch Ambassador has given a vigorous description of one of these drives in the following letter: *'His Highness, only accompanied with Secretary Thurloe and some few of his gentlemen and servants, went to take the air in Hyde Park, where he caused some dishes of meat to be brought, where he made his dinner, and afterwards had a desire to drive the coach himself, having put only the Secretary into it, being those six (grey) horses, which the Earl of Oldenburgh had presented unto his Highness, who drove pretty handsomely for some time. But at last, provoking those horses too much with the whip, they grew unruly, and ran so fast that the postillion could not hold them in; whereby his Highness was flung out of the coachbox upon the pole, upon which he lay with his body, and afterwards fell upon the ground. His foot getting hold in the tackling he was carried away a good while in that posture, during which time a pistol went off in his pocket: but at last he got his foot clear, and so came to escape, the coach passing by without hurting him. He was presently brought home and let blood; and after some rest taken, he is now pretty well again.'*

When England after the death of Cromwell changed government and became a kingdom again, many things were altered, but facilities for the citizens as regards parks and open spaces were not diminished. Charles II was himself 'a good sport' and he took his exercises, tennis, pall mall, and especially walking, quite publicly. He walked so fast that the courtiers could hardly keep up with him, 'Walk with me,' said the Merry Monarch to Prince George of Denmark, who was complaining of incipient corpulency, 'hunt with my brother, and do justice to my niece, and you will never be fat.' His favourite resort was St. James's Park. That was also one of the former hunting grounds from the time of Henry V, originally a swampy meadow intersected with little ponds and dotted with trees. Immediately after the Restoration Charles II began to improve the Park. It is said that the famous Le Nôtre was the King's adviser in laying out

The Mall in St. James's Park 1751. Engraving by H. Roberts

St. James's Park, but that is doubtful. A Swiss gentleman wrote at the end of the century: '*I have been told that King Charles II wished to render St. James's Park more beautiful, and for that purpose summoned from Paris a clever man, the same who had laid out the gardens of the Tuileries. But this man was of opinion that the natural simplicity of this Park, its rural, and in some places wild character, had something more grand than he could impart to it, and persuaded the King not to touch it. Thus the Park remained as we see it now — that is to say, a rural and beautiful spot, of which I think one will not easily get tired, just because there is neither art nor regularity about it.*' — The park *was* touched, however. The Mall was laid out as a broad avenue with four lines of trees. It was not planned as the stately approach to Buckingham Palace, but as a place where the King could play pall mall. '*"Pall Maille" is a game wherein a round bowle is with a mallet struck through a high arch of iron (standing at either end of an alley), which he that can do at the fewest blows or at the number agreed on, wins. This game was heretofore used in the long alley near St. James's and vulgarly called "Pell-Mell"*'[1] This first Mall was already at the time of Charles II a street bordered with fine houses.

[1] Thomas Blount's *Glossographia*.

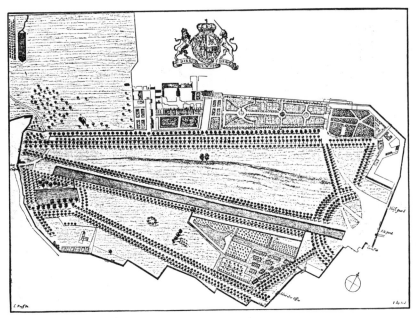

St. James's Park at the time of Charles II

The different waters and springs were united into one long pond, 'the Canal', 28 feet broad and 100 feet long. The purpose of this is not very clear. It had apparently no architectural relation to the avenue and the surrounding buildings, as one would expect of a canal in a Royal garden of the time of Louis XIV. An old Dutchman, Sextus Arnoldinus, who visited London in 1660 tells us that the King frequently swam in it. Possibly this regular canal, like the Mall, was meant as a sporting place for the King, a swimming pool. The ideals of Charles II were in many ways in conformity with those of Louis XIV, who was also a fine sportsman. But characteristic of the behaviour of the English King was his unambitious way of taking exercise in a park where he could be seen by all his people, even without his clothes on. In the comparatively democratic Denmark the Royal garden of Frederiksberg was opened to the public in the beginning of the eighteenth century, but there small enclosures were reserved into which ordinary people could be driven, when it pleased the Royal family to take the air in the garden. But in St. James's Park it was considered good form to lie down in the grass beside the walks. July 15th, 1666, the snobbish Samuel Pepys 'walked' to the Park, and there '*it being mighty hot and I weary, lay down upon the grass by the canalle, and slept awhile*'. It was a common entertainment to see the King feed his ducks and walk with the dogs. He had so many of them, that he every now and then had to advertise the loss of one of the pets in *London Gazette* or *Mercurius Politicus*. We get a vivid impression of life in St. James's Park from Tom Brown's journalistic description of 1700: '*The green Walk afforded us variety of discourses from persons of both sexes. Here walked a beau bareheaded — here a French fop with both his hands in his pockets, carrying all his pleated coat before to shew his silk breeches. There were a cluster of Senators talking of State affairs and the price of Corn and Cattle, and were disturbed with the noisy milk folks — crying — A Can of Milk, Ladies; A Can of Red Cow's Milk, Sir.*'

As we see, the Londoners had already in the seventeenth century acquired a number of open spaces each with its peculiar character. There was *Moorfields* with its 'Walks' and open fields for archery and games. There were the gardens at *Gray's Inn* and *Lincoln's Inn*, there was *Spring Gardens*, laid out with many green enclòsures which are said to have been the scene of many a gallant adventure. There was *St. James's Park* where the King and the Court took exercise; and there was *Hyde Park* with 'the Ring' and a delightful 'wilderness' into the bargain. And yet the citizens invaded at their own free will the fields of the farmers round about, shot with bows and arrows, played games and bleached their linen as they chose!

BOOKS OF REFERENCE

Fitz-Stephen's descriptions of London of the twelfth century are quoted in *John Stow's Survey of London*, a book containing much useful information explaining the origin of the open spaces, for instance on Moorfields. In *Strype's* edition (1720) of *Stow*, there is a considerably amplified chapter on sports and pastimes, from which the Proclamation by Edward III to the Sheriffs of London is taken. In a book which is now rare, *Jacob Larwood: London Parks* (Chatto and Windus, London, without year), there is among numerous anecdotes a great deal of interesting information on the history of the parks of London. *J. J. Sexby* has also collected a number of interesting facts in *The Municipal Parks, Gardens and Open Spaces of London*, 1905. The history of Lincoln's Inn Fields is related in *The Survey of London III*, published by the London County Council. The story of Dr. Barebone and Red Lion Square is to be found in Narcissus Luttrel's Diary, June 10th, 1684, and is taken from *The History of Squares of London*, by *B. Beresford Chancellor*, 1907. Detailed information, quotations and references to other books on the various localities of London and their history are contained in *London Past and Present*, by *Henry B. Wheatley* and *Peter Cunningham*, 1891, which is arranged in alphabetical order. The account of Cromwell's drive in the Ring is from the article on Hyde Park. *Evelyn's* and *Pepys's Diaries* give most vivid accounts of daily life in the parks in the seventeenth century.

TOWN-PLANNING SCHEMES IN 1666

THE GREAT FIRE, 1666, DESTROYED ALMOST THE WHOLE CITY. London was already a very great populated town. No census had yet been made but the number of inhabitants must have been about 400,000 when Westminster, Southwark, and all the new quarters outside the walls were counted. Paris was probably still the most populous town in the world, but London was gaining on it.

Many foreigners who visited the town in the seventeenth century have given enthusiastic descriptions of it. It must have been a wealthy and interesting town. The quarters inside the walls were crowded and still quite medieval. In former centuries only a few aldermen — and the Jews — had, as we have seen, stately stone houses. The rest of the inhabitants lived in small cottages as a kind of leaseholders. We get an idea of how badly they were built from the oldest building regulations from 1189 and 1212 requiring new houses to be built more solidly than before and prohibiting thatched roofs. In the course of centuries the houses had, from their too narrow sites, risen to several corbelled stories. As late as in the seventeenth century the greater part of the houses were still half timbered with pointed gables facing the street. Now the stone houses were the property of the rich companies and guilds. It had proved vain to prohibit projecting parts of the façades. As in all medieval towns where the houses were built on small sites the streets showed a tendency to grow more and more narrow. London inside the walls was a town packed full of pointed framework houses sprinkled with numerous churches with towers and spires — there were 109 in all! Over it rested the huge body of the Gothic St. Paul's Cathedral. The houses stood with their steep façades right out into the Thames and even London Bridge was overhung by piles of narrow houses four or five stories high. The narrow alleys were bazaars with a variety of hand-made things and fine fabrics and costly

Waterhouse by Illington.   W. Hollar delin et sculp: 1665.

Landscape from Islington, north of London, 1665. Etching by Hollar

merchandise coming from all parts of the world. One could look right into the booths which opened on to the street. All streets were crowded with pedestrians, sedan-chairs and carriages which could hardly move along. Pepys relates how his carriage swept two pieces of meat from a booth into the dirt in a narrow street.

The attempts to prevent the overcrowding of the houses had not succeeded. Poor people lived under the most terrible conditions. A small house in Dowgate Ward is said to have housed eleven married couples and fifteen single persons. A house in Silver Street with ten rooms was inhabited by ten families of which several had lodgers.[1] And this was in a town without common sewers; the dirt was simply poured into the street!

Outside the walls were large open quarters of a somewhat different character. The streets were broader, in many places with regular brick houses, and in between them were green squares and gardens and parks where everybody was allowed to walk. The ideal of later days: open spaces like air

[1] W. G. Bell, *The Great Fire of London* in 1666, London 1920, p. 14.

100

W. Hollar delin: et sculp: 1665.   By Islington.

Landscape from Islington north of London 1665. Etching by Hollar

courses running from the middle of the town out to the open
country was carried out already in the seventeenth century
in London without any definite planning. Both Moorfields
and Gray's Inn Walks were carried farther on into the beautiful countryside which we know from the etchings of Hollar.
It is an open, undulating landscape with streamlets which
here and there were dammed to form calm millponds.
Towards the north the town was encircled by the heights at
Hampstead and Highgate which in the hazy London air
looked like distant blue mountains. And still they were so
near, that it was easy to walk out there and see the big town
lying at one's feet. St. James's Park, a real garden, was
continued into Hyde Park, a piece of uncultivated land. But
the best of all the air courses was the Thames, which in those
days was a smiling river right up to London, full of fish and
boats and swans and bordered with gardens and stately
mansions.

The City was the residence of the old families of merchants
and craftsmen. But the nobility had left the narrow stinking
streets where their coaches could hardly move and had taken

up their residence in the royal city of Westminster, where they settled in the new, open quarters. Towards the end of the seventeenth century only two or three noble families lived within the walls. But even the citizens longed to get away from the town out into the country. The development which was gradually to change the character of the City completely, when all residences were moved out to other quarters, had already begun. Many wealthy families, who still had their houses in the old city, had at the same time country houses to go to on holidays. *Strype*, who in 1720 published an enlarged edition of Stow's *Survey of London*, says, that when the Great Fire spread so quickly one of the reasons was that it broke out on a Saturday night, when many of the magnates of the City, merchants and others had left for their country houses so that only the servants were left to take care of the town residence.

The fire broke out late in the evening of September 1st. It spread quickly and at first people did not know what to do; they only tried to save their possessions and left the town to the flames. Not until the fire had raged several days and entire quarters had been levelled to the ground, were belts of houses methodically pulled down to stop the fire. It ceased on *September 6th*, but soon broke out again. It is difficult to say when it stopped definitely. The accounts say that it smouldered for months.

On *September 10th*, when the fire had hardly stopped, the King received Dr. Christopher Wren, who handed him a plan for the rebuilding of the town. Wren must have worked hard, and we know that he said himself, that it was important to him to be the first to present a plan. On *September 13th*, that is to say three days after, his friend John Evelyn also presented a plan, but found — as he writes in a letter — that '*Dr. Wren got the start of me*'. On *September 20th* Captain Valentine Knight handed in a plan and finally on *September 21st* Professor Hooke brings in his. Probably there were more plans, but they are not known to us.

Strange it is that all these four men were amateurs. Christopher Wren was then hardly 34 years of age, but he was already a scientist of reputation. As a youth he had distinguished himself by his eminent mathematical talents and had

Old St. Paul's, 1616. From John Visscher's View of London

Hollar's Map of London, 1666, showing the area devastated by the Great Fire

at 25 been appointed professor of astronomy. He corresponded with the most prominent scientists and was already author of a series of treatises of high standing. In 1662, only four years before the Great Fire, he had taken up architecture. In those days, however, it was not a far cry from scientist to artist. Moreover, a series of new problems within architecture were of mathematical and scientific nature. It had dawned upon the architects that several static problems could be solved by the exact sciences. The rules of perspective, which were of such great importance to the artists of those days, were descriptive geometry, and there were a whole range of questions which the scholar could solve better than the craftsman. At any rate Wren showed great superiority in the handling of the problems put to him. His scientific knowledge proved advantageous to him in all constructive, economic and acoustic matters, and his synthetical faculty, trained through his knowledge of mathematics, made him at the same time a solid planner. His knowledge of architecture he had mostly acquired from books. During the Great Plague which devastated London the year before the Fire he had been in Paris where he studied as much as possible of the new architecture — the Louvre was then being built — with great energy. But besides that he had seen no architecture outside England.

At that time no English architect had so great a reputation as that of Inigo Jones (who died in 1651). Wren occupied an office as Deputy Surveyor of His Majesty's Works. Officially he was under Sir John Denham, but practically he was one of the most trusted officials although he had not yet the opportunity of carrying out any great task. In the year of the Great Fire the King had asked him to work out a plan for the restoration of St. Paul's Cathedral, which was in a state of decay, and he sent in his proposal in May that same year.

To Wren the Great Fire represented the great opportunity of his life for carrying out some of the architectural ideas he had acquired on the Continent about the forming of a modern town. The plan he laid down while the fire was still raging is a rather abstract product of a great intellect. It is clearly the mathematician who, starting from certain definite

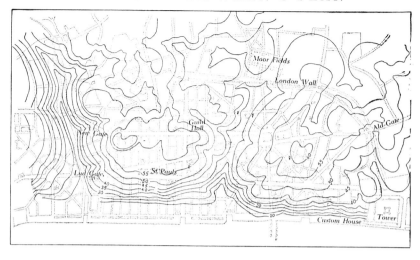

Contour map showing how Christopher Wren's plan would fit in with the actual ground level in London. Figures give height in feet

postulates, has solved an interesting geometrical problem. To him it was a given thing (1) that the entrances to the town were its gates and its bridge; (2) that a town is composed of rectangular houses; (3) that all street corners should preferably be rectangular; (4) that the entrances should give easy access to the different parts of the town; and (5) that the centre of commerce, the Stock Exchange, and the religious centre, St. Paul's, should have a dominating position. The problem was the plexus of streets. This he solved by means of common form ideals of those days.

During the last centuries there had been many theories about town-planning, and a considerable literature had appeared on ideal plans. In fortified towns newly laid out and formed as regular polygons the plexus of streets radiated from the centre marked by a tower. The effect of many streets which in this way meet in one place was one of the favourite devices in town-planning and was used in different ways. It was almost a matter of course in a system of streets with a gate as starting point. The greatest example was the Piazza del Popolo in Rome with three streets intersecting the city. During the reign of the French king, Henri IV, that is to say in the beginning of the seventeenth century, a fan-shaped system of streets was planned in Paris radiating from a bridge over the Seine with a crescent surrounded by uniform buildings. The plan was never carried out, but Wren may have seen an engraving of it; at any rate it was a plan which was quite natural for the period. Wren has used it in his design: from London Bridge radiates four main streets: one leads to the Stock Exchange lying in a spider's-web of straight streets just as the tower in an ideal town; from the gate on the west, Ludgate, two great main lines issue; and in the very acute angle between them, St. Paul's Cathedral was to be situated as a dominating feature. The whole plan is thereafter filled in with a net of streets which as far as possible meet at right angles. Sites for churches are indicated at certain intervals. — It is unknown whether Wren had time to write an explanation of the plan. After his death his son has rendered an account of his father's ideas (in *Parentalia*, published in 1750 by his grandson), but it is difficult to decide whether this description is based upon facts which Christopher Wren had written down or communicated to him personally, or if it is simply an explanation for what the son saw in the plan.

Wren was an ardent admirer of Bernini (see page 202) and many years later he made a scheme for the square in front of St. Paul's Cathedral which shows his interest in Bernini's Piazza di San Pietro in Rome. But at the time when he hurriedly executed the plan for London he had not yet discovered the monumental square as an architectural element in town-planning. The squares indicated in his plan are all mere extensions of street junctions. Not a single quiet and monumental square is indicated on it. So far his plan is more in contact with the garden architecture of the period as represented by Le Nôtre than with the great town-planning of the Baroque period.

Evelyn's plan is quite different. John Evelyn was the typical wealthy, well educated nobleman, who could live entirely for his hobbies and who divided his time equally between aesthetic and practical subjects. On his journeys in Holland, Belgium, France, and Italy, he had had the opportunity to see much more contemporary architecture than Wren. In his plan he has proposed a series of large and

Piazza del Popolo in Rome with the three streets intersecting the city
From Nolli's plan 1748

Place de France, Paris. Project. Engraving by Castillon 1610

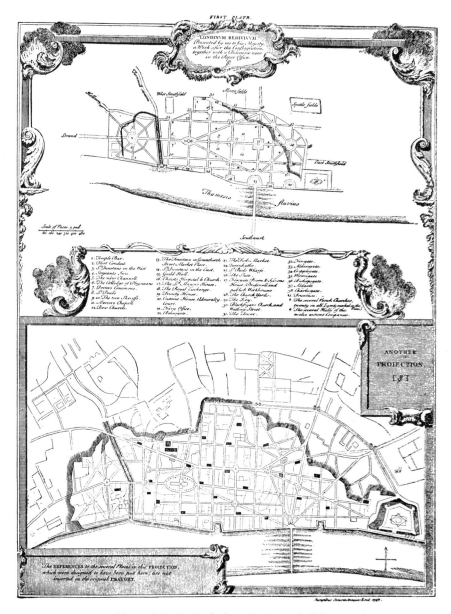

Above: John Evelyn's first plan for re-building
Below: A subsequent project of John Evelyn's showing more consideration for earlier conditions. From *Vetusta Monumenta*, 1789

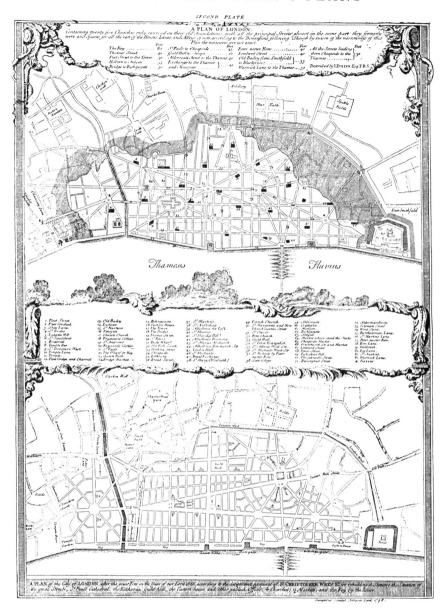

Above: John Evelyn's third plan for re-building
Below: Christopher Wren's project. From *Vetusta Monumenta,* 1789

regular squares, indicating the centres of gravity in the symmetrical system he has built up. He composed a description of his plan and fortunately it has been preserved (in manuscript in the Guildhall Library, London). It shows a careful and sensible man, who has used his eyes well when travelling and who now puts down a series of practical and aesthetical details which he recommends as suitable for London. It is characteristic of his reasoning that there is not the slightest explanation of the great lines of the plan itself but plenty of indications how it ought to be carried out in details right down to paving, arrangements of waste-pipes and gutters and decoration of town-gates. With regard to the aesthetic of the plexus of streets he says: '*In the disposure of the streets due consideration should be had, what are compitant breadths for commerce and entercourse, cherefullness and state; and therefore not to pass through the city all in one tenor without varieties, usefull breakings, and inlargements into piazzas at compitant distances, which ought to be built exactly uniform, strong, and with beautiful fronts. Nor should these be all of them be square, but some of them oblong, circular, and oval figures, for their better grace and capacity. I would allow none of the principal streets less than a hundred foot in breadth, nor any of the narrowest than thirty . . .*' His design shows a chessboard-plan in which he has introduced four diagonals connecting the main entrances to the town and wherein the most important junctions take the form of what he calls piazzas. According to his description markets were to be held there. These squares might also be used for 'parking' and he proposed their embellishment by fountains. The plan, of which the blocks were too large and the intersections of the streets bad, was unsatisfactory, and Evelyn, who could not give up his idea, has twice tried to improve it by introducing a more sensible scale and by basing it more on the plans of the old London. But he kept the diagonal streets which mercilessly intersected the chessboard-plan. This way of forming a town-plan which — just like Wren's — is closely related to contemporary plans for forests and gardens was really quite revolutionary and has apparently influenced L'Enfant's plan for Washington (1791).

Robert Hooke like Wren was a mathematician. His plan has been lost. But it is known to have been a very regular

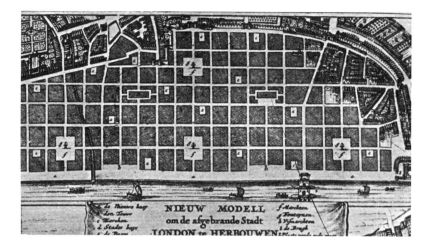

Robert Hooke's plan (?). From *A View of the Fire*, by Doornick

gridiron plan. A Dutchman, who made an engraving of the
Great Fire, has in one corner inserted what he calls '*a new
model for the rebuilding of the city London, destroyed by fire*'. It is
quite possible that it is Hooke's.

Valentine Knight's plan deserves more attention than it has
hitherto attracted. In contrast to Wren's and Evelyn's
proposals it consisted only of a description on a large printed
broadside dated September 20th, 1666. It gives directions
as to the rational parcelling out of the area devastated by the
fire. Wren and Evelyn had worked at the streets and had let
the blocks turn out as best they could without considering
how they were to be parcelled out (it would always be
possible as in old London to divide up by alleys blocks that
proved too large). Knight on the contrary designed the
whole town divided up in long, narrow blocks which easily
could be parcelled out without waste. First, he places two
60 feet broad main streets running from west to east parallel
with the river. Then he inserts six cross streets of the same
width at a right angle to the river. Each large block arising
between these main streets is divided up by secondary streets
only 30 feet broad, ten parallel with the river and one at a
right angle to it. This will produce blocks of an average size of
500 feet by 70 feet, just big enough to allow two rows of

houses separated by a narrow yard. On such lines, which give a maximum of houses with minimum of street space, an economical parcelling out will always be reasonable when special conditions do not prevent it. A number of sites had already been parcelled out in this way outside the City and it was going to be typical for London's future street houses in quarters where no space was laid out for open squares. Knight proposed that pavements should be placed in arcades on the ground floor of the houses and also that a great canal ('*A Cutt of 30 foot*') should encircle the City, permitting the ships to sail from the Thames right up to warehouses for which there was no room on the quays.

None of the plans were executed. They did not even reach Parliament or the City Corporation for discussion.

Wren's plan has been greatly admired by posterity. It is hardly ever spoken of without regret about it not having been carried out. It is generally considered a foresighted piece of town-planning which might have made London a magnificent town, still more beautiful than Paris, if the narrow-mindedness and the shortsighted politics of those days had not prevented its execution. To a modern, less aesthetically determined view things appear a little different. Wren's plan, finished in a few days, *is* a fine example of a certain type of town-planning — that type which is now going to be abandoned. It is the town-planning of Absolutism, which — as far as the exterior is concerned — has given such imposing results at the same time as the monumental form suppressed the vital functions of the towns. Paris, that has been admired as a most beautiful city, is a striking example of a great city, the natural growth of which has been checked. The government has constantly checked its expansion development, with the result that houses have grown higher and higher, and it has been possible to lay out grandiose streets and squares. The reverse side of the radiant medal is the disappearance of recreation grounds and too crowded and too populous quarters, a breeding place for the most dangerous type of populace. According to modern ideas it is impossible to give a town a definite and fixed form. A town plan is no longer a beautiful pattern of streets which a clever man can design in a day or two. Nowadays it is an outline for a sound development of the town based on thorough investigations concerning prevailing conditions. Nobody dreams of making designs for the moulding in detail of a whole town. A programme is given for its growth in words just as much as in drawing (rather like Knight's proposal) in order to gain the end that all functions of the town may develop in the best way, a programme which necessarily must keep pace with the growth and in process of time change together with the town. That Wren's ideas are *old fashioned* as seen by modern eyes is not surprising, and it might seem out of place to introduce the subject of modern views in connection with these old plans if the further history of the rebuilding of London had not shown that England in the days of Charles II actually possessed men who in many aspects were astonishingly *modern* in their conception of town-planning. That the King had to give up the plan immediately is but one of the numerous expressions of the failure of Absolutism in England. It is another confirmation of the picture we have got of the relations between London and the monarch. From our point of view the rejection of Wren's plan is not a fault but rather a new triumph for what might be called the idea of London. For there *was*, as we have seen, an idea in the apparently incidental growth of the town. Through the whole history of London we find a latent power, a desire to make the town healthy and it has been able to act because London in contrast to other capitals was self-governing and independent of the Crown, and no standards for her development could be forced on her. This local government was the vital nerve of the town — more important than any plans. It may sound like a paradox to say that there is more true town-planning in the unrestricted growth of London than in contemporary Continental towns that developed according to plans.

In itself Wren's plan was absolutely impossible to carry out. Not one street nor one building was kept in its old place. And even if all the houses were burned down yet something far more immovable than stone and wood existed, namely, the sites with their boundaries. Each of the citizens could exactly point out where his house had been and how far his site went. Its value was not only determined by its size but also by its situation. If Wren's plan was to be carried out it would be necessary that all individual property was united into one large piece of land which thereafter might be parcelled out to the hundreds of proprietors. It might be possible in our days through an extensive expropriation by the government, but was hardly possible at the time of Charles II. Modern banks were unknown. The town was impoverished by plague and fire and the government could not provide such enormous sums as would be necessary. Moreover they had not yet the practice in valuation which has been acquired during the following centuries. It is, therefore, not surprising that the plan was rejected; for a sober examination would demonstrate that it *could* not be carried out. The interesting thing is, however, that it was given up *so soon*. When Wren on September 10th was received by the King, His Majesty examined the plan with great interest. To Charles II, who for years had lived at the French Court, it must have been a very attractive idea to have London rebuilt as a monumental capital. That same day William Morice, one of the private secretaries of the King, wrote the following letter from Whitehall to London's Lord Mayor: *'My Lord — His Matie being informed that some persons are already about to erect houses againe in the Citty of London upon their old foundations, hath comanded mee to signify his pleasure unto your Lordship that you inhibit and straightly forbid both them and all other persons whatsoever that they presume not to build any dwelling houses till further order, his Matie having before him certaine modells and Draughts for re-edifying the Citty with more decency and conveniency than formerly. And if notwithstanding this advertisement, and the signification of his Matie's pleasure herein, they shall yet proceed to build without order, your Lordship may assure them (as undoubtedly it will come to passe) that whatever they raise in such manner will be demolished and levelled again. — I am, Your lordship's most humble servant, Will Morice.'* — This communication gives an impression of the Absolute King sitting at his table studying the plans for the rebuilding of his capital and paternally considering how it might be done so as to become an ornament to his realm. In a letter from a certain Dr. Oldenburg, Secretary to The Royal Society, it is said: *'. . . Dr. Wren has since my last drawn a modell for a new citty, and presented it to the king, who produced it himselfe before his councill, and manifested much approbation of it.'*

But already *three days later the King has entirely given up Wren's plan*, a fact that is clearly shown from a proclamation dated September 13th. We do not know what happened in the meantime. But from the proclamation we get the impression that the King has been influenced by representatives from the City. It seems likely, that the Lord Mayor of London — startled by the first letter and the rumours about Wren's plan — had been to the King to assure him that it would be absolutely impracticable to carry out an ideal plan. Anyway it sounds as if the King refutes all through his proclamation the view that he might intend to violate the sacred right of possession. On September 13th when it was issued, Evelyn, who was no fool, but a man of the world, had not got any further in his conceptions of conditions in London than to go to the King and show him *his* plan, that had just as Utopian a basis as that of Dr. Wren.

Also note the *tone* in the King's proclamation. It is no more the Absolute King who commands. It is rather like a proclamation from the Tudor days, like one of Elizabeth's reasonable communications to the citizens. He starts quite naturally by saying: '*As no particular Man hath sustained any loss or dammage by the late terrible and deplorable Fire in his Fortune or Estate, in any degree to be compared with the loss and dammage We Our Self have sustained, so it is not possible for any Man to take the same more to heart, and to be more concerned and sollicitous for the rebuilding this Famous City, with as much expedition as is possible: And since it hath pleased God to lay this heavy Judgment upon Us all in this time, as an evidence of his displeasure for Our sins, We do comfort Our Self with some hope, that he wil upon Our due humiliation before Him, as a new instance of his signal blessing upon Us, give Us life, not only to see the foundations laid, but the buildings finished, of a much more beautiful City than is at this time consumed; . . .*'

The whole proclamation is full of common sense. It says that it is impossible to lay down rules for the rebuilding of the City, but attempts must be made to avoid the annoyance arising from a premature rebuilding of individual houses. Therefore it is forbidden to commence any building until further directions have been given. It continues: '*And because no men shal complain or apprehend that by this caution or restraint of Ours, they shal or may for a long time be kept for providing Habitations for themselves, and for the carrying on their Trades, though We make no question, but in a short time, with the assistance and advice of the Lord Mayor and Court of Aldermen (who have besought Us for some time to put this restraint) to finish the whole design, even before any men can make provision of materials for any valuable Edifices: We do declare, that if any considerable number of men (for it is impossible to comply with the humour of every particular man) shal address themselves to the Court of Aldermen, & manifest to them in what places their Ground lies, upon which they design to build, they shal in a short time receive such order and direction, for their proceeding therein, that they shall have no cause to complain; and so We proceed to the setting down such general to which all particular designe must conform themselves.'* It is already established in the proclamation what was later to become law, that the houses in the future *must only be built of brick or stone.* As to the breadth of the streets it is declared that: *'Fleet Street, Cheapside, Cornhill, and all other eminent and notorious Streets, shal be of such breadth as may with Gods blessing prevent the mischief that one side may suffer if the other be on fire, which was the case lately in Cheapside, the precise breadth of which several Streets, shal be upon advice with the Lord Mayor and Aldermen shortly publish'd, with many other particular Orders and Rules, which cannot yet be adjusted; in the mean time We resolve though all Streets cannot be of equal breadth, yet none shall be so narrow as to make the passage uneasie or inconvenient, especially towards the Waterside; nor wil We suffer any Lanes or Allyes to be erected, but where upon mature deliberation the same shal be found absolutely necessary . . .'* As the extent of the fire is greatly due to the congestion of small, wooden houses along the Thames, a fact which made it impossible to utilize the water from the river for the extinction of the flames, it is enacted that a broad quay be built along the river. Concerning the houses along the Thames the proclamation says: *'. . . nor shal there be in those Buildings which shal be erected next the River, which We desire may be fair Structures, for the ornament of the City, any houses to be inhabited by Brewers, or Diers, or Sugar-Bakers, which Trades by their continual Smoaks*[1] *contribute very much to the unhealthiness of*

---

[1] In 1661 John Evelyn had composed a treatise, *Fumifugium,* about the smoke nuisance, proposing expedients as to how it might be remedied. According to his diary for September 13th and October 1st, 1661, the King was very interested in the matter. Even in Westminster the smoke was very annoying when the wind was east. The King wanted the Parliament to pass a law based on Evelyn's proposal, but nothing was done.

the adjacent places; but We require the Lord Major and Aldermen of London upon a full consideration, and weighing all conveniences and inconveniences that can be foreseen, to propose such a place as may be fit for all those Trades which are carried on by smoak to inhabit together, or at least several places for the several quarters of the Town for those occupations, and in which they shal find their accompt in convenience and profit, as wel as other places shal receive the benefit in the distance of the neighbourhood, it being Our purpose that they who exercise those necessary professions, shal be in all respects as wel provided for and encouraged as ever they have been, and undergo as little prejudice as may be by being less inconvenient to their Neighbours.' — The proclamation is upon the whole astonishingly modern. It is a true piece of town-planning, a programme for the development of the town. Also the expedients indicated at the end are quite modern. Officials will be appointed for the surveying of the sites and to establish what belongs to each single person and the individual value: *'... that so provision may be made, that though every man must not be suffered to erect what Buildings and where he pleases, he shal not in any degree be debarred from receiving the reasonable benefit of what ought to accrue to him from such Houses or Lands, there being nothing less in Our thoughts, then that any particular persons right and interest should be sacrificed to the publick benefit or convenience, without such recompence as in justice he ought to receive for the same: And when all things of this kind shall be prepared and adjusted by such Commissioners, and otherwise, which shal be found expedient, We make no doubt but such an Act of Parliament wil pass, as shal secure all men in what they shal and ought to possess.'*

Poor *Valentine Knight* had not understood at all which way the wind blew. In his proposal he had carefully laid down a plan for the financing of the rebuilding, and therein he proposed that each inhabitant was in the future to pay an annual rent to the King proportionate to the size of his building-site. The very considerable sum (£223,517 yearly) thus obtained was to be used for the maintenance of the King's Army and Navy (Knight was a captain in the King's service), yet each person who had suffered losses on account of the Fire had to receive damages from the money collected to an extent fixed by Parliament. The King, certainly, wanted nothing more than a large annual sum for which he could maintain an army, but he had seen that Knight's plan was Utopian and understood how dangerous it would be to publish it. At any rate he had the imaginative captain arrested and took the opportunity of a little preaching to his subjects, '*as if*' says the *London Gazette*, September 27th — October 1st: I, '*his Majesty would draw a benefit to himself from so public a calamity of his people, of which his Majesty is known to have so deep sense, that he is pleased to seek rather by all means to give them ease under it.*'

The other projectors had better luck although they too had not fully understood the exigencies of the time and their plans had also to be abandoned. Evelyn continued as the confidential but unofficial adviser to the King in many matters. And when the King hastily appointed a committee for the rebuilding of London it was composed of Sir *Roger Pratt*, Mr. *Hugh May* and Dr. *Wren*. They had to make a survey of the town and make proposals as to regulations concerning its rebuilding. This committee was joined by three other men among whom was the above mentioned Professor *Hooke*. From Sir Roger Pratt's memoirs, which have been published but recently, it is possible to see how they worked. They worked quickly and their proceedings are worthy of being taken for a model. The former state of the City was examined and surveyed exactly, thus forming a basis for the outlines of the London of the future. It was admitted that the streets had been too narrow. But the committee did not fall into temptation of demanding the same great widths for all the streets. This is worth noticing. Wide streets were desirable not only for practical reasons after the development of coaches, they also corresponded with the aesthetic ideals of the period. Many town-plans from the sixteenth and the seventeenth centuries show all streets of the same width. There is a temptation to do so for apparently it costs no money and it leaves every possibility open. In reality it is just as bad to have too much street area as too little. All money spent on extravagant streets must be recovered through a more extensive utilization of the buildings; and that means an increase of the average height of the houses and an unnecessary crowding together of the people.

Already at its third meeting the Committee decided that they would have to reckon with a whole series of different

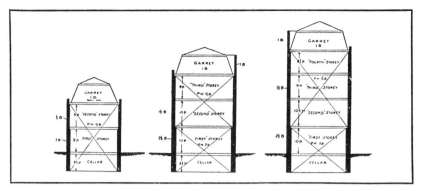

Types of houses of the size allowed after the Great Fire 1666, in side streets and alleys, in more important streets and main streets respectively

types of streets whose width would vary from 16 to 100 feet. During the autumn Parliament worked at high pressure to complete the building laws for the City. They were passed on February 8th, 1667. When one bears in mind that they were passed while the City was still in a state of panic, it is almost inconceivable that they should be as just and right as they are — seen from a modern point of view. They allow for the various types of streets and the corresponding types of houses such as are shown in the diagram (drawn by Mr. W. R. Davidge). It was only permitted to build comparatively low houses in the narrow streets which had no through traffic, and where the light was scarce, while taller buildings might be erected in the broader streets. Much can be learnt from the way in which the project was intended to be carried out. As was promised in the King's proclamation, the rights of the owners before the Fire were to be respected and no one wished to make any alteration in them. It was, however, evident that some changes must take place and that it must be possible for the City to buy ground which, on account of its situation, formed an obstacle in the way of a favourable project. Where this was the case, an impartial jury was appointed to judge its value and the town had to pay the private owner. At the same time it became evident that the plan was to the advantage of many of the landlords, and consequently they had to pay to the community which had occasioned the rise in values. Here we have an instance of how highly developed the English social system already was

Staple Inn, High Holborn (September 1930). Typical house
before the Fire

in those days: that among other things the solution of such
delicate questions concerning private property was attained,
without having recourse to absolute methods, by putting into
practice the institution of the jury.

There is one provision in the law of the rebuilding of
London which deserves special attention. It says here that if
the owner has not built a house on his site within three years
after the Fire, it would become the property of the town,
which must pay full compensation according to the valuation
made, and has then the right to sell it to others who do wish
to build. Behind this lies the idea that land can never be
considered as entirely private property. By right the land

Dr. Samuel Johnson's House, Gough Square. Typical house
from after the Fire

belongs to the community and a private individual may
acquire the use of it, but if it lies without being made any use
of, then he loses his right to it and must make it over to others.
On the other hand, he who has been able to make his land
productive, acquires a special right over it of which he cannot well be deprived. (It was therefore impossible, according
to the English way of thinking, to carry out a plan like
Wren's, according to which all citizens who had suffered
from the Fire must give up their private property to be joined
together in a large piece of public property, such as had
actually been brought before Parliament during the debate
on the building-law by Colonel Birch.) It corresponds quite

well to those conditions whit which we have become acquainted, concerning the right of the people to use open spaces for games, even if they were private property. That also is productive employment of land and when it once has become an established right it can no more be taken away than the right to build a house on the land.

In the ensuing years London was rebuilt as a city of bricks and stone instead of perishable timber as in former times. New streets were laid out and the old ones widened and a broad new road with a quay was built along the Thames. Even if the rebuilding was not accomplished in the three years with which the Law reckons, still London appeared now as a wealthy and powerful city, capable of rising again after the terrible catastrophe in a new and better form.

CHAPTER SIX

BOOKS OF REFERENCE

The Great Fire 1666 and the rebuilding of London is fully described in *Walter George Bell: The Great Fire of London 1666.* London 1920. The plans of Wren, Evelyn and Hooke and their story are discussed by *Sydney Perks* in an article, *London Town-Planning Schemes in 1666* in *Journal of R.I.B.A.*, December 20th, 1919, p. 69 ff. The best historical account of the rebuilding of London is given by *T. F. Reddaway* in his *The Rebuilding of London after the Great Fire.* Cape, 1940.

Wren's original plan is in All Soul's College, Oxford. In *Parentalia* (1750) is a description of the plan but as mentioned above it is unknown whether it is authentic or not. Wren's plan is — somewhat altered — shown in *John Gwynn: London and Westminster Improved, 1760.* Wren's plan and three of Evelyn's plans are published in *Vestusta Monumenta*, II. 1789 (Society of Antiquarians of London). John Evelyn's description to his plan is published in *John Evelyn: London Revived*, edited by E. S. de Beer. Oxford, 1938. The reproduced plan ascribed to Hooke is seen on *A View of the Fire* by Doornick. Concerning the Committee for the rebuilding of London see *The Architecture of Sir Roger Pratt*, Oxford, 1928, p. 12 ff. About Colonel Birch's plan see Pepys's *Diary*, February 24th, 1667.

INTERCOMMUNICATION IN LONDON

LONDON ALWAYS KNEW HOW TO USE NEW MEANS OF TRANSPORT. It has become an absolute necessity because of the enormous area over which the city spreads. The great distances aroused a keen interest in all possibilities for the improvement of the traffic and fewer stumbling blocks were put in the way than in other cities. Improved carriage of passengers led to the town spreading still more, and the greater distances ensuing demanded still greater facilities. On reading Pepys's famous *Diary* (1660-1666) one gets a lively impression how widely spread London was as early as the seventeenth century, and with what ease the citizens covered the distances. Pepys often went far, to Hampton Court to the west and Greenwich to the east, without a word of complaint about the inconvenience of it or the time spent in continual riding, driving and rowing. It was not only when on business that he undertook such long journeys, but frequently merely for pleasure. After a busy day, beginning with his office work at five in the morning, he thought nothing of going at night to Vauxhall Gardens with his wife and other ladies.

The story that Shakespeare's first work at a theatre was that of a stable-boy, gives one an insight into the life of Elizabethan London. It is true that students of Shakespeare doubt the veracity of the legend, that is to say they do not doubt that there *was* a boy at the theatre to look after the spectators' horses during the performance, but the question is, was it he who became the great poet? Distances were far too great then to be covered on foot, so one rode to the theatre — which at that time was for men. For longer journeys, the so-called Long Wagon was used, an elongated vehicle with broad wheels suited to the rough roads. It was drawn by six or eight horses or more, and could carry up to twenty passengers. There was a regular service between London and Canterbury, Norwich, Ipswich, Gloucester, and other towns. Most travellers, however, rode on horseback. The Long Wagon was used for the transport of goods and of those who either could not or would not ride.

Private coaches were introduced in the middle of the sixteenth century. It was considered a great event when Queen Mary, in 1553, at her coronation, rode in a chariot drawn by six horses, and followed by another containing the Lady Elizabeth (later Queen Elizabeth) and Lady Anne of Cleves. In 1565 a Dutchman presented Queen Elizabeth with a 'coach' which was supposed to be a very great improvement on the chariot used at the coronation of Queen Mary. It was greatly admired, but nevertheless it must have been anything but agreeable to drive in a coach without springs. The story runs, that Queen Elizabeth in 1568, while conversing with the French ambassador, told him 'the aching pains' she was suffering in consequence of having been 'knocked about' in her coach a few days previously, when it was driven too quickly through the streets. — It was greatly to the advantage of the new means of transport that the Queen continued to make use of it, in spite of her sufferings. In this way it became the fashion to drive in a coach, and it soon became general among the upper classes. As early as 1598 Stow wrote about the terrible number of coaches which were unknown in the old days, now 'the world runs on wheels', an expression which rapidly became popular in describing the enervating restlessness of the time. Coaches met with serious opposition from the more conservative citizens in general and from the Thames watermen in particular. The Thames was the silent highway connecting the various townships, the whole of the widespread colony of London. A lawyer going from the Temple to Westminster went by boat instead of driving or riding along the rough and muddy roads of the Strand and Charing Cross. All the great processions went by water. At the annual Lord Mayor's Show, the Lord Mayor of London was rowed in his richly decorated water barge from the City to Westminster, where he was received by the King. One gets an impression of the importance of the river traffic on hearing that in 1613 the number of the watermen and their families amounted to 40,000, in a city whose entire population hardly exceeded

200,000. By means of propaganda, they made war on all other methods of transport, by wagon or by coach, but it was of no use. In 1601 they succeeded in getting a Bill passed in the House of Commons *'to restrain the excessive and superfluous use of coaches'*. This was, however, stopped by the House of Lords and in 1614 the House of Commons refused to pass a similar measure.

In other Royal residences the number of coaches was on the increase, but in London private coaches for the members of the noble families did not suffice, as in Paris. In 1625 already hackney coaches made their first appearance. They of course met with still greater opposition than the private coaches had done, but the development was not to be checked. Again the watermen appeared on the scene and explained how much better it would be if people would go, for instance, to the theatre by boat. From 1634 it was permitted for hackney coaches to ply in the streets for hire. Then a public stand appeared in the Strand where there were four coaches with coachmen in livery.

The broad type of coach with wheels projecting far out on each side was, as a matter of fact, a great inconvenience in the narrow medieval streets. It is no wonder that a narrower vehicle which took up less room, the sedan-chair, was eagerly welcomed. When the Duke of Buckingham was first seen being carried about in a chair, loud and indignant protests were heard against permitting one's countrymen to be used as beasts of burden. But in 1634 the privilege was granted to a certain Sanders Duncombe to use, and to let, covered chairs in London and Westminster, in order, as was expressly stated, to prevent the unnecessary use of coaches. They came to play the same part in the traffic of London as the Baby Austin motor-car does in our days. The sedan-chair had not merely the advantage of taking up less room than a coach, but it was much more comfortable in streets with uneven pavement. They were in use for a very long period. As late as 1821 sedan-chairs were still for hire in London and to this day the 'Porte chaise' may still be seen standing in some of the old homes, although only used as a porter's seat or a telephone box.

Horse traffic had to encounter great difficulties for a long time. It was naturally an encouragement that it was considered both costly and fashionable to drive, but at the same time it occasioned a certain amount of ill-will. It was considered 'a mere engine of pride' — as the great champion of the watermen, the Water-Poet, John Taylor, wrote, the streets and lanes were by no means fit for driving in, and the more one drove on them, the worse they grew. Anyone could see that. So the best thing to do was to restrict the evil, that is to say, the traffic, as much as possible. That the roads were there for the sake of the traffic was an idea which had never yet entered anyone's head! The system of laws which was evolved in order to protect the roads already in existence from destruction grew more and more complicated. Cunning brains invented vehicles which rolled the road as they drove on them, and would thus benefit them instead of causing damage. A proposal was made in sober earnest that only these rollers might be employed, and even if the measure was not put into practice, it had so much influence on the legislation, that during several years a series of regulations were issued as to the equipment of the coaches, even to the very nails used. — In London an attempt was made to limit the number of coaches. According to a Royal Proclamation of 1635 no driving in hackney coaches was allowed unless the distance was three miles at least out of London. In 1637 the number of licensed coaches was fifty. But it is easy to see of how little effect the regulation was, as a new one was passed in 1652 according to which there must only be 200 coaches for hire in the streets. In 1654 the number was increased to 300. As they still continued to increase, attempts were made to check them in other ways. In 1660, the watermen persuaded Charles II to issue a proclamation that no coaches could be hired in the streets for the future. On the very day, however, in which the proclamation came into force, our meticulous friend, Samuel Pepys, notes down in his *Diary*: '*yet I got one* (hackney-coach) *to carry me home*'. They became organized like the watermen, and their organization was recognized, and now competition between them began in earnest. In 1694 there were 700 licensed coaches; in 1711, 800. In 1739 the population of London was 725,903, and there were 22,639 horses, 2484 persons who kept their own carriages, and besides that 1100 carriages for hire, 800 larger ones and 300 smaller. Driving coaches and horses soon became a passion with the wealthier classes. The nobility and gentry who loved hunting and were keenly interested in horses now began to take an interest in driving as well. An instance of this is Cromwell driving in the Ring in Hyde Park. Driving thus became the sport of those to whom expense was no object, and so coaches were continually improved and their speed increased. It lasted a very long time, however, before the laying-out of suitable roads was taken in hand. On longer journeys people usually drove with six horses, so that they ran no risk of sticking in the mud; but even then progress was slow. Prince George of Denmark, on a journey in England in 1702, took six hours to drive nine miles, that is to say a mile and a half an hour! In 1728 a widow who had put down in her will that she wished to be buried in Preston, adds characteristically *'if she should die at such time of the year as the roads thereto were passable'*.

In 1752 a man wrote in *The Gentleman's Magazine* that the roads were still *what God left them after the flood,* and he continues, *'Nothing piques me more than that a trumpery despotic government like France should have enchanting roads from the Capital to each remote part of use.* The difference between the French roads and the English was exceedingly great in the eighteenth century. The Absolute government of France, the mother-country of mercantilism, had made the most vigorous efforts to complete a system of roads which would serve the whole of the country. It was partly out of regard to military interests and partly to commercial. Troops could easily and speedily be transported to any part of the kingdom and His Majesty's couriers could carry messages just as quickly. The system of roads of Absolutism had, however, no real influence on the situation of the towns. They had merely to connect one point of strategical or commercial importance with another, in a direct line if possible, but neither the townspeople nor the farmers used them. (In Denmark it was even strictly forbidden for the farmers to drive on the Royal roads, only in the dark of night did they dare to steal on to the good main roads with their carts.) Arthur Young, describing his journey in 1787-89 says that in France it was practically only the noblemen and officials who used coaches. It was easy for them to get to their châteaux from the capital. But in the environs of Paris, outside the clearly defined boundaries of the city, there was very little traffic to be seen — except along the road to Versailles, where, according to Taine, there was an uninterrupted succession of coaches running in both directions in the morning and the evening.

It was quite different in England. The roads were bad, without any general plan, and very differently administered by the local authorities. In a poor parish there would hardly be any trace of a road, while in a wealthy neighbouring parish it would again appear. The roads in existence, however, were always in use. London had no clearly defined boundary. The population moved farther and farther out, and there was a constant stream of traffic from the surrounding ring of suburbs to the capital. The citizens had many kinds of vehicles at their disposal: hackney coaches and sedan-chairs, mail coaches running regularly on the longer routes and post-horses which could be hired and changed at fixed stations. Along the road there were inns and hostels, some of them large enough to accommodate two or three hundred guests with their horses and carriages. For those who wished to travel slowly and cheaply there was the 'long wagon' before-mentioned, which also carried freight. And those who were in haste could travel by the Flying Coaches, started as early as 1669, which connected London with Oxford and Cambridge. They covered the distance in a single day, which was quick. To begin with, the speed was considered excessive, and even scandalous; but very soon, however, Flying Coaches were put on other routes as well.

The old state of things, according to which each separate parish had to look after its own respective roads, could not be kept up in the long run. Another method had to be found to cope with the increasing traffic. It was manifestly right that those who made use of the roads ought to contribute to their maintenance, instead of the respective parishes which, as a rule, would have preferred to be rid of the through traffic. In 1663 a beginning was made and a law passed that travellers should pay a little toll when using a certain road which passed through a very thickly populated district. Later, there were turnpikes on many of the roads. Although it was in reality a means of easing the burdens of the country people, they were to begin with extremely indignant about this new-fangled arrangement. Popular agitators went about the country to stir up the farmers, telling them that the turn-pikes were part of a plan concocted by the government to deprive them of their freedom and reduce them to slavery. It led to open resistance which had to be suppressed by armed force. Not until the last half of the eighteenth century did the system become popular and turnpikes were then in general use. When one looks through the legislative work of Parliament at this time, one meets with hundreds of regula-tions regarding the roads. Between 1760 and 1809, 1514 laws were passed concerning the turnpike roads, many concerning the main roads in the immediate neighbourhood of London. The old system of Roman roads was improved and supple-mented with a number of new ones. But all this legislation shows no sign whatever of aiming at one settled purpose, like the roads of French Absolutism — or those of the Danish either. The construction and repair of the roads was carried out piecemeal here and there when there was need of it, but it led to many new roads being laid out near London and that encouraged the spreading of the town.

The construction of a new road which proved of the great-est importance to London was sanctioned in 1756. It was simply called the New Road, and ran in a long curved line north of the City. Old maps show that it was right out in the country when first laid out, far from all the buildings. It crossed fields and connected several villages. This was in very deed a road on a grand scale. The roadway itself was 40 feet wide and future houses were to lie another 50 feet away from it, so that the entire width would be 140 feet. This New Road is now an old one and is completely built in on all sides. But the foresight of their forefathers was greatly to the benefit of the Londoners of to-day, as it left them a broad open road in this part of the town. As the construction of the road, however, had been sanctioned by Parliament, it was necessary to find some motive proving the need of it. This is clearly set forth in the comments on the Act, 1756, which

'The New Road' (above) from John Rocque's map. Middle of the eighteenth century.

found out that as traffic increases, the passage through the
narrow streets of the town grows more and more difficult
and therefore an attempt should be made to divert some of
the traffic to the City by means of a roundabout road avoid-
ing the most thickly populated quarters. Attention is called
in the bill to the special difficulties of the time. The roads
were not only cut up by the many vehicles for the transport
of passengers, but the large herds of cattle which were
necessary for the daily food supply of the City were most
destructive. The New Road was to absorb these various
currents and take them straight through to the market-places.
It is characteristic of the state of things in England that an
enterprise of that kind had not only to be sanctioned by a
body of men elected by the people, but efforts were made on
all sides to prove the utility of the measure. In a contemporary
newspaper, *The Public Advertizer* of February 20th, 1756,
there is a lengthy article on the advantages of the New Road.

Now that the money for the upkeep of the roads had been
procured in a rational manner by means of the turnpike-
money, a more practical method of construction than that

which was hitherto known, became general. About 1800, several British engineers arrived at excellent results in this special sphere of activity. The best known of them was a Scot, McAdam (1756-1836). Like many of his contemporaries he considered the question of the roads to be of primary importance to the community. In 1814 he had travelled 30,000 miles. In his time Parliament began also to realize what an important matter it was, and in 1811 a Select Committee was appointed to look into it. McAdam sent in a lengthy and detailed report. It was so clear and so much to the point, that his ideas attracted general attention, and he was allowed to try the methods he proposed. In 1827 he was appointed Surveyor-General of Roads, and had a great number of the roads 'macadamized'.

Londoners were not slow to utilize the possibilities which the new system of roads offered. In quarters lying many miles distant from the centre of the City, there are interminable rows of houses from the end of the eighteenth century. They are typical London houses, not built for local tenants whose work lay in the small towns outside London, but for well-to-do citizens who wished to live outside the town and had no objection to going in and out every day. When Queen Victoria ascended the throne in 1837, London traffic resembled to a certain extent that of a modern city, though mechanically driven vehicles were still so rare that they were of little account. There were a number of mail-coaches keeping up the connection with the most distant parts of England with an average speed of about eight and a half miles an hour, and the fastest could do about ten. Among other public conveyances there were, besides the mail-coaches, a number of so-called stage-coaches, 600 of which were licensed to run between London and towns within 19 miles of it. There were fixed routes starting from 123 stations in London and these coaches could carry 68,000 passengers in and out of town daily. At that time, the population of the City proper was only 123,000 in all. A contemporary author writes: 'The enormous traffic between London and the suburbs within a twelve miles radius of St. Paul's is interesting to watch.' That was still considered the compass of London before steam traffic and the motor-cars came into use. Many who could not afford the daily sum of two shillings which it cost to drive that distance settled far outside all the same. When the weather was fine they walked in and out and only went by coach when it rained.

Contrary to the prevailing conditions in other countries, the traffic in and out of London was allowed to develop quite independently of all municipal boundaries. The City proper was such restricted territory that the idea of hindering people from moving away from it was out of the question. The wealthy merchants who governed the City had moved away from it long ago to the more open quarters, and as the expansion of the town was not due to incorporation but to the building of one little independent township after the other, there was no question of preventing removal from one part to another, as in other countries, on account of the technicalities of taxation.

If the London of the eighteenth century had had to do without a clearly defined system of roads, as existing in France and other absolute monarchies, then on the other hand, in the nineteenth century, the town enjoyed to the full the benefit of the problems of traffic having been left to private initiative. The private enterprises of the London traffic proved far easier to handle and were much quicker in profiting from the advantages of technical progress than the official enterprises of the State and the municipalities usually were. In the nineteenth century it was particularly the means of collective transport which made progress: the railroads, underground railways and the omnibuses and tramways. A first attempt was made with an omnibus introduced by the coach-builder Shillibeer. He had been living in Paris engaged in the work of building omnibuses, and it occurred to him how useful they would be in his widely-spread native town. In 1829 he settled in London, and started with a single omnibus, which ran from Paddington Green to the Bank of England, for the transport of the tradesmen who lived in the new quarters and went into the City every day. This first bus, which carried eighteen passengers, was followed shortly by others and numerous omnibus routes were opened. To begin with, attempts were made to render them more attractive by providing books and papers — a praiseworthy custom which was, however, abandoned as soon as the omnibus had become a popular feature. Already in the 'fifties a large number of 'buses were in use. In 1856, the London General Omnibus Company was started; it bought up 600 of the omnibuses already running and had to pay £250,000 to the owners for the right of letting them run on the routes already established. This co-operation occasioned forthwith the introduction of cheaper rates and a much more efficient service.

In the meantime, however, a new means of transport had made its appearance, and was of immediate benefit to the long-distance traffic of London — the railway. The first line, begun in 1834, ran from London to Greenwich, four miles to the east of the City. It was opened in 1836. To begin with it was regarded as a great attraction for tourists, and there were orchestras playing at the stations and provision of other forms of entertainment. In the first year, half a million passengers travelled by it.

On the Continent the development was quite different. On the first appearance of the railway attempts were made in Paris to keep it outside the boundaries of the town. No one thought of it then as connection between the suburbs and the heart of the City. The new railroads were merely intended to connect one big town with another, in the same way as the main roads of Absolutism. The military authorities feared the railways which ran right into the heart of a city, and no one had any desire to provide the citizens with an easy means of access to zones where they could escape from taxation.

In England the new means of transport met at first with as obstinate a resistance as all the others. Both the canal-owners, who competed with the railways, and the landowners whose ground they ran through, were certain to oppose them. Towards the middle of the century, however, ill-will was transformed into a complete mania for railways, and the most incredible projects were formed. In 1849 Parliament had sanctioned the construction of 1071 railroads. In 1845, 19 were projected in London itself!

In 1854 the building of the first underground railway was sanctioned. It was 21 miles in length and ran for the whole

London: Area built over 1840

of its length under the above-mentioned New Road, which was now entirely lined by houses. Like all the other English railroads, it was built by a private company, the Metropolitan Railway Company. But as the City expected that the streets would be relieved of a great deal of traffic by this means, it put a lot of money into it. The Underground was a great success, and the result was that Parliament in the ensuing years was beset with projects for underground railways — so many, it is said, that if they had all been carried out, half the town would have had to be demolished.

Just at this time it was literally true that half of a large city was being pulled down on account of the traffic — the city of Paris. In 1862 the town consisted of 66,578 houses, and when the construction of the boulevards planned by

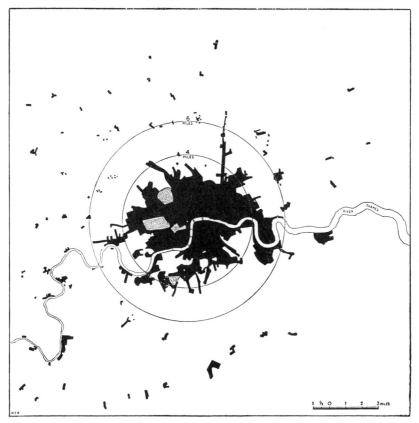

London: Area built over 1860

Napoleon III and Haussmann was carried out 27,000 of them were demolished. The object of this, however, was not, as in London, to give access to the suburbs from the middle of the town by means of the underground railways, but only to facilitate circulation within the boundaries of the city. The railways were kept outside the town and the lines coming from the other towns were connected into a circle which hindered rather than it furthered the extension of the town. In London, too, the expediency of allowing the railways to cut into the heart of the City in order to reach the terminus appeared very doubtful. In 1846 already a Royal Commission determined that all railways within a certain radius were to be underground. The first stretch of underground railway was soon continued to the east and to the west and

135

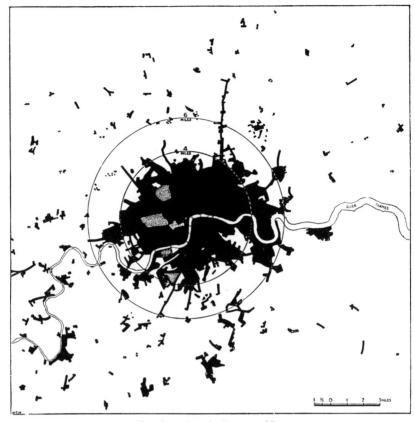

London: Area built over 1880

carried on until the circle was complete, in 1884. It did not however, as in Paris, form a ring encircling the City as the walls had done formerly and the boulevards later. In London it should rather be compared to an ellipse with one focus in the City and the other far out to the west, as it was carried on round Hyde Park. It penetrated the planetary system of the City like the orbit of a comet. It connected the railway stations and at the same time as it radiated in various directions, it was also a circular railway. It had long ago sent out small spurs. The first, to Earl's Court and West Brompton, was built as early as 1869. It was, however, only in the very thickly populated districts that the railway ran through tunnels. As soon as it reached the more open spaces, it was carried on, at much cheaper cost, between embankments.

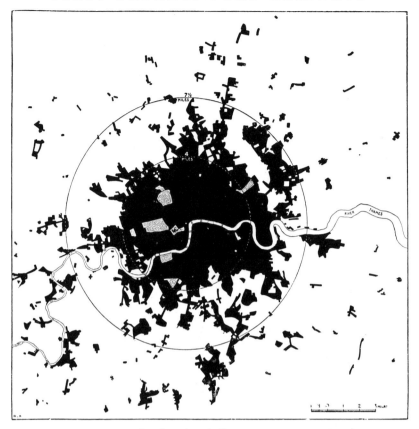

London: Area built over 1900

It extended farther and farther to the west. In 1874 it reached Hammersmith and in 1877 Richmond, far out in the country, about nine miles from the City as the crow flies.

As an important link of the building policy of the government, which always encouraged the spreading of the residential quarters, measures were taken to ensure cheap rates for the working classes using the railway. In 1861 a beginning was made by an Act according to which the North London Railway and the Metropolitan Railway pledged themselves to run two workmen's trains a day in each direction, and the price of the tickets was not to exceed a penny a mile. In 1864 the Cheap Trains Act was passed by which the Board of Trade can enjoin any railway to provide cheap and sufficient trains for workmen. At first they ran before seven in the

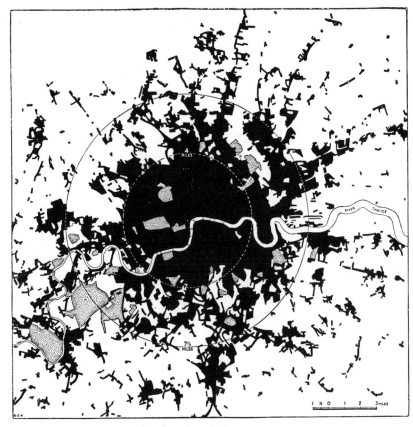

London: Area built over 1914

morning, but since 1900, there are several which run at eight.
The price was and usually is a halfpenny a mile.

Other methods of transport had made their appearance.
In the 'sixties tramway cars had gradually begun to be seen
in the streets — drawn, of course, by horses — but they were
of no real consequence until after 1870. They never developed
as freely as the railways had done. They encountered at the
beginning considerable opposition. The municipal authorities would not build tramways themselves, but neither would
they allow others to do so. They were afraid of granting to
private capitalists a monopoly of anything which had become
a vital necessity to the City. (A somewhat similar thing had
happened to the railways. Attempts had even been made to
run parallel lines so that they could compete together.) By an

138

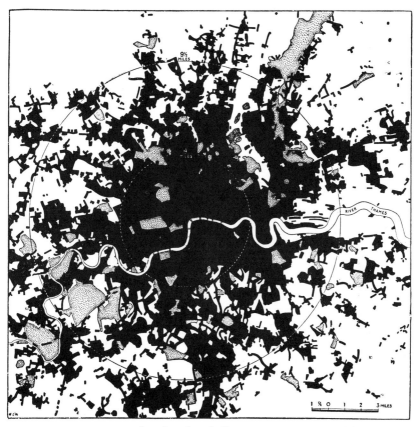

London: Area built over 1929

Act of 1870 extensive rights were granted to the local authorities concerning the burdens they might lay on the Tramway Companies which desired permission to use the streets. It was called 'An Act to Facilitate the Construction and to Regulate the Working of Tramways', although, as has since been asserted, it should rather have been called 'An Act to discourage the Construction of Tramways'. If a private company were to construct a line it had first to obtain the sanction of the local authorities in each of the areas through which it had to pass, and each one of these had the right to veto it. (A dispensation could, however, be obtained if two-thirds of a line were already sanctioned.) If a concession were granted, it was only valid for 21 years. At the end of that period, the town had the right to buy the entire plant and all

139

the stock at the appraised value, regardless of the revenues of the company at the time. The result of this arrangement was that the company had to earn as much as possible in the 21 years allotted to them and they troubled about nothing else. As the end of the time approached, they refused to spend a farthing on repairs and employed shaky and dilapidated cars with the paint worn off and drawn by wretched old horses. For at any moment the company was liable to have to sell all as scrap-iron. Foreigners visiting London could not conceive why the tramways were so far behind those of other cities. It gradually became more and more difficult for the private companies to run the tramways. If a company applied to some loca authority for the assent to construct a tram-line, the answer would be that permission might perhaps be granted, but that something must be done in return for the favour. The local authorities obliged the companies to keep the streets in repair, to build public lavatories, or whatever else they might need. It was still more difficult at the beginning of the new century when electric power was introduced, and far more capital was needed, capital which was to yield interest and to provide a sinking fund within 21 years. Strangely enough, there was no lack of private enterprise but the terms proposed were wellnigh unacceptable. In 1904, a company wished to construct a tramway line about 18 miles in length, through the western suburbs of London. In order to obtain the assent, it offered to spend about £200,000 on the streets and bridges. This did not prove sufficient, however, the authorities demanded also that the company, in order to obtain the assent, should spend another £600,000 on local enterprises. And then the plan was abandoned.

It is easy to see that under such conditions the tramways had to follow *after* development. No line could be constructed unless it were absolutely certain to pay. While the Underground and the omnibuses went ahead and opened up the way for new quarters, the tramways appeared later in districts already invaded by the builders.

In the twentieth century, now that the underground railways are being electrified, omnibuses have become motor-buses and the various companies have amalgamated so that the working is safer, cheaper and far more effective. The facilities of transport in London are improving and increasing enormously. But that is another chapter.

CHAPTER SEVEN

BOOKS OF REFERENCE

IN *Werner Hegermann's* book, *Der Städtebau II*, Berlin 1913, pp. 285-300, which has been referred to before, there is a brief but brilliant account of the history of London traffic with numerous important references to other books on the subject. Among the books on travel from the eighteenth century, *Daniel Defoe's A Tour through the Whole Island of Great Britain*, 1724, *Arthur Young: A Six Weeks' Tour through the Southern Counties*, 1769, and *A Six Months' Tour through the North of England*, 1770, by the same author, deserve mention. In chapter III of his *History of England, Macaulay* writes on English Traffic of the seventeenth century. For London traffic under Victoria, see *Laurence Gomme: London in the Reign of Victoria*, 1898. The history of traffic in England is treated at length in *E. A. Pratt's A History of Inland Transport*, 1912. *The Story of the King's Highway* is written by *Sidney and Beatrice Webb*, 1913. *Coach and Sedan, Pleasantly Disputing for Place and Precedence*, 1646, reprinted 1925, gives an amusing picture of the period.

THE ENGLISH LANDSCAPE GARDEN

THE ENGLISH LANDSCAPE GARDEN IS NOT CREATION OF ONE MAN.
English writers, from Horace Walpole to the present-
day authors of books on landscape architecture, have
pointed out the architect and painter *William Kent* (1685-
1748) as its originator. But as a matter of fact nature-gardens
had existed in England long before his time. Even in the
Middle Ages the country gentlemen were acquainted with
fenced-in areas of uncultivated land, not only as large
hunting grounds, but also as smaller enclosures, 'wilder-
nesses', in connection with the more formal gardens.

Sir Francis Bacon (1561-1626) in the beginning of the seventeenth century has given in an essay his ideas of a princely
garden of thirty acres. It is divided into three sections, one
of which is a great lawn surrounded by avenues of trees,
another the garden proper with flowers and fountains and
sculpture, and the third finally is 'heath' and 'desert' — that
is a piece of wild land. This essay shows *that the sixteenth
century already appreciated the aesthetic effect of the contrasts between
formal and landscape gardens.*

The nature-garden was still popular during the Stuart
period. The French garden was of course the fashion of the
time, and in front of the east block of Hampton Court
Charles II laid out a real spacious French garden with a long
straight canal and big avenues, all pointing at the same centre
and forming the popular *patte d'oie* pattern. Contemporary
engravings, especially those of the Dutch engraver *Kip*, show
us numerous other French gardens laid out by English
noblemen at their country houses. But side by side with the
formal garden the nature-garden lived on and the King's
favourite park was St. James's Park, which as we have seen —
with the exception of the canal and 'the Mall' — remained
untouched, perhaps by the advice of *Le Nôtre* himself,
because '*the natural simplicity of this Park, its rural, and in some
places wild character, had something more grand than he could impart*

Hampton Court: The canal opposite the east front of the palace

to it . . .' (See above, page 95). The King had the right instinct that the French garden was not in its place in England. As a matter of fact he could not afford such expensive gardens as Louis XIV, and Charles II, who was a very sensible man, preferred to live on good terms with his subjects and enjoy a free and merry life in and about St. James's Park under less ceremonious forms rather than to be king living in great style and risking to have to *'set out on his travels again'* as he jokingly said.

England soon turned away from the French garden, as can readily be understood. It could hardly be detached from Absolutism, and the English considered themselves the people that had broken the force of despotism. It seems more strange, that the gardening of Holland, the home of Protestantism and burgher life, should not have had a more lasting influence on English gardens. For a while there was an apparent approach to Holland. It can be traced back to the time of Charles II, although he was himself much more inclined to favour French civilization. It was for the greater part due to the clever diplomat and politician *Sir William Temple* (1628-1699). For several years he was England's

143

ambassador in Brussels and later in The Hague where he eagerly promoted the Triple Alliance between England, the Netherlands and Sweden. He was a personal friend of de Witt and the young Prince of Orange, and it was he who in 1677 brought about the marriage between this prince and Princess Mary, a marriage that in 1688 resulted in the Dutch stadtholder mounting the English throne. As in 1681 Temple acknowledged that he could not carry through his politics, he retired first to Sheen and then to Moor Park in Surrey, where he spent his time gardening and writing essays. Though a born Londoner he settled far from the town, as soon as he found a chance. This is typically English; Temple is only one of the innumerable men who during ages have sought the pursuits of country life, which in England were always considered more fashionable than those of the city. In order to acquire a social position for himself and his children the Englishman who has made his fortune must buy land and rise to the class of the landed proprietors. In France the absolute kings encouraged the nobility to leave their estates and join the court. A nobleman who did not appear often enough at the court of Louis XIV was disgraced. The King said coldly, that he did not know him. In England, on the contrary, the most absolute of English kings, Charles I, the somewhat older contemporary of Louis XIV, encouraged the nobility — in a Royal proclamation of 1632 — to remain on their estates and not waste their money on living in London. Like most well-intentioned Royal decrees it had but little effect and did not prevent the nobility from building palaces in the new suburbs of London. But it is nevertheless characteristic of the difference between French and English life. The English ideal is and has always been the life of the well-to-do *country gentleman*. They favour country life instead of that of the city. It is typical that the illustrated magazine for and about the English upper ten is called *Country Life*. For hundreds of years there has been a continual stream of rich people going from the offices and shops of the city to the green pastures of the country, that are the paradise of the sporting man. It has been possible to carry out the ideal of English country life as the country has been opened up more and more owing to the gradual moving of the centre of gravity of England's economy from agriculture to the industry and trade of the cities. Already at the time of Sir William Temple, town life was considered the dark side of existence, a centre for business life and industry, from which one tried to get away as soon as possible to realize the dream of country life. He who could not afford an estate contented himself with a less magnificent life — but just as free and unrestrained — in a *country house* surrounded by nature. Macaulay writes as follows about Temple's leisure: '*Temple had made a retreat for himself at a place called Moor Park, in the neighbourhood of Farnham. The country round his dwelling was almost a wilderness. His amusement during some years had been to create in the waste what those Dutch burgomasters, among whom he had passed some of the best years of his life, would have considered as a paradise. His hermitage had been occasionally honoured by the presence of the King, who had from a boy known and esteemed the author of the Triple Alliance, and who was well pleased to find, among the wilds of Surrey, a spot which seemed to be part of Holland, a straight canal, a terrace, rows of clipped trees, and rectangular beds of flowers and pot-herbs.*'

Here he found time to write his essays on politics and constitutional questions. In an essay *Upon the Garden of Epicurus* (1685) he joined the number of great Englishmen who have dealt with the art of gardening. In this essay he also wrote about the Chinese garden style, as he had heard about it from other people. It is especially interesting to read this essay so many years after, when everyone knows the influence the Chinese style was going to have on English landscape gardening. As a man of the world he will not deny that it may be all very well for the Chinese, but on the whole he objects to its lack of order. Temple, who loved plants, was well aware of the effect of contrast, that could be obtained by the grouping of different specimens, but he would hardly advise anybody to experiment with such gardens in England: they are '*Adventures of too hard Atchievement for any common Hands and tho there may be more Honour if they succeed well yet there is more Dishonour if they fail, and 'tis Twenty to One they will, whereas in regular figures it is hard to make any great and remarkable Faults*'.

During the reign of William III the popularity of the Dutch

'The Dutch Garden', Kensington Gardens (September 1931)

garden made great progress in England. In Kensington
Gardens there is a small enclosure surrounding a rectangular
pond, known as 'the sunk garden'. It pretends to be William's
own Garden, although Londoners will remember its construction about 1906. Dutch gardeners came to England but their
influence did not last long. England collaborated with Holland
for as long as it suited her politics, but there was never a really
fertile relation between the two forms of civilization. It soon
became evident that the Londoners were just as hostile to Dutch
influence as they had been to the French. The attitude of the
English people towards William of Orange is characteristic.
King William never became popular. This genius, whose
politics had made England a Great Power surpassing all Powers
of the Continent, was always considered by the English as rather
a spoil-sport. He never won their hearts. Charles II, who
readily betrayed his country to France, when he could enrich
himself by doing so, had been popular because he understood
how to disguise his intrigues with a cheerful carelessness and a
certain charming insolence. On the other hand, William was
a Dutchman; he did not speak their language too well: he
was dreadfully serious-minded and in his wit — for he could
be witty — he was cynical and un-English: and always liked
to make somebody into his butt. The robust Charles II at

146

least had been a 'sport' and could always be seen in St. James strolling among his people. William III, on the contrary, might be a hero, a warrior, but to the Londoners he remained merely the delicate prince who could not stand the foggy climate. His military progress did not impress them when they found he couldn't stand London and must reside at Kensington or Hampton Court. The fact that he had been *elected* by the English ought to have ensured the popularity of William of Orange. But it was not so. A hereditary king, monarch by the Grace of God, had much more prestige than an ordinary leader who had been elected by Parliament, and who could therefore be deposed without fearing the vengeance of God.

During the reign of William of Orange the English took rather a dislike to the Dutch burgher-civilization, and English poets and philosophers turned against it. They sought the classics again, sought Italy. An English gentleman generally once in his life made the grand tour through France to Rome. The gardens of the Italian Renaissance had always been greatly admired. They had already fallen into a state of decay, and growing wild, formed fine surroundings for villas built in a simple, classic style. After having seen them the English connoisseur considered the French garden too stiff and regular. All the set phrases about the affectation of the French garden-style had been invented already by the beginning of the eighteenth century. But they despised Dutch gardens more than ever. They despised the little enclosures where flowers were finically and neatly ordered in regular beds surrounded by yews and box and cut in hedges and figures like the playthings in a nursery — like chickens and pigeons, like balls and cones and spirals. In such an idyll, delicate William would have been able to bask in the sun without fearing London fog and wind. But the English wanted something else. They wanted to build up an unaffected landscape gardening. They never wearied of making fun of gardeners who clipped and trimmed bushes.

The movement started as a literary one. It is determined politically (as already mentioned) by a reaction against French and Dutch influences. But it has a no less outspoken philosophical note. The taste changed from the closed to the free and open. One of the originators of the movement was *Shaftesbury* (1671-1713), who as early as 1709 (in *The Moralists*) opposed the beauty of nature to '*formal mockery of princely gardens*'. Like William Temple he has written about the English Constitution. To him it was the foundation of the liberty of the individual. In England 'Constitution' and 'Liberty' were on the whole the favourite subjects of the time. The English people, long before any other people, had regarded itself as a nation, but now it considered itself a chosen people, carrier of a political idea. England had resisted tyranny, and shown that there was another state-craft beside that of despotism. It had been strong enough to take over the supremacy in world politics from France, the country of Absolutism. This manifested itself in many ways. One of the most important results for the capitalists of London was that England, the country of liberty, by the Treaty of Utrecht, wrung the monopoly of the slave-trade from despotic France. Now English merchants for at least thirty years could make millions on the slave-trade with America. To the spiritual world the political development was no less advantageous, most of all to English philosophy, to which Shaftesbury's pantheism and worship of nature belongs. By means of magazines the movement was spread by an en-lightened journalism to the upper circles. *Joseph Addison* (1672-1719), one of those who had admired the Italian gardens in their beautiful decay, wrote a few essays upon landscape gardening in his magazine the *Spectator*. He is especially critical as regards the Dutch garden and much in favour of a new and quite free form of landscape gardening. *Alexander Pope* (1688-1744) followed him in 1713 with an article in the *Guardian*, and he tried to carry out his ideals in a garden in Twickenham, where trees and bushes and plants grew pell mell just as they chose.

Such experiments as Pope's could not lead to any real *art* in gardening. When an English garden-style at length came into existence it was due to persons who had far more artistic ideas and who understood how to handle the means that already existed, especially in French art. Englishmen wanted to get away from the enclosed gardens of the Dutch. They wanted to create a grandiose open landscape based on the

Kensington Gardens, looking over Hyde Park (September 1931)

ancient sporting and open-air traditions of the nation. But this artistic aim is already latent in Le Nôtre's gardens. The genius of Le Nôtre combined the Italian garden — mounting up by terraces to a height from whence a fine view could be enjoyed — with the level garden of the Dutch, where the flat ground was widely laid out with canals and avenues continuing beyond the boundaries of the garden into flat, infinite country. He had understood also the new ideas in the art of painting, that which could be called the Dutch standpoint — namely the low horizon and the wide view. It was not a garden in the real sense of the word (for in English, as well as in many other languages, the word garden really means enclosure), for he opened up the view as far as the eye could reach. Seen from the palace the garden of Versailles is a *landscape*. From an artistic point of view it is of less importance that it is a *formal* landscape, that the trees are clipped and all lines keep straight. Formality in gardening was an old feature, what was new was the spacious, horizontal terraces and the grand vistas. It was an attempt to articulate an open space reaching to the horizon instead of dealing with small enclosures. The 'garden' of Versailles is a cultivated *park*

Kensington Gardens, view of Hyde park in the distance (September 1931)

with enormous distances, to be traversed on horseback or in coaches. The junction of many roads forming a circle — which later were used also in town-planning — originate from forestry. In this park the artist has always of course counted upon the contrast between the stiff, architectural forms and the organic growing of the plants. Behind the clipped hedges were seen shrubberies and detached trees. Even the geometrical forms were as a matter of fact alive: they were living plants. Where the scale was more modest than in Versailles it was necessary to open up the garden to the surrounding country in order to obtain the desired effect of width. The English gardener *Bridgeman* understood this, and when he laid out *Kensington Gardens* in 1730, he made a sunk fence or *ha-ha* between this park and Hyde Park — which might be considered as uncultivated land — so as to make the boundary invisible from Kensington Gardens; in this way the landscape-park enlarged the wide perspective of the architectural garden. *William Kent* (1685-1748) went a large step further: he brought the landscape garden right up to the building. But the landscape garden was not — as Pope had conceived it — a chance piece of land with scattered; trees it was a carefully *arranged* landscape. Kent was both a painter and an architect, a great admirer of Claude Lorrain. In his gardens he tried to create from living material, from trees and houses, what Claude had created with his brushes. But when all details are taken away from the *heroic landscape* only the purely architectural skeleton remains: it is a stage, plainly built up, with the depth of the vista marked from the wings, constructed as they are from a fixed plane. On the other hand the *architectural* French garden forms *landscapes* in the style of Claude when it is allowed to grow untrimmed. This is how we see the garden of Versailles to-day: the tops of its trees have grown a second time and have become as great and full as any painter of the eighteenth century could wish.

The English thought that they could find in antique culture the right foundation for a certain noble simplicity in which— as they conceived it — the civilization of the French court was lacking. English architecture was classic in a Palladian style in a period when that of other countries was baroque. The most pronounced classicists were the most ardent partisans of the nature-garden. It may seem strange, but in those days — and also at a later date — people saw no contradiction in the combination of classic buildings and nature-gardens. This combination was well known from the heroic landscape, and was known also from the numerous Roman *vedutas* — known, that is to say, from those very landscapes which show a garden architecture gone wild.

A true classical garden architecture was impossible, for no one knew what the gardens of antiquity were like. The bucolic poetry of antique literature gave certain romantic ideas of villas and temples in arcadian landscapes, where dark and sombre groves alternated with sunny, green lawns. But this was exactly the sort of landscape typical of England after the vast areas of former arable land in the sixteenth century had been converted into pastures. The spacious parks of the great landowners formed the most beautiful and most obvious example of landscape gardening. Had not English philosophers and essayists of the time pointed it out over and over again! The English ideal: that is to say the intimate life in nature of the individual with a passive receptivity of its beauty like that of the shepherd on the hill, was put forward as a contrast to that centralization of state and society implied in the ideas of Absolutism. The English garden never became a formal wood for riding or driving only, like the French park. It had always a more pastoral character. It was even intended for lonely and dreamy walks, and it is possible to trace in the English park, and what it stood for, that desire for an intimacy with nature which led at the end of the century to the Lake School of Poetry.

In this period solitary trees were characteristic of the English gardens. The evergreen trees and bushes, which had been the foundation of the architectural garden, disappeared. On account of their gloomy appearance Pope called them 'never green', and he — and many other writers — encouraged people to prefer the English flora which was lively and testified so unmistakably to the changeability of Nature. The *solitary* tree was cultivated, the tree was allowed to develop in freedom to its full and most harmonious form. But in practice it is artificially produced. Left to itself a solitary tree would sow itself and form a community of trees. These isolated trees were the remnants of cut groves, just as the scattered population of shepherds were the remnants of a former peasant population driven from their homesteads to the trades of the cities. Results of this kind symbolized for the philosophical essayists of those times nature pure and free. — Had not the shepherds *also* an aesthetic object? In the heroic landscape-painting both shepherds and trees helped to articulate the whole and render intelligible the perspective of the picture!

The landscape garden is by nature a changeable work of art subject to constant transformation, and yet some English parks remain to give us an idea of the great style of the eighteenth century. Prior Park near Bath is a good example. From the portico of the big Palladian main building there is a wide view over theatrical scenery in a valley. The trees stand as settings round the cup-shaped hollow. From a letter dated 1756 we know with certainty that they have been planted in order to produce exactly this effect. One solitary tree stands out from the others to make the distance more perceptible, and at the bottom of the valley is the mirror of a silent pool. The idea of the classical architects about the landscape garden have found an adequate expression in a book by *Isaac*

Prior Park, Bath. View from the main building on a summer evening (June 1927)

Ware: A Complete Body of Architecture (1756) in the chapter on gardens. '*The original idea of a garden*', he says, '*was much more on the principles of truth than the forms which followed*', for '*this first taste was the selecting a good piece of ground that had the varieties of hill and valley, sun and shade, if then the proprietor cut here and there a hedge to form or planted a few trees to terminate his vistas, he thought all was done that nature could effect, and that art could prompt for her improvement.*' This form of garden, which is represented as illustrations of nature gardens of the Middle Ages, was, says Ware, only enclosed fields, not gardens; and he continues: '*But here nature, though too much herself, was infinitely better than where every step savoured of art, and every tree bled from the sheers. We now despice these; and have between the two extremes of absolute wild nature and precise art, hit upon a very just method: we need only pursue the same principles, and we shall bring it to perfection. What we propose now in Gardens is to collect the beauties of nature; to separate them from those rude views in which her blemishes are seen, and to bring them nearer to the eye; to dispose them in the most pleasing order and create an universal harmony among them: that every thing may be free, and nothing savage; that the eye may be regaled with the collected beauties of the vegetable world, brought to-gether from the remotest regions, without that formality which was once understood to constitute the character of a garden: and that the farther views be open to the horizon. Thus the eye delights itself at its own choice with the charms of the particular object, or the vast assemblage of the whole: philosophick mind is detained upon the construction of a flower; while the free fancy of another turn is charmed with hill and lawn, and slope and precipice; and sees in one great view beyond the limits of the bounding walls, all those charms that can arise from wood and water, burnt heaths and waving forests.*

Our gardens are thus more regular than those of our ancestors; in effect more extensive; and throughout agreeable: everything pleasing is thrown open; everything disgustful is shut out, nor do we perceive the art, while we enjoy its effects: the sunk wall prevents your knowing where the garden terminates; and the very screen from unpleasing objects seems planted only for its natural beauty.'

The fancy for romantic arrangements increased gradually and was strongly furthered by another classicist: *William Chambers* (1726-1796). When a young man he visited China as a merchant, and when he afterwards took up the profession of an architect this knowledge of the Far East became very valuable to him, as *chinoiseries* were the fashion of the day. Among other works he published a book on Chinese gardens: *A Dissertation on Oriental Gardens*, 1772. In this book he lays down the most romantic ideas of gardening of those days, pretending that they were Chinese. He constantly points out that the book is merely descriptive, and says that we should not imitate everything that pleases the Chinese but try to make ourselves familiar with it and choose the best. The book, however, is rather to be considered as one of the fictive accounts of travels of the time using an oriental apparel to give the author opportunities to exhibit his own views in an entertaining way. Chambers had only been to Canton and had never seen the beautiful imperial gardens of Hangchow or Peking which seem to be the subjects of his description. On the other hand it must be admitted, that he has grasped the central idea in Chinese garden-architecture, and I am sure that it in fact has had a fructifying influence in England in the same way as Chinese furniture had.

Chambers's book is the climax of romanticism in garden-architecture. In his opinion the aim of the lay-out was to make it a dramatic adventure to walk in the garden. In the previous nature-garden everything had been arranged round an open space, but Chambers wanted to create a series of smaller vistas which gradually reveal themselves to the visitor. Each of them should have its own character and express a special spirit. He asserts that the Chinese have three different kinds of gardens: the pleasing, the horrible and the surprising gardens, and he gives a very realistic picture of the horrible gardens, where there are bats, owls and vultures, where wolves, tigers and jackals howl in the forests, while from the paths of the garden you see gibbets and wheels and other instruments of torture; where you pass monuments with pathetic inscriptions about tragic events and many acts of cruelties. The surprising gardens are no less strange: through dark caves with colossal figures of dragons and devils you arrive at a place where there is a sudden violent shower of artificial rain or explosions or small earthquakes. As a contrast to these exciting gardens there are idyllic scenes where you can sit on a bench and enjoy the beauty of lovely landscapes so much the more after the horrors from which you have suffered. Chambers's dramatic description altogether reminds one constantly of the romantic works of the following decennaries, for instance, Schikanader's and Mozart's 'Magic Flute' and of the nineteenth-century fairy-tales of Tieck. In other matters his book is very sensible; he says, for instance, that the Chinese '*in their crooked walks carefully avoid all sudden or unnatural windings, particularly the regular serpentine curves, of which our English Gardeners are so fond; observing, that these eternal, uniform, undulating lines, are of all things, the most unnatural, the most affected, and most tiresome to persue . . . if a river, the sea, a wide extended lake, or a terrace commanding rich prospects, present themselves, they hold it judicious to follow them in all their windings . . . but on a plain, either open, or formed into groves and thickets, where no impediments oblige, nor no curiosity invites to follow a winding path, they think it absurd, saying, that the road must either have been made by art, or be worn by the constant passage of travellers; in either of which cases, it cannot be supposed that men would go by a crooked line, where they could arrive by a straight one.*'

Chambers's book was unfavourably criticized and the most extreme ideas were ridiculed by contemporary writers, but the affectedly romantic garden style had nevertheless an enormous success — perhaps even more on the Continent than

Kew Gardens, London. The Pagoda, by William Chambers (August 1930)

in England. As an architect to the royal family he was entrusted with the construction of a number of small pavilions in *Kew Gardens*, each of them with its own character. Among his designs, published in 1763, are found buildings so different as a Chinese pagoda (which is still to be seen in Kew Gardens), a Turkish mosque, a Moorish Alhambra, a Temple of Solitude, a Gothic churchfront, a number of small bowers in the shape of

Kew Gardens, London. Temple, by William Chambers (August 1930)

Greek and Roman temples, an aviary and many others.

In England Chambers's romantic ideas had only a temporary influence, while the more grand and simple style — of which Kent was the representative — continued. The development, that had started as a pronounced reaction against French taste, resulted therefore in an English continuation of the grand style created by French painters and garden architects.

157

The lake in Regent's Park (August 1931)

It appeared that even if culture was driven out by force it would always return — and from England it once more spread over Europe. The philosophical and political ideas from which the creation of the landscape garden had sprung came

158

Regent's Park, looking towards Cumberland Terrace (August 1931)

to exercise an enormous influence over the intellectuals in France. What was natural and a matter of course in England, the Encyclopaedists and other apostles of enlightment on the Continent changed into maxims and theory. That 'Back to Nature' which the English philosophers had proclaimed about 1700 returned at the end of the century to England from the Continent with renewed strength. Rousseau had made an international fashion of the enthusiasm for country life, which now also reached the middle classes in England. When the courtiers and the wealthy merchants of London went to the fashionable town of Bath to take the waters, the less wealthy discovered that in the immediate neighbourhood of London there were many delightful places with wells situated in beautiful, rustic and primitive surroundings. People went to Greenwich, to Islington, to Hampstead and numerous other places, where 'Spas' sprung up with their inns and parks.

People felt a strong desire for natural parks and about the year 1800 the Crown satisfied it by laying out *Regent's Park*, a typical English park both in origin and in form. The numerous large grounds which since the days of Henry VIII had been used as royal hunting-grounds were still lying untouched near the town. Among these was the big Marylebone Estate north

Regent's Park. Airphoto looking north. Aerofilms Ltd.

of Westminster with an area of 543 acres. The Duke of Portland had leased it from the Crown. When the lease had
nearly expired at the end of the eighteenth century the City
had spread so near to the park, that it had to be considered if
in the future the ground should not be utilized in a more
profitable way. Already in 1793 the Treasury has offered a
prize for the best plan for developing Marylebone Fields.
Although the prize was considerable — £1000 — only three
schemes were received, all of them by the same person. After
this failure the Crown preferred to let its own architects make
projects and a plan by *John Nash* was accepted. He proposed
to leave the centre of the vast piece of ground as open country,
laying out about from two to three hundred acres as a park
with large lawns and solitary trees, to be surrounded by
groves and shrubberies and the whole park circumscribed by
a broad promenade for equestrians and carriages. Along the
outer side of the road there were to be sites for fashionable
houses in long monumental rows called *terraces*. There people
could enjoy town life and still feel as if they were in the country.

Hyde Park, London: Marble Arch Entrance. Aerofilms Ltd.

The rest of the land was used for quarters laid out round rectangular squares where markets might be held. On his first design Nash had indicated an enormous circular row of buildings in the middle of the park surrounded by a fine road. The road was laid out but instead of houses it is now surrounding a botanical garden.

It is worth noticing that the Crown might have used the whole area for building purposes. At the same time as Nash's plans were published another proposal parcelled out the whole of Marylebone Park into lots for small houses round squares and in allotments for cottages. This proposal of course would be much more profitable to the Crown. But George, Prince of Wales, the Regent, had to decide and his ideals were so English and so aristocratic that of course he preferred to create a new Hyde Park. It was named after him and called *Regent's Park*, but it became the people's park.

The virtues of the English garden become most obvious by

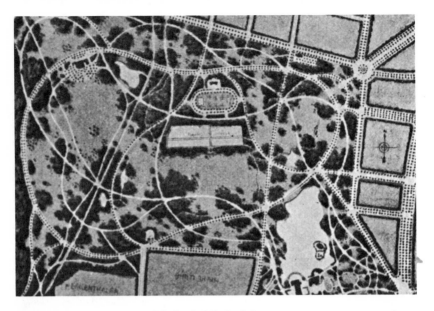

Lindenthal Park, Cologne

studying how the English garden style has been adopted on the Continent. Before it had developed to its definite form in England there had been a lot of formulas and designs trying to find an expression for the style of the 'free garden'. For some time the landscape architects thought that they might reach their aim in replacing all straight lines of the French garden with curved ones. More theoretical artists, like *William Hogarth* (1697-1764), have philosophized over the superiority of the serpentine line compared with any other: it presents to the spectator constant variety and new impressions. A garden style determined by undulating ground would in the design necessarily show a number of curved and irregular figures. But after the victory of Kent's landscape garden the English understood that the curved line was not the main point. We have seen how Chambers tried to ridicule it. But for the people on the Continent the curved line was to become the symbol of English landscape architecture. When they tried the impossible, to give formulas for the natural and unrestricted garden, the result would invariably be a plan formed of more or less elegant curves. While in England the undulating form of the ground and the plant material more and more became subjects of interest, the problem of the Continent developed into a mere question of pattern. In this caricature the English landscape garden was to conquer the world. In Denmark there is hardly any provincial town that has not got a park in what we call English style, that is a garden traversed by too broad, curved roads along oval lawns, here and there with shrubberies and trees and perhaps even a few flower-beds dotted about. All over the world such parks are to be found, everywhere representing the same hackneyed landscape idea. But it is as far apart as it can be from the idea of English landscape gardening, where it is not the gravel that counts but the lawn. The lawn is always the base of the large,

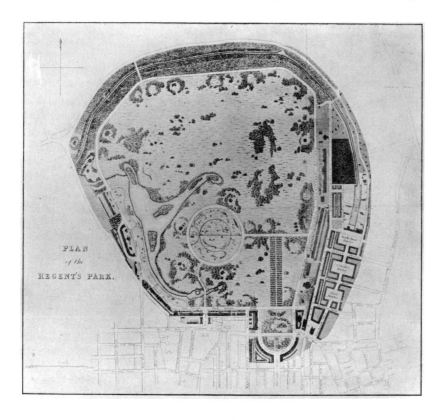

Plan of Regent's Park, 1826

beautiful space which is an English garden; roads and paths are secondary matters that are placed at the borders, if they are not artistically indifferent as narrow, straight lines through the green. The English garden is not *designed*, it is *planted* in the country, it *grows*.

CHAPTER EIGHT

BOOKS OF REFERENCE

THE author will recommend the following German books: *Marie Louise Gothein's Geschichte der Gartenkunst*, Jena 1914; and as the chief work on landscape gardens: *Franz Hallbaum's Der Landschaftsgarten*. *Hans Rose's Spätbarok, Studien zur Geschichte des Profanbaues in den Jahren 1660-1760* is also of importance. *Sir William Temple's* treatise *Upon the Gardens of Epicurus* is to be found in *Miscellanea*, published in a series of editions about 1700, the first in 1688. The above-mentioned articles by *Joseph Addison* are in *The Spectator*, Nos. 414 and 477. *Alexander Pope's* essay was published in *The Guardian*, September 1713, No. 178. Mention must also be made of *A Dissertation on Oriental Gardens*, 1772, by *William Chambers*, and *Plans, Elevations, Sections and Perspective Views of the Gardens and Buildings at Kew*, 1763, by the same author. The passage from *Isaac Ware* is to be found in *A Complete Body of Architecture*, London, 1756, p. 637.

LONDON SQUARES

THE XVIII CENTURY CREATED QUARTERS OF REFINED HOUSES. All the nobility and many other wealthy families left the narrow smoky town inside the walls and moved to the new open quarters nearer the parks and the country — and also nearer the Court, and at the same time more and more people from all parts of the country flocked to London. To all of them London was *the* town, the only town that counted. In the days of Charles II the population of London was more than seventeen times the population of Bristol or of Norwich, and London's population taken as percentage of the entire population of the country, has been constantly increasing from the Middle Ages to the present day. The increase was greatly noticeable in the seventeenth century. *John Evelyn* wrote in 1684, that the town had grown to twice its size since he was born. The prosperity of London was not due merely to the trade and industry of the town but increasingly to its position in social life: it was England's social centre.

When the magnates purchased houses near London it was not town-houses in narrow streets but country-houses with a series of different buildings and vast gardens. The arrival of each noble family increased the population not only by the family itself and its many servants with their relatives but also by merchants, artisans and others who lived on the aristocracy. Besides London, the town of producers, the capital of the world-trade and industry, there arose another London, the town of consumers, the town of the Court, of the nobility, of the retired capitalists. Where a little room was left between the big mansions the middle classes settled in groups of smaller houses which sprung up as best they could. But very soon the proprietors discovered the chance of using the areas for considerable housing enterprises which would provide suitable quarters for people of quality. In the long run the development of the town made it impossible to leave large areas as private gardens. On the other hand, when an earl or a duke *did* turn his property to account he wanted to determine what neighbours he got. The great landlord and the speculative builder found each other and together they created the London square with its character of unity surrounded as it is by dignified houses, all alike.

The first real square was *Covent Garden Piazza*. Covent Garden was formerly a convent garden, ecclesiastical ground, belonging to the Abbey of St. Peter. Henry VIII confiscated all estates belonging to the monasteries and in 1552 Covent Garden was given to John Russell, who had been of great service to the Tudors and therefore in 1550 was created first Earl of Bedford. Among other fashionable houses belonging to the nobility he built *Bedford House*. Almost a century later, about 1630, the surrounding quarters had so greatly developed, that Francis Russell, the fourth Earl of Bedford, decided to use part of his ground of seven acres for building purposes. *Inigo Jones* (1573-1651) was chosen to design the plan. He proposed to place the new houses round a large rectangular square, one side of which was to be dominated by a monumental church. About twenty years earlier the French king, Henri IV, had built the *Place Royale* in Paris, the present *Place des Vosges*. This was also a regular square surrounded by tall but narrow houses, all alike, and destined for the courtiers. The pavements were placed under arcades all round the open square, which was used for tournaments and pageants, as may be seen from an engraving of the festivities at the marriage of Louis XIII. It soon became popular with the nobility and was highly admired and much spoken of by *tout le monde*. The Earl of Bedford probably had the *Place Royale* in his mind when he decided to build *his* aristocratic square. But while the French model with its low and heavy arcades and the many pointed roofs of its narrow houses was still quite Gothic, the London square was built in the Classic style, Italian even in its name 'piazza'. When John Evelyn visited Leghorn in 1644 he wrote in his diary: '*The piazza is very fair and commodious, and, with the church whose four columns at the portico are of black marble polished, gave the first hint to the building both of the church and piazza in Covent Garden with us, though very perfectly pursued.*'

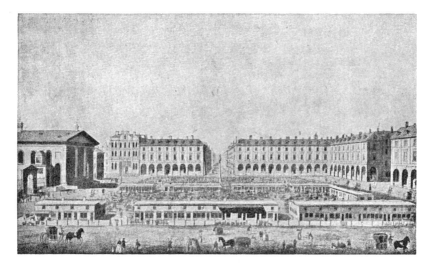

London: Covent Garden Piazza, 1751. Engraving by Thomas Bowles

The original scheme by Inigo Jones is to be found in Vitruvius Britannicus. The square was not completed, as the south side was never built, after all the Earl would not sacrifice his garden. Instead of arcades and Roman frontages there only came a garden wall. (See plan on page 168.)

Paris: Place des Vosges. Tournament in honour of the marriage of Louis XIII, 1615

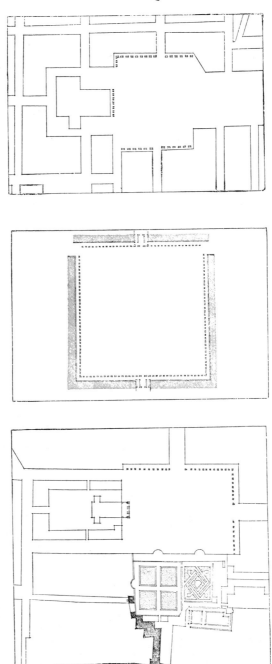

Church Square, Leghorn, Place des Vosges, Paris, and Covent Garden, London

London: Covent Garden Piazza Arcade, built 1878 by Henry Clutton following the lines of the original buildings (November 1928). Now demolished

Paris: Arcade of the Place des Vosges (August 1931)

Nicolas Poussin — The Rape of the Sabine Women, Louvre

The appearance of the square as it is to-day gives but little idea of what it looked like when newly built 300 years ago, but even that which is left is very striking. The effect of Inigo Jones's church is perhaps especially due to it being situated in London, the town that has so many large buildings, but so few that are truly great. It has been slightly altered (after a fire 1795) and the level has been raised about one yard so that the large portico — which at the beginning was attained by a flight of steps — now stands with its heavy columns right on the pavement. But this has only added to its force. — The English have not always known how to appreciate the great simplicity of this building. In order to excuse the famous Inigo Jones for having built a church so little decorated, the story goes, that the Earl of Bedford said to him, that he wanted a chapel for the parishioners of Covent Garden, but added he would not go to any considerable expense: in short, said he, 'I would not have it much better than a barn.' 'Well then,' replied Inigo Jones, 'you shall have the handsomest barn in England.' Yet it is much more probable that Inigo Jones was entirely at liberty to carry out his artistic ideas.

Inigo Jones — St. Paul's, Covent Garden: Portico facing the Square

Covent Garden Piazza is just the monumental square which a classically trained artist of those days would want to create. It is an antique forum governed by the large one-cell-building of a temple, akin to the one which the contemporary of Inigo Jones, the painter Nicolas Poussin, has shown in his picture of the rape of the Sabine women. The two artists have worked at the same problem, namely, to make the low central building dominating. But while it is obvious that Poussin has exerted himself in order to give his temple a broad and heavy effect, Inigo Jones has reached his end without exaggerating the proportions. He has followed the indications of architecture-theorists (Vitruvius) for 'a temple of Tuscan order of columns' and has given the building enormous eaves. But it cannot be said that this powerful architecture is based on literature rather than on experience.

The large portico with the swelling entasis of the antae and columns is not, however, the entrance to the church but simply, a shelter belonging to the square and not at all to the church. On an old engraved plan of Covent Garden there is a notice on the portico reading: 'Here the members for Westminster

St. Paul's, Covent Garden, in February sunshine, 1930

are elected', which seems to indicate that it really has been a sort of forum, a meeting-place for the people. The entrance to the church is at the other end of the building facing a small, quiet churchyard, surrounded by houses.

The print in Vitruvius Britannicus gives the impression that the buildings surrounding the square had only the depth of the arcades, but of course it has never been so. They were individual houses with varying depths and breadths hidden behind the homogeneous pilaster architecture of the frontage, which – just as was the case with the front of the church – rather belonged to the square than to the buildings it covered. This proved to be the right conception: the arcades became very popular, always full of people who were on their way to the

172

Dwelling houses in Covent Garden (February 1930). Now pulled down

coffee-houses of the neighbourhood or to the theatre situated in the north-east corner, or only walking to and fro discussing the topics of the day; the arcades were so popular that the foreign word *Piazza* soon became synonymous with the arcades instead of with the square.

It was fashionable to live in the stately houses. Even a hundred years later, when the place was already growing degraded, Covent Garden was inhabited by the highest society in London. Even so long ago the London papers published Fashionable News. One of them (*Morning Advertiser*, March 1st, 1730) reads as follows: '*The Lady Wortley Montagu, who has been greatly indisposed at her house in Covent Garden for some time, is now perfectly recovered, and takes the benefit of the air in Hyde Park every*

173

Front view of St. Paul's, Covent Garden (February 1930)

morning by advice of her physicians.' It is, however, strange that
the genteel occupants had not long ago left the place. The
Duke of Bedford (for now the Earl had been created Duke)
had certainly done nothing to encourage them to stay. From
Charles II, who was always in need of money, the Duke had

Side view of frontage of St. Paul's, Covent Garden (February 1930)

in 1671 obtained the right to have a daily vegetable-market in Covent Garden, which did not in any way embellish the noble square. Early in the morning people arrived from the country with their carts and baskets and the whole morning Inigo Jones's Roman piazza rang with street cries and screams and

175

it was overflowing with cabbage leaves and radishes. And if it was untidy in the morning, it was — in the seventeenth and eighteenth centuries — really dangerous to pass there at night. In this part of the town — between the City and Westminster — there was hardly any police up to the nineteenth century, and robberies and assaults were commonplace events. The middle of the square was filled with stalls and sheds which later — in the beginning of the nineteenth century — were transformed into permanent market halls. They are still there. The houses on the north side are altered and a whole story is added to the original buildings. The east side has been pulled down and the remaining houses look shabby and decayed. The fruit-market spreads all over the surrounding quarters where the streets are blocked up by carts arriving at midnight and remaining there till long after noon. — To a foreigner it seems remarkable that an institution of such importance to the public as a vegetable market still remains in private hands. It is strange that market rights according to Royal prerogatives dating back to the Middle Ages could be granted to a nobleman in the seventeenth century, but it is still more strange that this right is respected as a private one even to this day. In this century the Duke of Bedford sold Covent Garden and its market rights to a limited company, and it is still in private hands. In England there seems to be a general aversion against making any institution public which can by any means be run by a private enterprise.

Aerial view of Covent Garden showing morning traffic. Aerofilms Ltd.

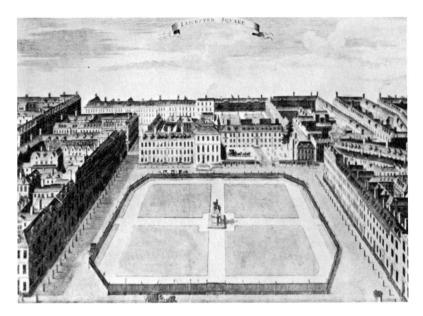

Leicester Square, *circa* 1754. Engraving by Sutton Nicholls

When Covent Garden Piazza became fashionable the London square was recognized as a suitable town residence for society and in the following hundred years many other squares were built, though none so fine as Covent Garden Piazza. Only four years later (1635) *Leicester Square* was laid out in front of Leicester House as a somewhat irregular square surrounded by houses of an individual type. In a similar way the Earl of Southampton succeeded in preserving the free situation of *his* residence at the same time as he utilized his estate by laying out a square in 1665, the present *Bloomsbury Square*. In a previous chapter we have already seen how the speculative builders — compelled to do so by the demand for the preservation of open spaces — had been obliged to lay out *Lincoln's Inn Fields* as a very large open square and *Red Lion Square* in its neighbourhood as a smaller one (1684). The Plague (1665) and the Great Fire (1666) greatly furthered building in the West End. Before the end of the century a number of squares had been laid out, *Soho Square* (1681), *Grosvenor Square* (1695) and *Berkeley Square* (1698). The most regular was *St. James's Square* (1684), which has always been

St. James's Square: looking east (November 1928)

a very fashionable place.[1] It is completely square and by a street corresponding to one of its axes it is connected with Christopher Wren's church, *St. James's, Piccadilly.* For some time it was embellished with a circular pond where the statue of William III now stands surrounded by trees.

[1] An old rhyme says:
> She shall have all that's fine and fair
> And the best of silk and satin shall wear;
> And ride in a coach to take the air,
> And have a house in St. James's Square.

178

In the course of the eighteenth century it became quite a fashion to build rows of houses all alike as joint building-enterprises, but until the end of the century we have no instance of a combination of houses in great architectural schemes. *Adelphi*, near the Thames, just between the City and Westminster, is one of the biggest and most extraordinary examples. The Greek name reminds us, to this day, of the gifted Adam brothers who built it. Three of them were architects and the fourth a banker. In 1768 they jointly leased a piece of land called *Durham Yard* from the Duke of St. Albans on a long lease of 99 years. It was situated south of *the Strand* and there were only small and dilapidated houses. It sloped down towards the Thames whose banks here were so untidy and malodorous that the neighbours repeatedly complained. This neglected property, which the brothers Adam had acquired at a very low price, was now to be transformed into one of the most fashionable quarters in London by means of a grand building enterprise. All the possibilities of the place were to be utilized. The banks were to be straightened and made secure by a quay in order to make a suitable landing-place. The adjoining sloping area was covered with large vaulted warehouse cellars facing the Thames with a row of huge gates. In this way a high brick terrace was created on which dwelling-houses were built, high above the dirt of the quay and with a splendid view over the river. They were united into a broad block of buildings like a palace front with a centre and two side-wings with pilasters. Here the occupants lived as if on a rock without being disturbed by the warehouse traffic below. The cellars ran 265 feet into the obscure underworld below the buildings and streets. In later years the banks were moved further south when the Thames Embankment was laid out and the warehouses have consequently no access to the quay any longer, but the strange subterranean warehouse-streets still exist. The air enters only through a few round apertures which hardly allow a suspicion of grey daylight to filter through. In the beginning the cellars were probably lighted by torches. Later there was a drowsy gas lantern at the angle of the subterranean streets.

The Adam brothers had hoped to get the government to hire the extensive vaults for an arsenal, but this plan failed

Vaulting under the Adelphi (August 1930). Demolished

completely. The quayline was a little too low, so that the river
entered the vaults at high water, and it proved very difficult
to let the costly cellars, these cellars which in their magnificence reminded us of old Roman works. For many years they
were hardly made use of, a shelter for the worst refuse of the
town. The architects also met with unexpected difficulties in
letting or selling the splendidly situated houses and the bold
enterprise threatened to ruin the brothers. But they were
saved: Parliament sanctioned a lottery and thereby they
found a way out of the crisis; the individual houses were set in
as prizes and there was a great run on the tickets.

This enterprise is very characteristic of England. It shows
us a grand speculation with enormous profit in view but also
enormous risk. It is quite different from speculations in real
property on the Continent, which are generally mere speculations in a rise of ground value. This is speculation in fictitious
values, attempts to profit from the varying valuation of the

Street under the Adelphi. A motor car by the third bay (1930). Demolished

ground, independent of its use. The English enterprise is an attempt to convey to a ground — which in itself is not worth much — new and real value through the buildings erected on it and then take the profit of what has been produced. It is a purely productive enterprise. In the case of the Adelphi the *commercial* idea is no less grand and full of imagination than is the *artistic* one. The scheme is a fantasia upon antique motifs: the enormous subterranean vaults, the terrace on to the river and the simple classical houses with their Pompeian decorated pilasters executed in terra-cotta — in 1757 Robert Adam had been in Spalato and in a very short time he had surveyed the ruins of the huge palace of Diocletian (his drawings were published in 1764). But Adelphi was not only a dream of antique architecture, it was just as much a finance-fantasia over risk and profit; the financier was an artist and the artist a financier. This creative speculation is something very English, and it is no less typical, that when it turns out a failure

The Adelphi: A peep down two flights of area steps

the enterprise is saved by a lottery—an appeal to people's gambling instinct — business adventure and excitement in another form. This spirit is typical of many of the big building enterprises in London during the eighteenth, nineteenth and twentieth centuries. It also renders possible the financing of the means of transit and thereby furthers the enormous decentralization of the town. There have always been people who were willing to finance large productive enterprises rather than bury their money in ground-speculation. That fact has given London its activity and rendered possible its free growth.

Robert Adam had since 1762 a secure and satisfactory position as Sole Architect to the King and the Board of Works, but in 1768 he gave it up in order to devote himself entirely

The Adelphi: John Street (August 1930)

to the Adelphi speculation, in which he and his brothers
risked everything they possessed and also were ready to bear
the blow when things went wrong. They had to sell their art-
collections and all they could spare. This, however, did not
spoil their reputation in society, they still belonged to the
upper classes. It is strange to see how the stratification of the
community is plainly shown in the construction of Adelphi
itself: the fine although plain houses for the upper classes
built on two dark basements containing kitchens and rooms
for servants and below these again large vaulted cellars, where
the poorest classes sought refuge. Bernard Shaw and H. G.
Wells lived for a while in Adelphi, and from this pile of human
dwellings, one class over the other, Wells may have got the

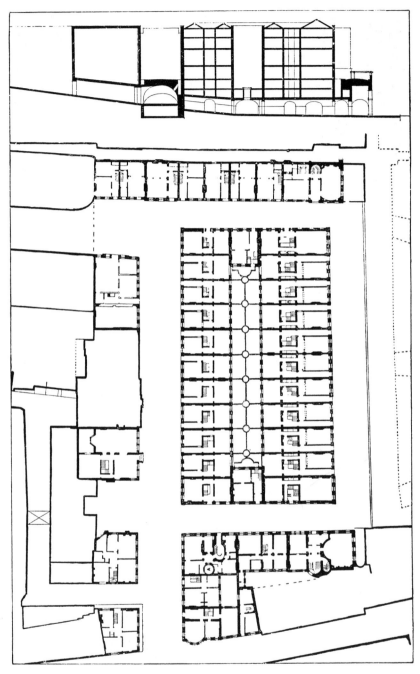

Adelphi: Ground floor plan. Above, Section showing the streets underground. 1 : 1000

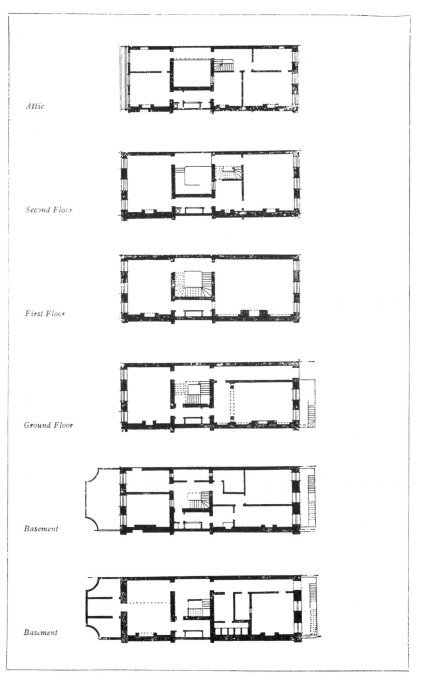

Attic

Second Floor

First Floor

Ground Floor

Basement

Basement

Plan of the six stories of a house in the Adelphi. 1 : 400

idea of a strange vision of the future, which he has described in a short story called *The Story of the Days to Come*. In this he gives a terrible picture of what the city of the future will be if capitalism and mechanization continue as they have begun. 'In the nineteenth century,' he says, 'the lower quarters were still beneath the sky; . . . In the twenty-second century, however, the growth of the city story above story, and the coalescence of buildings had led to a different arrangement. The prosperous people lived in a vast series of sumptuous hotels in the upper storys and halls of the city fabric; the industrial population dwelt beneath in the tremendous ground-floor and basement, so to speak, of the place.' He then describes how these toilers must always live in artificial light without any chance of enjoying nature. This is the apotheosis of the Continental metropolis, the English ideal is the Garden-City.

In the nineteenth century old Adelphi did not exactly suggest the idea of a Babylon in the manner of Wells, but at the time when it was built it was very imposing and was by contemporaries considered to represent the very idea

The Adelphi in its original form seen from the Thames

186

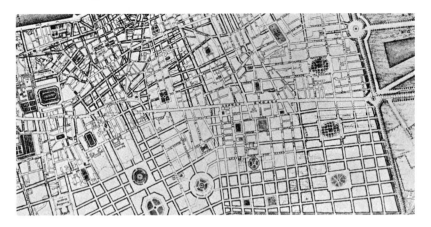

John Gwynn — Part of project for new quarters in London (1760)

of the great modern city. (The huge block of buildings, Somerset House, by William Chambers had not yet been built — it was not begun until 1776.) But in those days there were plenty of great schemes for the improvement and extension of London. Best known is a book by John Gwynn: *London and Westminster improved*. It sets forth a number of proposals for wide thoroughfares through existing quarters and the laying out of new quarters, propositions that the author would not live to see carried out. Many of them were, however, executed in the nineteenth century. The new quarters of the town are planned with regular buildings intermingled by open squares, octagons and circuses. Gwynn writes: 'It is essential for the architectural effect to secure a similar appearance of all buildings belonging to the same scheme', and he refers to the fine results obtained in *Bath*. In this city, much frequented for its hot mineral springs, two architects both called *John Wood*, father and son, had carried out considerable undertakings similar to the Adelphi of the Adam brothers. But instead of a 'quarter' they had built a whole town. *Bath* had been discovered by *the upper ten* in 1702, when Queen Anne went there on the advice of her physician. The first great building enterprise was Queen's Square. John Wood the elder got the land on long leasehold for 99 years (1727), built the houses and leased them for 98 years. From this rectangular square Gay Street (built between 1750 and

187

Bath: The Circus and Royal Crescent. Aerofilms Ltd.

1760) ascends to the *Circus* (1754). It has three regularly
placed entrances each pointing towards a concave frontage.
The ground is regulated to make the Circus lie like a horizontal hollow in the sloping ground. The unity of the architecture is perfect: the façades are embellished by three rows
of columns one above the other. It resembles the façade
of a Roman amphitheatre which has been turned outside
in and made concave instead of convex. From one of the
exits another street ascends to the *Royal Crescent* (commenced 1767), a huge concave row of houses which in the
plan forms a semi-ellipse and which opens towards the slope
with a wonderful view over the old town in the valley. The
elevation shows a simple colossal order of columns, Ionic
columns spanning over two stories and standing on the
rustic plinth of the ground floor. The visitor feels as though
he had come from the Colosseum to the Marcellus Theatre.

Bath: Royal Crescent. Aerofilms Ltd.

Other streets mount the hillsides with recurring semicircles of buildings, *Camden Crescent* and *Norfolk Crescent*, squeezed into the slope and facing the town beneath. Besides these monumental constructions there is a number of more modest building enterprises consisting of houses in classical style. This aristocratic architecture, making use of the site of Bath and of the local 'Bath stone', could not be transferred to London. In London the new ideas were carried out in a series of squares on the same level and instead of the elaborate, classical fronts of Bath-stone the London houses had to be built in bricks with less rich detail.

At the end of the eighteenth century the Duke of Bedford began to parcel out an estate of 112 acres of land north of Oxford Street and began by laying out twenty acres as gardens for the use of the lessees. The idea was to group the buildings

Photo of Bloomsbury taken from the air. Aerofilms Ltd.

round the greens which were spread over the whole of the area. In this way a series of squares were laid out — some of them quite square, some oblong, some semi-circular, but all with a central garden of grass and plane-trees. *Bedford Square* was one of the first built (between 1775 and 1780). The name of the designer of the lay-out is not known. The original designs are not in the possession of the Bedford Estate. It is not known whether the scheme was originally planned either by the owner (that is to say Bedford Estate) as a programme for those who wanted to build, or by an enterprising builder (as in the cases of Adelphi and Bath) after he had leased the area on long leasehold: but it is certain that the lots surrounding the square have been leased for building purposes and that all the houses are almost uniform. They are not absolutely alike (they differ especially with regard to the interior arrangement), but they resemble each other so much that it is probable that the Bedford Estate has either put forward or recognized a model for the frontages which all the lessees had to copy. Within these outlines houses could be built with varying accommodations suitable for different purchasers.

By following the history of one of these houses from about 1780 we apparently have a means of studying the development of London property during 150 years. It is of special interest to follow the increases in the ground values each time the lease expired. But the history of the different houses varies so much that it is impossible to draw general conclusions from the experiences with a single building. It is to a foreigner especially strange that there is no means of getting accurate information of ground value itself at different times. To begin with, each lot was leased for 99 years at a fixed annual sum. As to Bedford Square, it was — as far as I have been able to ascertain — £3. After the expiration of the first 99 years' lease the Bedford Estate became owner not only of the ground but also of the buildings which during this period had been erected on it. The whole property (ground plus building) was again leased for a certain time and a new annual rent was fixed. But it does not give us the slightest indication of what the new leaseholder had to pay for the ground and what he had to pay for the building, and strangely enough the office of the Bedford Estate, by which the rent was fixed, has not realized the value of the ground in itself. It has continually considered the property, that is to say *the ground plus the building* as an indivisible whole. Therefore the prices of the houses in Bedford Square varied considerably already at the time when the price for the second lease had been fixed. One building was richly decorated and in good repair, another was badly built and perhaps in disrepair — which is often the case in the last years before the expiration of a lease. After the first lease of 99 years the new leases were made for much shorter periods, generally from twenty to fifty years. In fixing the length of the period the following considerations were enforced: if a future lessee intended to undertake considerable and costly rebuildings or improvements of the building he would get a lease for a comparatively long period so that he might get the benefit of his expenses before the lease expired; otherwise the lease was a short one — yet generally not less than twenty years — so that the price might be raised at the first opportunity. After 150 years, therefore, these houses which are externally as like as peas will be of quite different value and the increase of the ground-value cannot be deducted from the rent which includes also the buildings. Some houses have been leased for twenty years, others for fifty, some are cheap, some are expensive, and the leases expire at different dates. The office of the Bedford Estate considers it one of its principal tasks to see that they never expire at the same time. If all the leases expired in the same year and it happened to be a year of depression only a low rent could be obtained which would then be binding for the following twenty years at least. In making the leases expire at different times the effect of good and bad years will be eliminated. Bedford Estate evidently carries on a very cautious policy without speculations in ground value and without reckoning with the possibility of new and bold enterprises. The fact that the leases expire at different times will on the contrary render impossible any plan for radical changes and prevent any sudden increase of the rent in a place like Bedford Square. That explains why it has remained for 150 years without any considerable changes taking place in spite of its being in the vicinity of some of the most important arterial roads of the town.

The big hotels have now taken possession of Southampton Row; the British Museum has filled up the whole of the block reserved for it; the London University is swallowing up more and more of the old houses, and this quarter — which the Duke of Bedford laid out for good domestic houses — has taken on quite a different character. But there is still so much left, that it is possible to get an impression of how people lived in old Bloomsbury. The green squares were quiet and calm, away from the traffic of the main streets. The approaches from the great arteries like Euston Road and Oxford Street were closed by gates, and people who had no business in Bloomsbury were not admitted to the quarter. The grocer could not even send his errand-boy across to Bedford Square, he had to bring the goods himself in order to get in. This lasted until 1893 when an Act of Parliament was passed enjoining that the gates should be abolished. Many houses had stables and coach-houses situated behind the row of houses; they were approached from a back street, 'the mews'.[1]

---

[1] *Mew*, originally a cage for hawks; as royal stables were often built on the site of the hawks' mews, the word *mews* has now got the sense of 'stables' arranged round open yards or back streets.

Bedford Square (September 1931). The flagged pavements are clearly seen with the circular covers over the apertures leading to the coal cellars, which stretch from the area in front of the house right under the street.

Bloomsbury: Cartwright Gardens (August 1931)

There are very strict rules for each square. If one of the leaseholders in Bedford Square should put a signboard on the railing round the area of his house it will not be long before a letter arrives from the Bedford Estate to tell him to remove it. It may be well designed — English signs often áre — but that is not the point. In the contract it is clearly stated that the leaseholder must not use the house for a shop or a restaurant and that he must not put up signs of any kind. It is strange to observe that while the leaseholders are very strongly bound by their contracts, the owners — in this case the Bedford

Bloomsbury: Bedford Place seen from Bloomsbury Square (August 1931)

Estate — have not assumed any obligations whatever to keep the square up to the same standard. They could — whenever they liked — lease any of the houses for some purpose which would not at all suit the refined aspect of the rest of the place. But it is taken for granted that this does not happen. The Bedford Estate would not for a possible small gain risk the value of the rest of the houses. There is something ideal and also something abstract in this. It may seem strange to foreigners that the Duke of Bedford, the Duke of Westminster and other great landowners own enormous estates and can do

195

Bedford Square (June 1927)

Torrington Square (June 1927)

The Temple: Pump Court (destroyed 1941)

whatever they like with them. But it is only in appearance that a single person deals as he likes with this trust (which is literally a 'trust', for in reality he holds it as a feoff from the Crown). The estates are administered by impersonal offices and the leaseholders hardly know whether they hold their leases from a duke or from the State itself.

The London square is very different from the grand continental squares of the Baroque period. The architecture of the Baroque square is generally united into a grand crescendo. It leads the vision of the spectator from one place to the other, the whole lay-out has a distinct tendency and an architectural climax, a monument or a monumental building. Each square is a subordinate element in a great composition. The English square or crescent, on the contrary, is a restricted whole as com-

Torrington Square (June 1927)

plete as the courtyard of a convent. They form fine geometrical figures in the town plan, they are regular and completely uniform on all sides, and a series of such squares may
be linked together in any order. The English solution is, however, a very clear expression of the English problem. A French
or a German Baroque square was intended to be a monument
for Absolutism and consequently must have a climax in some
monument or other, it had to lead the eye to some public
building, a castle, a church or whatever the monument might
be. The English square, on the contrary, was merely a place
where many people of the same class had their houses and it
was therefore perfectly in keeping that it should be like the
courtyard of a convent.

In walking through the courtyards of the *Temple* — which

originally were ecclesiastical buildings — and continuing through *Staple Inn*, through *Gray's Inn* to the beautiful squares round the site of the *Foundling Hospital*, through *Queen's Square* to the other squares in *Bloomsbury: Russell Square, Torrington Square, Bedford Square* and all the rest of them, one can tell that they belong to the town. It is as if the traditions of the Middle Ages had been handed down to the present day in the squares, these domestic quarters. But the narrow courts of the old town have been transformed into the open squares of the newer quarters.

These quarters are London's contribution to town-planning in the eighteenth century. In the beginning of the nineteenth century new quarters were laid out on the same lines, blocks of houses intermingled with squares with fine gardens and still preserving a distinct urban character. This form for laying out was continued until the Victorian romanticism led to the extinction of the old Georgian classicism and more villa-like buildings came into fashion.

But already in the eighteenth century in England it was possible to standardize a type for a house which would suit every family with a certain income. Uniform houses were just as natural as uniform costumes. The pronounced reserve of these simple houses and their likeness one to another corresponds with the reserve of English manners already in those days so strongly developed.

Green trees and grass were fitted into the urban surroundings with great ease. People liked to see something green for everybody had country tastes. But here, where circumstances demanded closer building, the villa ideals were given up and the vegetation was arranged in large units with the houses as a neutral frame. The trees in the squares of Bloomsbury are never pruned. The plane trees develop as freely as if they stood in the country. From the windows there is always a view of green foliage, a fine vision of the trees growing. By putting them all in the middle of the square, any shadow on the houses has been avoided. The gardens and the streets are distinctly separated just as everything-else in this quarter of the town is defined and accentuated.

On a summer day when the sun is shining you can walk for hours from one square to another under fresh green trees and see thousands of little circular spots cast by the sun on the green lawns. But in the dark season the old squares are no less attractive. In the afternoon, when lights begin to appear in the houses, when the tea is served — a rite so sacred to the English — when London is being swallowed up in the moisture and fog of the same yellowish colour as the tea, the London square appears to be at the bottom of the sea under branches whose indistinct outlines form a pattern like seaweed floating overhead.

CHAPTER NINE

BOOKS OF REFERENCE

FOR London Squares see *Beresford Chancellor's The History of the Squares of London*, 1907. For the Adelphi and Adam Brothers *J. Bolton: Architecture of Robert and James Adam*, 1922. On the occasion of the laying of the Foundation Stone of the new London University, June 16th, 1933, a beautifully printed little pamphlet on the Bloomsbury site was issued, with a series of maps of Bloomsbury which were hitherto unpublished, and an historical account by Miss E. Jeffries Davis. There is excellent and reliable information on London houses and squares in the volumes published by the London County Council, the *Survey of London* which describe them house by house.

DOMESTIC ARCHITECTURE

LONDON'S CONTRIBUTION TO ARCHITECTURE IS SIMPLICITY. In almost all periods English monumental architecture has been ordinary and conventional in character as compared with that of other countries, while English domestic architecture always had a stamp of its own.

While other countries have contributed more to the art of painting, sculpture, music, or monumental architecture, the English have cultivated everything connected with daily life: they have made it an art to live in the right way. Sport is the music of the Englishman; he has cultivated his clothes, his furniture; he has created a language which is modern and supple, an instrument equally suited for the lawyer, the orator, the journalist or the author. Also in architecture the Englishman understands best all that is most intimately connected with his daily life, that is to say his house. This is the impression we receive from the works of modern architects, whether it is a Norman Shaw towards the end of the nineteenth century or an Edwin Lutyens during the twentieth. Their great monumental works are dull compared with the fine country houses they have created. The same is the case with most English architects of the past. We admire even Sir Christopher Wren much more for his simple and dignified houses in the *Temple* than for his most striking academic monumental buildings. And yet there is no doubt that he was keenly interested in the great tasks he undertook. We know that he, when he was in Paris in 1665, eagerly studied everything concerning the building of palaces. He had the privilege of meeting *Bernini* who was in Paris just at that time, invited by the French king in order to make a design for Le Louvre (a plan which was never executed). Wren was allowed to have a look at it, but Bernini would not permit him to copy it, although Wren, as he himself describes it, 'would have given his skin for it'.

Wren had prepared himself as well as conditions permitted for becoming a great palace builder. He also succeeded in obtaining the confidence of the English kings. And yet it was not he but the architect of the Swedish king who (in the Royal palace in Stockholm) was to carry out the ideal of Bernini: the huge four-winged *palazzo*. England — governed by a parliament — had no use for royal castles, the grand symbols of Absolutism, and in spite of several attempts Wren was never to succeed in building a large royal residence. It is interesting to study the great schemes for a royal palace, to see how they arise and how they disappear, and to watch the interest in English architecture in the eighteenth century shifting from public monumental architecture to the building of private houses.

Wren's first great plan for a palace was intended for Winchester. Charles II, the 'Merry Monarch', who apparently lived so unconcernedly in London surrounded by his favourite dogs and his favourite mistresses, secretly entertained plans for building a palace, where a hereditary king could be more independent of Parliament — and of the wealthy bourgeoisie in London — than in Westminster. He, who was in such close connection with Louis XIV, knew quite well that the French king, after the insurrection of the Fronde, left Paris and enlarged Versailles (1668) in order to make it the seat of the Court and the Government. How convenient to do the same thing in England! And so it happened that the old problem of the Middle Ages: *the commercial town versus the royal town* was once more embodied in *London* and *Winchester*.

Winchester had dropped behind in the competition with London; it was but a small town that mostly lived on its great past represented by the cathedral and the old school. But even if it were not as rich as London it had still the idea, that it was a town especially connected with the Crown. From the choir of the cathedral, where the coffins of the old kings lie, emanated an imperceptible odour of the Royal frankincense which penetrated the whole city. Its inhabitants had been loyal to Charles I long after the shopkeepers' town of London had turned its back upon him and sided with the rebellious Parliament. Winchester had tried to resist the 'Ironsides', but had to retreat before numbers. It was therefore quite natural that Charles II in remembering the fate of his poor father and his own unhappy youth should want to move his residence to

Winchester. In 1682 a beginning was made and Christopher
Wren began to work out the plans for the new palace. It has
been called a *miniature* Versailles. The whole undertaking is
rather obscure, but from all that we know about the plans it is
evident that even this first commencement was anything but
diminutive. It is most clearly seen in comparing its size with
that of the palace of Versailles, which had also been smaller
in its early stages. Historians do not agree about the scope of
the Winchester plans. It is, however, quite clear that it would
have suited the King to leave London, where he had seen some
of his most faithful partisans lay down their lives, and move to
Winchester. It was situated near Southampton, then the
chief port for France. From Southampton the King got sub-
sidies from Louis XIV and also got advice how to rule England independent of Parliament. At any rate the erection of
the palace was carried on energetically and Wren did wonders
— until the death of Charles II in 1685 put an end to it. The
palace was never finished; part of the building materials were
used for the enlargement of Hampton Court, while the buildings already completed were transformed into barracks which
still exist as a huge block in the small town. It is a plain
building on the barren brick surfaces of which enormous
architectural details are laid in, grandiose stone columns
which Wren had designed for the palace of Charles II. After
the accession of James II the Winchester plans were consigned
to oblivion, and the King's resistance to Parliament was so un-
wise and obstinate that he soon had to leave the country (1688).
Any attempt to move the seat of the government after the
example of the French was henceforth impossible.

Wren also worked out plans for a palace for the successor of
James II, William III, but the result was only an addition —
however grand it might be — to the already existing Hampton
Court. It tells a great deal of the England of the eighteenth
century, that although Wren was always favoured by the
Monarch the only monumental building scheme which he
completed was a Hospital for Invalids, while on the Continent
there sprung up one great royal palace after another. *Greenwich Hospital* was originally a palace, but after the death of
Queen Mary her husband, William III, decided to finish it in
grand style as a naval hospital, a monument for the beloved

Winchester Palace from *Milner's History of Winchester*, 1798

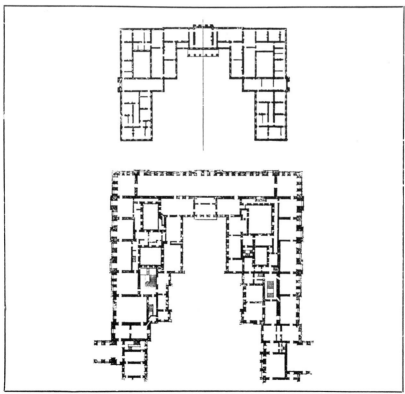

Proposed plan of Winchester Palace and the plan of the centre of the Palace of Versailles in the same scale

Queen. Regarded as a hospital it is an absolutely fantastic building, the very dream of an academic architect: enormous white stone buildings bordered with rows of gigantic columns. It reminds one of the Winchester scheme but represents a much more ripe and clarified style of achitecture. On Wren's old plans there had been some strange buildings with small pediments and columns not quite developed, at the narrowing of the buildings. On the more recent plan there are domes in the corresponding position which stand out, towering over the buildings, and surrounded by porticos on each side of the long perspective, which points towards the low, Palladian villa of Inigo Jones, called *The Queen's House*. The strange awkwardness of the Winchester scheme has been succeeded in Greenwich Hospital by irreproachable academic assurance. The vista from the Thames is marvellous. These rows of columns, the domes and the abundance of all sorts of classical details became to the English mind the ideal architecture of public buildings. Over and over again architects have repeated this magnificence — which leaves the spectator more and more indifferent each time it is repeated. But we need not walk far from this place to see how the English were able to create the fine house with the simplest means.

From Greenwich Hospital we can follow a road along the west side of the park until we reach the top of the hill at *Blackheath*. Here, so near each other that we can take them in at a glance, are three houses, which clearly illustrate three of the chief phases in the history of simple, English architecture of the eighteenth century. The first — the oldest of the three — is called *The Manor House*: in its present form it dates from about the year 1700. According to an unconfirmed tradition it was designed by Sir Christopher Wren himself. It is not at all unlikely. This great amateur in architecture — at the same time as he built Greenwich Hospital in what he considered Italian Renaissance — might have designed this neat little private house in a thoroughly Dutch style. But it may just as well have been designed by a Dutch architect. This cannot be determined now. Only one thing is sure: it has not the particular stamp of an *English* house, it might belong to any country where Dutch architects of the time were at work. The second house, on the contrary, is purely English. It is

The Manor House, Blackheath (February 1930). Badly damaged, 1941

called *The Yews* and dates from the end of the eighteenth century. It solves exactly the same problem as the first house; the simple five-bay fronts of the two brick houses might cover exactly the same plan; yet how different they are! The effect of the first one is gay with its varied colours, with the broad, white windows in the red wall, executed in two different sorts of bricks, and with the shadow of the white wooden cornice falling between carved brackets. The other one is bare and sharp

'The Yews', Blackheath (February 1930). Now demolished

in its puristic cubic form. The windows are merely rectangular holes cut into the brickwork, and the large roof, which on the first house — the Dutch one — projects as a shading cap over the front, has on the second house — the English one — entirely disappeared and only a horizontal covering remains, one single little thin square moulding. It is a house which seems to represent the most simple solution of the problem. But even if it has no decoration whatever it is all the same a building of a very refined taste; it bears a stamp which immediately shows the connoisseur that it is an English house from the end of the eighteenth century and not a child of the present day Modernism. The third house, *Clifton House*, from the beginning of the nineteenth century has — like the two others — a quite

'Clifton House', Blackheath (August 1930). Now demolished

simple front with five windows, but it is all the same in a richer style than *The Yews*. It is not so stripped. The brick-work is covered with plaster that is oil-painted, the windows have frames with a dainty relief, and the doorway is quite a little portico with Dorian columns. English architecture is again under the influence of foreign style and this has stamped the house, but it is not Dutch any longer, now it is considered to be Greek. It is the period of *The Greek Revival*. When we descend from Blackheath and enter the old streets of London, the buildings we see confirm our conception and the rough outline of London domestic architecture which we have traced in the three buildings is supplemented by many interesting details.

Kew Palace or 'The Dutch House', Kew Gardens (August 1930)

The gable-architecture of former days, which had been characteristic of the London of the Tudors, and which suited the narrow one-family-houses so well, disappeared during the reign of the Stuarts. It was simply prohibited to build half-timbered houses, and the pointed Gothic style went out of fashion. Now everything had to be solidly built and be classic in style, either Italian — as the architecture of Inigo Jones — or Dutch. This last style was very appropriate for London where brick was the local building-material. Palladian houses had to be either plastered or to be built of the expensive Portland stone, but the Dutch way of building could be transferred directly. To begin with the houses were built in a sort of Baroque style with all details executed in brick. The so-called *Kew Palace*, also called *The Dutch House* (1631), is a fine example of this style. Its columns with capitals, cornices and gables, its flowing lines and the elaborate mouldings are altogether — from plinth to gable — made of red brick, hewn and cut in all these beautifully modelled shapes. The effect of its texture is extraordinarily homogeneous. In *Cromwell's House*, Highgate, the brickwork is also admirably fine. But the portico is white like a foreign body inlaid in the plastic, red brick relief.

Kew Palace, or 'The Dutch House', Kew Gardens (August 1930)

The so-called Cromwell's House at Highgate (August 1930)

The so-called Cromwell's House at Highgate (August 1930)

At the end of the century the severe homogeneousness of material and colour was given up. Now, on the contrary, important features were emphasized by executing in special materials and special colours. Red houses had white mouldings and square, white corner-stones and white bracket-cornices; and in order to give the whole of it still more variety the light joinery of the windows was articulated in broad, elaborate casements, covering the counterweights of the sash-windows now in fashion. Typical for this period is a house in Lincoln's Inn Fields, No. 66 & 67. We know for certain that it has been built by a Dutchman. It corresponds obviously in style with The Manor House at Blackheath. The bold relief was still very popular but architects worked no longer — as they did in the old houses — with the whole surface as a plastic mass, but concentrated upon special decorative details. A favourite motive was the large, curved shell which is to be found over the entrance of The Manor House. Here it has apparently been difficult to manage all the different motives: the beautifully carved brackets, the projecting hood and the large shell. In other English houses the problems have been solved in a more elegant fashion by letting the cornice of the hood circumscribe the shell in a semicircle.

By the irony of fate this style — which is so obviously adopted from Holland — is in modern times considered to be the most English of all! It is called Queen Anne's style, and that is supposed to be the real old one. According to English law *ancient architecture* may be protected and preserved, and there are Royal commissions which examine it and write books about it. By Act of Parliament it is decided that all that is more recent than the death of Queen Anne (1714) should have no right to be called ancient. From this it might be concluded that the architecture of periods following the lamented death of her most sacred Majesty was *modern* — and that is not altogether wrong. Yet it must be added, that during a romantic period of the nineteenth century many houses have been built which could hardly be called modern in any sense of the word. So it happened that during the reign of *Queen Victoria* far more buildings in Queen Anne's style have been built than during the reign of *Queen Anne* herself. Her own government put an end to the Queen Anne style in London. Through building

Lincoln's Inn Fields: No. 66 & 67, 1754. Strype's edition of Stow

regulations of 1708 it was prohibited to place joinery nearer than four inches from the wall front, and as the wooden cornices were also prohibited the most important attributes of this style so highly appreciated by posterity were simply made illegal in London.

215

Houses in Queen Anne's Gate, Westminster, *circ.* 1700 (September 1931)

But the change in style was not due only to building regulations. It was quite in accordance with the artistic ideas of those days. The Italian classicism, which had been introduced by Inigo Jones, had existed in England since that time side by side with the Dutch style. It was especially

216

Houses in Church Row, Hampstead (August 1930)

patronized by gentlemen who posed as amateur architects. The knowledge of Italian architecture was a consequence of 'the grand tour' which was part of a gentleman's education. In those days it was necessary for a gentleman to have a knowledge of the classics of architectural theory and also to be able

No. 6 Bloomsbury Square, by Isaac Ware (August 1930)

to design a façade in the classical style — a fashion far more agreeable to one's neighbours than that of later days which made piano-playing a criterion of education. The results were generally rather meagre: and it is a fact that the amateur's copying of recognized *motifs* has to a certain extent influenced English architecture. Certain details were learned by heart, such as casements, porticos and cornices, and these were then placed on lines across the bare surfaces of the front, just as children write letters on the blank pages of their copybooks. When for several reasons (which we have already studied in the chapter on the landscape gardens) the English at the beginning of the eighteenth century grew tired of Dutch civilization, the preference of the gentlemen amateurs for the

No. 44 Berkeley Square, by William Kent (January 1930)

'classic' Italian architecture had a decisive influence. In architecture it was impossible to go 'back to Nature' as in the art of gardening, but the classical architecture was considered nearly as sublime, something which represented a common human foundation, far from the affectation of later periods. The romanticism in gardening and the classicism in architecture were considered as styles belonging together and represented by the same artists, especially *William Kent* and *Chambers* (page 154). Kent built a town house in *Arlington Street near Piccadilly* (*No.* 17) and another in *Berkeley Square* (*No.* 44). Finer than these brick houses were *Devonshire House* (now pulled down) in Piccadilly and *the Horse Guards* (1742). *Isaac Ware,* a contemporary of Kent, built in a similar style

Chesterfield House, Mayfair, by Isaac Ware (September 1930). Now demolished

Chesterfield House and the brick-built *Bloomsbury Square* (*No. 6*).
It represents what might be qualified a 'hard' classicism as
distinct from the earlier more softly modelled Dutch kind.
Formerly the fronts had been handled as a relief, composed of
different materials in light and dark colours and of a different
degree of hardness. Now it was only regarded as a homogeneous block of brick and the joinery did not belong to the architecture itself. The walls alone constituted the architecture
and it could do without all wooden details as on the engravings
in architectural books, where the windows are indicated only
as voids in the solid masses. Neither was the roof of any consequence from an architectural point of view; it was a mere
technical necessity, architecturally just as indifferent as the
chimneys. It was preferable to disguise both with a parapet.
The fashion of style corresponded with the rules of the build-

The Horse Guards, by William Kent (September 1930)

ing regulations: the woodwork was eliminated as an effective part of the front. After the introduction of window-tax the area of the walls compared with that of the windows increased. It agreed very well with the new view on architecture where the heavy brick block was considered the main thing.

These simple buildings were the dwellings of the rich Englishmen of the eighteenth century. The English continued to accumulate riches, but they certainly did not spend them on the exterior decoration of their houses.

English architecture followed a line very different from that of the Continent. A few comparisons will illustrate the contrast. After the Seven Years War (1756-1763) Frederick the Great built *Neues Palais in Potsdam* as a somewhat late descendant of the Hampton Court fronts of Sir Christopher Wren, but larger and more varied, with light pilasters against the red brickwork, with an almost Tartarian splendour, a large dome crowning the enormously broad front. It is quite incomprehensible how this King, the great model of enlightened Absolutism, the vigilant governor and 'his people's first servant', could get the money for this exceptionally vast enterprise. By the vicissitudes of fortune (the death of the Empress Elizabeth of Russia) he escaped losing the Seven Years War, but Prussia was yet as impoverished as a country could be after so many years of suffering. It seems as if Frederick the Great wanted to show that he was not yet down and out, and had tried to increase his credit by spending eight million marks on a palace, an orgy of architecture, which was quite useless for the lonely old fluteplayer. The English did just the contrary. While the poor country of Frederick the Great held its own against its enemies England had snatched away Canada from France and also secured for herself the domination of India. In this way she wisely turned to her account — and further developed — the chances which the wars of William III and Marlborough had given her.

Thus the English profited from the war, and profited enormously. But the English king did not get the new palace which had been planned for more than a century, and the victorious English merchant had acquired such a feeling of superiority, that he might quite well live in a simple house. He was so rich, that he felt no need to advertise himself after the fashion of the Prussian king by palaces with pilasters and domes — and bad sculpture. In spite of all that had taken place since the Commonwealth, Puritanism seems to have had a lasting influence on English habits, and even rich people who in the eighteenth century in other ways lived luxuriously considered it right and natural to live in houses with hardly any decoration. It was considered refined.

The difference between contemporary English and Continental architecture in the eighteenth century is not sufficiently characterized by saying that the one is more simple than the other. They represent fundamentally different views on architecture. On the Continent architects worked with the house as a ponderous accumulation of heavy stones. Even when the building was comparatively slender they tried to give the spectator a certain impression of heaviness. The base

No. 1 Bedford Square, by Thomas Leverton (?) *circ.* 1780 (September 1930)

had to be especially heavy and large: rough square stones akin
to the sluggish soil out of which the buildings grew. Higher
up the house became less bulky, seeming to pretend that the
lower, rustic part enveloped the fine body of a building, which
grew up with its smooth fronts between pilasters crowned at the
top by a cornice which was not heavy in the least, developing

223

into the most delicate plant ornaments. The buildings might be simpler, but the artistic means was always the same, namely the relation between the 'weight' of the different parts. English domestic architecture was not based on these ideas at all. The house did not pretend to be especially heavy below and light at the top, it was but a shell round the rooms. While the Continental architect considered it his task to make the fronts of the building as imaginative as possible the English endeavoured to let them express what had to be said in the simplest and most concise way.

The English house from this period is in accordance with the principles of Industrialism which in England was developing already in the eighteenth century. Each building is not an individual work of art, but a refined industrial product brought to perfection through constant selection during repeated serial construction.

A few steps from the old Queen Anne houses in Queen Anne's Gate in Westminster is a row of large houses from about 1780 which are very good examples of the fashionable London houses of the period. Everything seems to indicate that they have not been designed by an architect. They were built by an enterprising master-mason, probably in co-operation with a carpenter. All the buildings are slightly different both in depth and breadth, but the outlines of the plans are exactly the same. This type was used as a matter of course when the building was begun and therefore an architect was unnecessary for the planning of it. Traces of architectural work are to be found in some of the houses, but only in a fine mantelpiece, a beautiful ceiling or some other detail which were provided by the inhabitants for the bare house just as they provided furniture, pictures and carpets. The virtues of this type of house are not to be sought in the expression of the elevation but in the brilliantly economical use of the narrow site. On the first floor the three windows of the front give light to a large room which occupies the whole breadth of the building; behind this is the large staircase with top-light leading to a drawing-room nine to ten yards deep and facing St. James's Park. This front towards the park arches out in a bay window. It seems as if the wall is distended from the inside by an expansive power of the narrow room. The staircase which

Houses in Queen Anne's Gate from the end of the eighteenth century (September 1931)

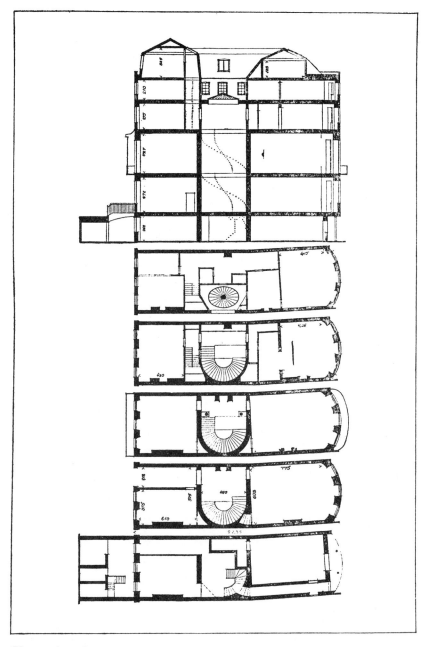

Plans and section of a London citizen's house in Queen Anne's Gate. 1 : 400.
Measured drawing by Niels Rohweder

Frontage of a house in Queen Anne's Gate. 1 : 200. Measured drawing by Niels Rohweder

ascends in the middle of the house — in a room which is also formed like a niche — is built up with beautiful marble steps, and the whole construction is so delicate and slender that one can hardly believe one's own eyes. It shows that the meagreness of the architecture has been cultivated not for the sake of economy only, but because of its intrinsic beauty — for simple

Staircase in a private house in Queen Anne's Gate

Staircase in a private house in Queen Anne's Gate

as it is, this staircase with its fine species of stone, its beautiful wrought iron railing is sumptuous enough.

These stairs all exactly alike form a propelling shape that ascends through the room in a fine curve as light as if the law of gravitation did not exist.

The tendency of these houses which remind us so much of modernistic experiments of our days, this modernism from about 1800, was by the contemporaries hardly recognized as a style. No books were written on it as on 'real' architecture. But it was nevertheless very much alive. The whole form of the houses is an adequate expression of the taste of the period. Just because they were executed as refined industrial products made for sale their aesthetic appearance was specially considered. In order to be sold they had to satisfy the prevailing ideas of beauty. People would choose a house as they nowadays choose a car. Even if they did not consider it an architectural work of art they were not at all indifferent to its appearance, but demanded exactly the lines, colour-scheme and material which at that moment were in vogue. In this

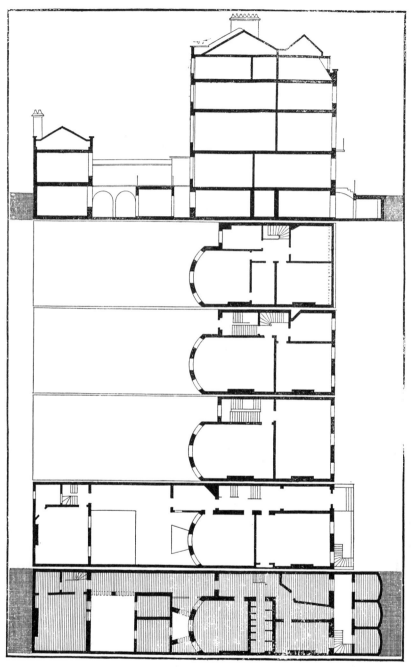

Plans and section of a typical house in Bedford Square. 1 : 400

Frontage of a typical house in Bedford Square. 1 : 200. Measured drawing by
Niels Rohweder

way the houses of the builders ranked with the more refined
products in shipbuilding, coachbuilding or the art of furniture
making. In their purified form they were much more akin to
these than to the classical stone architecture.

About the middle of the century architects had criticized the
unsymmetrical entrances of the town houses as being contrary
to the rules of classic architecture. But this had not much
influence on the actual buildings. It remained most common
to place the entrance as the outer of the three bays of the
narrow house because it permitted a better use of the space of

231

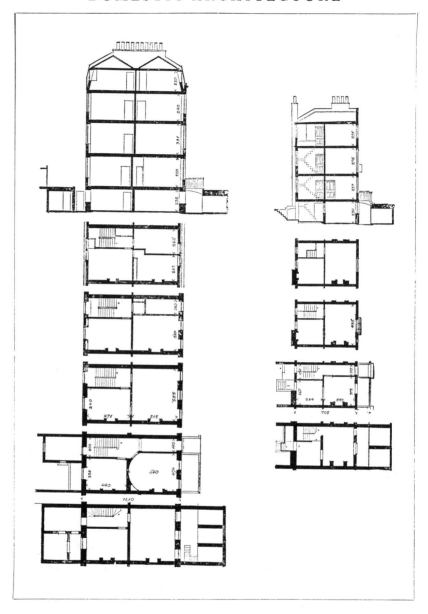

Left: a typical house in Doughty Street, Bloomsbury. 1 : 400. Charles Dickens lived in a house of this type 1837-9

Right: A typical house from Parkway, Camden Town, on the same scale. Comp. photograph of the house on pages 234 and 235. Measured drawing by Niels Rohweder

House in Doughty Street. Frontage. 1 : 200. Measured drawing by Niels Rohweder

the building. As a matter of fact there arose only a few types of buildings, which with their characteristic features were repeated over and over again in long rows of streets and they only varied in scale and in interior decoration. Facing the parks — St. James's Park and Hyde Park — houses were built as very narrow and very deep buildings of the kind which we have just mentioned. In the squares and places of Bloomsbury where the street front is the best the houses were less deep. The largest room on the first floor was a broad room facing the street, and facing the yard there were two deep rooms side by side; a narrow staircase and a dwelling-room which often projected like one huge bay window from the surface of the wall. This Bloomsbury house with its three bays we find in a large scale in Bedford Square. Here each room is as large as a ballroom, but in streets near by the same type of house is also to be found on a smaller scale, down to quite small dimen-

Houses in Parkway near Regent's Park, Camden Town, *circ.* 1820 (January 1930)

sions, as for instance the houses in *Doughty Street* where Charles
Dickens lived in No. 48 (1837-1839). Houses smaller than
these have become two-bay buildings, but little by little the
composition of façades as systems of bays was abandoned and
one large window for each room was considered sufficient.
In *Parkway* in *Camden Town* (about 1820) we find the most
simple form for a house: a large box of rooms. They look as if
they were made in one as a presentiment of the concrete buildings of later days.

A Londoner is so accustomed to them that he does not see

Backs of houses in Parkway shown on preceding page (August 1931)

anything strange in their form; but their simple lines are not a matter of course. On the contrary, they are results of pronounced aesthetic ideas. The façades in *Parkway*, for instance, are mere *aesthetics*. It is clearly seen in comparison with the back facing the courtyard. It represents a functional architecture with a chimney for each house and with steep roofs. In it we can see the narrow house of old Gothic London which has survived in the dwellings of the nineteenth century hidden behind the tall front wall. This tall front wall was intended to imbue the spectators with an idea of the sunny buildings of the

Georgian houses. Mount Vernon, Hampstead (November 1929)

Backs of houses in Hampstead shown on preceding page (August 1930)

Houses with two stories from a row in Southwark. Beginning of nineteenth century
(June 1927)

South with their flat roofs, roofs which in the materials of those days would have been quite impossible to employ in the English climate.

The artistic effect of the materials was cultivated at the same time as the simple, cubic form. Inside the houses of the rich

House with two stories. 19 Keats Grove, Hampstead, *circ.* 1820 (August 1931)

everything was at the same time very simple and very refined. The floors were parqueted in oak or in fine wood from the Far East. The walls were oil-painted mostly in a cream tone, the ceiling was plastered. The plain surfaces remained, without being divided by moulding. All the decoration was added

239

as isolated ornament. The fine mantelpiece with small inlaid reliefs in incrustation of marble was placed like a cameo on the pure, bright surface of the wall. In the same way the ceilings were decorated: vines surrounded small pieces of painting or reliefs, like antique gems enlarged to a big scale. In this somewhat naive way it became possible to create a certain effect of richness, without making the simple forms of the rooms less perceptible.

In his book *A Complete Body of Architecture* (1756) Isaac Ware had recommended grey bricks for the fronts instead of red ones, because they vary so little in colour from the stone which was used as decoration. This was correct as long as the buildings were new. But in London brick surfaces always turn black, while Portland stone, where it gets washed by the rain, turns white. The homogeneous appearance which Isaac Ware aimed at would therefore disappear in the course of the years. After some time it will be impossible to distinguish the details of the fine classic cornices, for where the Portland stone is protected from the rain it will turn black and the dark weather makes it still more difficult to distinguish what lies in the shadow. From an aesthetic point of view, it was consequently quite natural to give up such mouldings and try to create an effect by contrast in colours instead of in relief. This was also in accordance with the preference for slender and delicate forms. In the classic architecture of Italy the windows were dark holes in the light front. In London where the fronts could not remain light, but turned coal-black, architects chose the very strange method of making the holes appear light at the same time as the dark texture of the walls was made still blacker. The reveals were plastered and oil-painted in a cream colour, as if the refined rooms were carried through to the outside. The brick, which originally had been grey or yellowish, was now painted absolutely black, and in order to enhance the effect the dark joints were often inlaid with a new and perfectly white line of chalk only a quarter of an inch broad, known as the 'tuck point'. This is still the fashion and good houses in *Mayfair* are every now and then redecorated in this manner. The origin and date of this fashion is unknown, it dates probably from about 1800. It is the period of *Beau Brummel* when people learned to appreciate discreet effects in

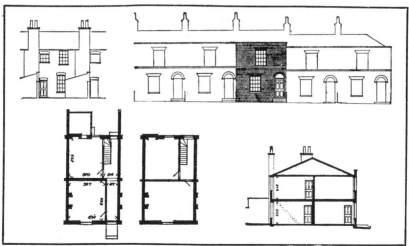

Houses in Keats Grove, Hampstead. Measured drawing by Niels Rohweder. 1 : 400.
(August 1931). Cf. page 239

241

Ornamental door. Bedford Square, Bloomsbury (September 1930)

clothes. The bright reveals in the black fronts were of the same elegant effect as his famous country bleached linen and white muslin stock against his dark cloth.

Classical architectural details were used out of doors as well as indoors in a rather superficial way, both literally and figuratively. All decoration is on many houses concentrated on the entrance. It may be executed in queer rustic stones, painted in a light colour showing up against the dark wall, as for instance on the houses in Bedford Square. It may also be quite a small portico, carried out as pedantically as a piece of furniture and added to the front of the building like a little isolated

Porch in Hart Street, Bloomsbury (September 1930). Now demolished

house. Strangely enough it is usual, both in London houses and in those in the American *Colonial Style*, to let the arch of the door penetrate into the pediment as it does in the Baroque style of Borromini. But no one troubled about such details. The decoration was not considered to be part of the pure form of the building, and all sorts of ornamentation was used without scruple — if only the effect was delicate and slender. The heavy shell of the Baroque style had been succeeded as a decoration by the sunshade of the Adam period.

Originally there was in the Puritan English style a pro-

243

Houses with balconies. Berkeley Square (August 1930). Now demolished

nounced tendency to get away from all that was pompous, and it still continues. This tendency was noticeable in the architecture of watering-places which arose at the end of the eighteenth century. George III went to Weymouth in 1789 acting on the advice of his physicians: people who could afford it went to Margate, Hastings, Brighton, Scarborough or one of the other fashionable seaside places every year. This fashion gave rise to a light and simple style of *holiday architecture*, corresponding to the more informal and free method of life of these places. The fronts of the buildings were

Houses with balconies. Berkeley Square (August 1930). Now demolished

covered with balconies protected by linen awnings or iron
sun-blinds and overgrown with creepers, vine and flowers.
This style again influenced the architecture in London which
at the same time had an obvious inclination towards Oriental
motifs. The balconies were made lighter and more slender,
supported by thin columns. By means of cast-iron the imaginary architecture of Pompeian wall-paintings had now become
reality. But the balcony frontage of a late Georgian London
house can also express a vision of Penang and Singapore, the
cities of the Far East from whence the fortunes came. Until

Spaniards Inn, Hampstead (November 1929). Now demolished

recently there was at Spaniards Inn a small house with an
outside staircase, the railing of which is quite Chinese and
covered by a canopy that reminds one at the same time of a
Chinese roof and an umbrella. Certain rich houses surviving

246

Private houses in Park Lane facing Hyde Park (November 1929)

in Park Lane are like pagodas placed in a row with one balcony over the other each with its own Chinese sunshade. Not only the style of the Orient was copied, the whole shape of the houses seemed to indicate that they belonged to a warmer

247

House in Downshire Hill, Hampstead. Beginning of nineteenth century

climate. They were provided with balconies although it was evident that no one would ever venture to sit on them. (They had generally rail floors, so that decency must have made it impossible for a lady wearing a crinoline to stand on them.) In sitting in the room and looking out of the large windows, people wished to have the same feeling of freedom as when sitting in the verandaed houses of the tropics. In the drawing-rooms of the house they wanted to feel in close contact with

248

House am Rupenhorn, Berlin (Gebr. Luckardt).   Beginning of twentieth century

the trees of the park or square. In housebuilding the precise
and the smooth, the plain and the refined was still their aim.
It showed what could be created by modern means, and as an
effective contrast to the barren block of the building the living
trees and plants were used, still more living against the concise
form of the dead cubes. The balconies were intended for
flowers and creepers which made the streets of London look
like the hanging gardens of Babylon.

Balcony in Mayfair. 14 Charles Street (September 1933)

Balcony in a house in Park Lane. Cf. page 247. (September 1931)

In all this we meet tendencies which are well known to us from the 'Modernism' of latter days: standardization of houses, simplicity of forms, cylindrical bay windows and balconies, perfectly bare walls without even a cornice, and having only the relief which the necessary voids in the solids will give, flat roofs, windows which during the whole period became larger and larger in order to get as much glass-area and as thin bars as possible, attempts to give an impression of freedom and openness even to the interiors of the houses and to connect the light, sparely furnished rooms with beautiful gardens outside. Also we meet an inclination to use the newest technical wonders, the most modern materials and to use colours in order to make it all look clear and precise. Where a Modernist from the twentieth century would put useless, bridgelike balconies on the corners, the late Georgian would suspend cast-iron balconies like cages outside the windows. Cast-iron was *le dernier cri* of that period as concrete is that of our days. But there is one essential difference between Modernism now and a hundred years ago. To-day the architects want to create something visibly new and unseen. But in those days they did not demonstrate any rupture with Classicism. On the contrary, they continued upon the basis of the antique traditions, adjusting them to the demands of a new age and at the same time utilizing the possibilities of modern inventions. The simplifications in architecture made it possible to execute purely technical constructions that went well with the houses of that era. (Examples can be seen in the simple and imposing warehouses built of brick east of the Tower and the street between them called Nightingale Lane.) But even when more decoration was wanted no one found any difficulty in the combination of formal architecture and engineering work. So an elegant iron bridge was suspended between two large triumphal arches which were not exactly Roman in style but at any rate had some pretension to antique grandeur. At the end of the eighteenth century Italian influence was succeeded by Greek and this led to *the Greek Revival* in English Architecture. *St. Pancras Church* in Bloomsbury by W. and H. W. Inwood is a compilation of exact copies of the Tower of the Winds in Athens and the Caryatid Hall of the Erectheion — the latter even in two replicas — etc. But in other less monu-

Suspension bridge at Hammersmith. Engraving 1827

mental buildings antique details were used more freely. To
the above mentioned church for instance belonged a house
(which is now pulled down) with a small portico squeezed in
between two enormous round projecting bays. In this house
the quite mechanical, precise, English domestic architecture
is combined in the most perfect way with refined, classicized
details, and the same may be said about a row of houses next to
it near *Woburn Walk*. They are houses of the same dimensions
as those which we have studied in Camden Town, but the

253

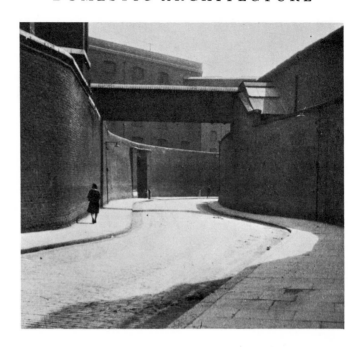

Nightingale Lane through the docks east of the Tower

Nightingale Lane through the docks east of the Tower

Houses with shops near St. Pancras Church, Woburn Walk (August 1930)

Shop in a passage near St. Pancras Church, Woburn Walk (August 1930)

Semi-detached, three-storied house, Mount Vernon, Hampstead (August 1931)

No. 23 Keats Grove, Hampstead (November 1929). Now altered

ground floor is entirely occupied by a shop with a projecting bay window carrying a large and fine iron balcony.

No English architect has furthered the so-called Greek Revival more than *John Nash*. He had been in charge of the regulating of St. James's Park which he had transformed into an English landscape garden and designed festival arrangements whereby he had attracted the attention of the Prince of Wales, later George IV who, as Regent, acquired very great influence. It was great luck for an architect to have this royal patron. Nash became adviser to the Crown on architectural matters, and since the Regent was very enterprising, he constructed a great many buildings. Nash put his stamp on the newest and most fashionable parts of the town. The houses which every visitor wanted to see when he came to London were those designed by Nash, and it therefore seemed as if London had become entirely changed under his hands. He left the old-established brick-style and introduced plaster fronts with fine classical details in stucco covered with a film of light oil-paint. Half ironically, half admiringly the gay new houses sang:

> Augustus of Rome was for building renowned,
> And of marble he left what of brick he had found;
> But is not our Nash, too, a very great master?
> He found us all brick, and he leaves us all plaster.

In oil-paint stucco even very fine details could be clearly perceptible: they did not weather like Portland stone, nor had they the rough texture. This architecture had the mark of dainty interior decoration, and went very well with the fine streets of a large city. People did not walk between rough walls of stone or of brick, but as if they were in an elegant gallery between delicately handled walls painted in a cream colour. There were then in London two typical ways of handling the walls: either the bare brick house which according to its nature had to be without cornices, merely a box made of brick, articulated by rectangular holes, or the plastered and painted house, which could be provided with all sorts of details. But even in this latter case the clear and simple form was generally preserved and only accentuated by mouldings, cornices and other details to the walls. The decoration was in no organic connection with the mass of the building. Therefore although

Oil-painted houses by John Nash. Munster Square (February 1930). Damaged during the war, demolished 1946

meagre Greek details could be stuck to it in one place and emaciated Gothic ones in another, yet the English house preserved a style of its own all the same. Besides other historical styles a sort of Gothic decoration came into fashion. Sometimes it is difficult to find out whether a thin cast-iron column with a foliated capital was meant to be Classic or Gothic. In England the Gothic traditions had been carried

Palm House, Kew Gardens, by Decimus Burton (August 1930)

right down through the different periods. The great architects of the seventeenth century had restored the churches of the Middle Ages and in the eighteenth century romantic tendencies had brought Gothic chapels and rustic Gothic houses in favour as decorations in sentimental gardens. Now in the nineteenth century a naive Gothicism might without difficulty be mixed with the classicized cast-iron romanticism with the Europeanized chinoiseries of that period — and with quite recently invented geometrical ornaments (Nash and especially

John Soane). The whole turned out to be mere patterns and trimmings which could be added to the simple forms of the buildings. Houses which are quite classic in their form have sometimes leaded windows with small diamond-shaped panes. This is one of the outcomes of the Gothic tendencies in domestic architecture of the nineteenth century. The modern tendency to utilize new materials shows itself mostly in balconies, in projecting bays with large curved panes and in the construction of buildings entirely of glass. It was considered the wonder of the period that a perfectly transparent house could be built in which people could enjoy the warmth of a heated room and yet feel themselves in touch with Nature outside. The large aristocratic town houses were often provided with a sort of glass room looking into the tiny garden with one or two languishing trees (see the description of Mr. Dombey's house in *Dombey and Son*), or there were long glass galleries leading to the rear building facing the mews. Sir Joseph Paxton (1801-1865) attracted attention by building a grand conservatory at *Chatsworth* in the garden of the Duke of Devonshire; it was 300 feet in length and 70 feet in height. The classical architect *Decimus Burton* used the same *motif*, the thin curved panes, in his beautiful palm house in Kew Gardens (1844-1848). So great was the enthusiasm for these houses made all of iron and glass, that when in 1851 the Great Exhibition was to be built in Hyde Park 238 schemes for the exhibition building were rejected in favour of Paxton's enormous Crystal Palace.

Sir Joseph Paxton's Crystal Palace in 1851, in Hyde Park. Afterwards re-erected at Sydenham, now demolished

Street scene, Pimlico, showing the backs of houses (September 1930)

About the middle of the nineteenth century domestic architecture in London was vulgarized. The temptation to stick—literally speaking—cheap ornaments on the oil-painted fronts was too much for the jerry-builders, and houses and villas were soon too richly provided with commonplace details. The classicism of the buildings proved to be only a varnish, not an expression of culture. That is very obvious in many London quarters from 1850-1870. The streets may be crowded with open stalls as they were in the Middle Ages, and where

264

Street scene, Pimlico, showing the front of houses (September 1930)

the backs of the houses are visible the effect is quite Gothic —
not in details but in the conglomeration of tall, narrow, and
perpendicular masses of brick. On the villas of that period —
often built as semi-detached houses — the classical varnish is
generally carried on only one or two feet round the corners of
the side fronts. Here all the cornices and plaster and oil-paint
and decoration stop and the back shows a simple and often
very neat Georgian brick house.

A reaction against the banalities of the builder's Classicism had to come, and after the middle of the century the fashion turned towards its antithesis. Now the front of the houses had to be Gothic, each having its own peaked Nuremberg gable. A row of houses had no longer to be uniform although they were all of the same size and contained quite identical dwellings. By means of projecting bays, flights of steps, irregular windows and all sorts of expensive masonry the fronts were shaped into a Gothic style, which had never existed in England during the Gothic period. Most important, however, was a movement that originated from a group of architects inspired by *William Morris*. One of them, *Norman Shaw*, succeeded in creating a new Queen Anne style, which was not a copy at all, and which really had style. William Morris had considered industrialization and mechanization as the root of all evil. He thought that a renaissance in architecture must be based on handicraft and the personal relation between the individual workman and his production. To him the question was social no less than artistic. He wanted to create new and small medieval communities, where each individual worked with an intimate love for his work. His efforts to carry out these Utopian ideals resulted in realities in English architecture and art industry which (with regard to quality) reached a very high standard. The born enemy, the machine, was now utilized to carry people out to virgin lands not yet infected by the malevolent influence of the great town. A small suburb *Bedford Park* (1877) was built near a station on the new Metropolitan Railway after a plan by Norman Shaw, in the right style and for people of the right faith. It got its own church and near the station also an imitation wayside inn with a front provided with an abundance of steep gables in a sort of Tudor style. According to the taste of the period this suburb should have consisted entirely of detached and individual houses, but for economical reasons there were built only nine different types, some of them built in long rows but accentuated with different gables. From a technical standpoint the whole lay-out was exactly as in the other quarters of London. It was as a sensible scheme of dwelling houses necessarily must be: long parallel streets with rather narrow and deep sites and comparatively few cross-roads. Still it was a little less stiff than a plan by a common surveyor. The big trees that were found on the site were made an integral part of the town-planning scheme and as much variety as possible was obtained.

Bedford Park has worn well. Even a modern man who is against revivalism in architecture must admire the stamp of unity of this suburb, the fine character of the materials and the simple appearance of the houses. It would be difficult in other countries to find a modern garden suburb with a similar mark of culture. The materials are rather coarse, responding to the somewhat rural character of the place with its many detached trees and bushes. Near the station there is still a distinguished old house in the very severe and purified style of the end of the eighteenth century. For those who have learned to appreciate the Georgian architecture and who have understood how modern it really was, it seems a little strange that the 'eighties considered it necessary to go back to a more primitive, somewhat rustic, phase in order to create something good. But in any case the result is creditable. Norman Shaw's red brick houses are as a matter of fact no better than those refined oil-painted buildings to which he was so strongly opposed, but they were just as good, in a different way. There are no means of proving that the aesthetic effect of one building material is better or more correct than another. It is the way the things are carried out that matters, and Norman Shaw's garden suburb has just as much unity of style as we find in the old Regent Street or the best parts of Bloomsbury. Instead of the cast-iron rails of the Georgian period all the sites are now fenced in by means of thin unfinished and unpainted oak-boards. They have turned a weather worn grey corresponding to the artistic effect of the coarse brick of the houses. As in the houses showing Dutch influence from the first half of the seventeenth century (not from Queen Anne's period) these houses have a very homogenous appearance because cornices and all details of the wall are executed in brick. Moreover the roof has been generously treated and has never been broken by dormer windows or attics.

Norman Shaw and his companions had had sufficient ability to make architecture a vigorous art again. At the same time the garden had a renaissance. Also here *the material* or rather the material effect was looked upon with fresh eyes. In the

'The Inn', Bedford Park, Turnham Green (January 1930)

Row of houses, Bedford Park, Turnham Green

Row of houses, Bedford Park

Semi-detached houses, Bedford Park (January 1930)

269

small garden the landscape-style had degenerated into hackneyed pattern. The different sorts of plants caught the interest anew and so did the effect of their colours and material, the nicely rolled and mown lawn spread out surrounded by beds with gaudy flowers. Clipped bushes and trees were again the fashion, just as were flagged walks and surrounding walls. Everywhere an effective contrast between dead constructions and living vegetation, as when the regular joints of the flagged paths are broken by green plants.

This garden style forms the right surroundings for the new romantic architecture, and it chiefly accounts for the fact that the modern garden suburb, as for instance *Hampstead Garden Suburb* (1907), is so fascinating (see the chapter on the Underground). Its buildings are designed by a number of well-known architects, but the planning is done by *Sir Raymond Unwin*, harmonized to a whole. Also this style has been hackneyed by jerry-builders. After designs by third class architects, houses bearing a stamp of historical romanticism have multiplied by thousands. The simple, plain and modern houses of the eighteenth century have been replaced by the badly built semi-detached houses of the twentieth century, houses provided with half timber work, gables and projecting bays, small crooked porches and twisting roofs.

CHAPTER TEN

BOOKS OF REFERENCE

THERE is one book on the London house of the period described here which every student of London history should know. That is *John Summerson: Georgian London*, 1945. Other authors write especially on detached houses, but Summerson gives a full account of the development of the typical London terrace house. The London County Council has published four small volumes about buildings which have been the homes of famous citizens, politicians, scientists, poets and artists. Nearly all of them lived in simple London houses. A very good example is the Prime Minister's residence, 10 Downing Street.

THE TRUE AND SAD STORY OF THE REGENT'S STREET

REGENT STREET IS A SECTION CUT THROUGH THE TOWN. It goes from south to north, from St. James's Park through the club quarter of Pall Mall, crosses the business quarter at Piccadilly and Oxford Street, and leads up to the northern residential part of the town round Regent's Park. Its history leads us through the development of London from George III to George V.

In a double sense Regent Street began at Carlton House. Here, at the beginning of the century, lived the Prince of Wales, later George IV, who was Regent from 1811. His residence was an old brick house built in 1709 for Lord Carlton. After coming into the possession of the Royal family, it had its main front which looked north faced with stone. The building lay where the Duke of York's column now stands; the garden to the south, where, in our time, a big flight of steps as broad as a boulevard leads down to St. James's Park. In front of the house George had a low wall built by his favourite architect, John Nash (1752-1835). The wall was surmounted by a row of columns, two by two, bearing a long architrave. Even at that time when the theatrical style of architecture was more general, the small columns had a comic appearance in front of the big ones and a little

271

joke was made, in Italian, of course, as the columns would not understand English. When asked: '*Care colonne, che state quà?*' ('Dear columns, what are you doing there?') the columns answered: '*Non sapiamo, in verita.*' ('Indeed, we do not know!') The Prince was not satisfied with Carlton House, however, which was too much of a town house, although charmingly situated by the Park. He wanted a real country house further out near the new Regent's Park which was being laid out according to Nash's designs. It was a beautiful spot, free and open, lying high and far from the crowded city, but it had one drawback, it was difficult to get there — from Carlton House especially. The way ran through quarters which had grown up according to no plan at all and in such a way that there was not one single road which was suitable for a royal procession. Here and there lay handsome houses with old gardens, and there were fine squares too, but between them lay a maze of narrow alleys where poorer people lived crowding together as best they could. Already in 1760, John Gwynn (see page 187) in his project for the improvement of London and Westminster, had pointed out the necessity of a main artery leading from St. James's Park to the open districts to the north. He imagined it as a prolongation of the Haymarket from the east end of the Mall up to a new and lengthy avenue running from east to west, which, according to his idea, should form the northern boundary of the town as a boulevard. The plan had never been executed, however, and indeed John Gwynn hardly lived to see one of his ideas realized. But his labours were not in vain. His far-reaching plans seem to have had an influence on much of the work since undertaken for the regulating of the town. They played a part in London corresponding to that which the plans made by the great *Commission temporaire d'artists*, in 1793, played in Paris, under both Napoleon I and Napoleon III.

Just as was the case with London's first square, Covent Garden square, the first square to be carried out architecturally has been executed under direct influence from France. When the French Emperor had the Rue de Rivoli built, the English Regent must needs also have a splendid thoroughfare. The First Gentleman of England, however, wanted the street

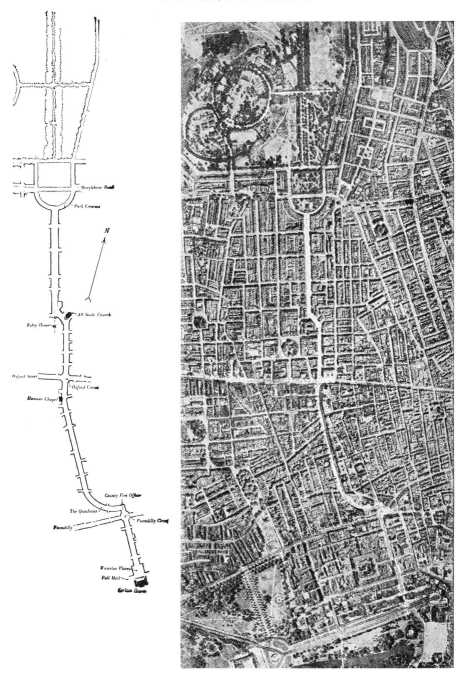

Regent Street from the air. Aerofilms Ltd.

to form an artery leading from Carlton House to the country house he had planned to build surrounded by the big park with its fine views. It was a great task, entailing difficult and extensive demolition of streets, and could only be carried out with the aid of a Parliamentary grant. In order to obtain this, there must have been some social aim in view, and the building of the new street was granted in 1813 as a means of improving the sanitation of the unhealthy quarters.

Near Regent's Park was a large area which could be fitted into the plan, Portland Place. While the surroundings were still quite rural, Lord Foley had built his country house there, Foley House, with a large garden surrounded by fields and meadows. In order to preserve the beautiful and extensive view over the fine stretch of undulating country to the north, he got the owner of the land, the Duke of Portland, to sign a contract not to build to the north of Foley House. When the town spread, however, and the ground was there ready for building, the Duke regretted his promise. What a lot of money could be earned by parcelling out the extensive area which was now lying idle there merely to please Lord Foley! The Adam brothers who, as we know, were equally clever as business men and as architects, found a way out of the difficulty: they drew a plan according to which all the ground belonging to the Duke could be built on except a strip of the same breadth as Foley House which was left open from the front of the House right up to Regent's Park. The result of this was that very fine thoroughfare, Portland Place, 100 feet wide, with houses by Adam on each side of it — more to the satisfaction of the Duke of Portland and of Adam Brothers than of Lord Foley, who, in spite of his contract, was now obliged to live with houses on three sides of him! It was this imposing thoroughfare that Nash wanted to carry right through to St. James's Park. He met with many obstacles however. For a time he had the offer of Foley House but had to abandon the idea of pulling it down and went round it instead. The street between Oxford Street and Piccadilly was still more difficult to negotiate. To avoid too great expense, the street had to be swung round for some distance. And thus Regent Street did not, like the Rue de Rivoli, become a thoroughfare with buildings of the same type, running in a straight line through

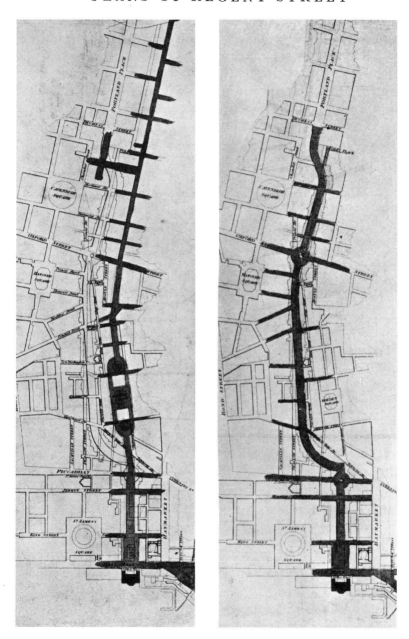

Two projects of Regent Street by John Nash. The straighter line in the plan on the left had to be abandoned for the curved street to the right

the town as if drawn by a ruler, but it was pieced together in sections of different appearance and different character, according to the quarter they ran through. Many years passed before it was completed. Nash did not merely design the street-plan but also most of the houses and he speculated largely in the buildings. For a long time difficulties continued to accumulate. But when at last Regent Street was finished, the money spent had been repaid over and over again.

In appearance, Regent Street was very different to the large new thoroughfares of Paris. But the difference in the importance of the streets to the quarters they traversed was still greater. The idea of the Paris streets was chiefly the embellishment of the city. Right back to the reign of Louis XIV the main object of the policy of town-planning in Paris had been to make the French capital a grand and imposing city, and the Empire continued, in this way as in so many others, to follow the Royalist programme. Napoleon I wanted, as he said, to make of Paris not only the most beautiful city in existence, but the most beautiful city which could ever exist. The models of the new Paris streets were the boulevards originally constructed along the boundaries of the ancient city, as the name tells us, a bulwark marking the boundary towards the open country. Just as John Gwynn had planned for London, the town was not supposed to spread on the other side of the boulevards, the line of which encircled Paris. Regent Street had quite a different mission, for it radiated from the very centre of the town and right out to the open country. It is true that the French Artists' Commission of 1793 had proposed carrying out new streets, which were to lead out to land which had hitherto not been built on, especially church lands which had been confiscated by the state during the Revolution. That was not, however, in order to provide easier access to open space but, on the contrary, to turn former gardens into building ground and transform them into a new and profitable residential quarter as soon as possible. Napoleon — who, before becoming the great general, had thought for a while of speculating on a large scale in building-ground — continued to follow the same policy. Unless they ran in a circle the new streets laid out by Haussmann under Napoleon III also led out to new quarters which were as closely built over as the old ones. Regent Street, however, formed an artery which gave access to the open country, which was to be preserved as an open area for the recreation of the people. The breaking through of big new thoroughfares in Paris chiefly occasioned a re-grouping of houses and traffic in the same place, as numerous narrow streets were replaced by broad ones, and small houses by tall ones. The English streets, however, facilitated removal to new and improved quarters and the houses in Regent Street were kept comparatively low so that building became less crowded than hitherto.

The project for the parcelling out of the Marylebone estate — the quarter round Regent's Park — is astonishingly far-seeing in every way. We have already touched on the remarkable fact that the Crown, although it could have made a very large profit by selling the whole for building purposes, left most of it lying as a park for the people. But the most remarkable thing of all is perhaps that the whole had been planned as what might be called a complete 'town cell'. Not only the park and the bigger houses of the well-to-do, the terraces, which had the benefit of the fine situation, but the lay-out of a quarter with smaller houses was also included in the plan. In this manner there was some compensation for the slums which were pulled down when Regent Street was built. These were also designed by Nash and were situated to the east of the Park around large regular squares intended for market places. A project for the so-called Regent's Canal also formed part of the plan and proved of great importance both from an aesthetic point of view, as it was led into the Park like the canal in St. James's Park, and from a practical one as it connected that part of the town with the Docks and the East End. In this manner an entire ideal suburb was founded on a small scale, which could provide for itself, with favourable conditions for its own industry, its own houses both for the upper and lower classes, its own supplies of goods, and its own large and beautiful park which was not only an ornament for the royal residential city but also a place in which the citizens could find recreation in playing games. The ideas embodied in the parcelling out of the Marylebone estate are modern to this very day. It is the

Waterloo Place in the foreground and Lower Regent Street mounting to the County Fire Office, which finishes the street. Engraving by Tho. H. Shepherd. *Circ.* 1825

The Quadrant. The County Fire Office on the right. Engraving by Tho. H. Shepherd. *Circ.* 1825

garden-city in embryo. Many designers of town-plans have formed their towns thus, on paper, by means of such unities, such 'town-cells', but few have been actually built on such far-seeing lines. The task allotted to Regent Street was to give access to this new and improved quarter and connect

278

Regent Street. Commercial buildings on the east side. Engraving by Tho. H. Shepherd. *Circ.* 1825

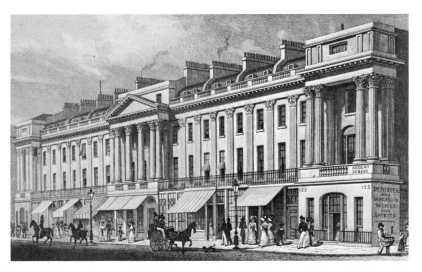

Regent Street. Commercial buildings on the east side (later 'Liberty'). Engraving by Tho. H. Shepherd. *Circ.* 1825

it with the main business thoroughfares of London. The first part of Regent Street, beginning at Carlton House, was in truly monumental style worthy of a royal residence. After passing Waterloo Place, which was wide, it grew slightly narrower. From this point it rose, flanked by buildings of a

Regent Street. Building the Quadrant. The County Fire Office on the right.
Water colour by unknown artist in London Museum

similar type fronted with columns, at a steep incline up to the
County Fire Office which, with its façade decorated with
columns and designed by Robert Abraham, was strangely rem-
iniscent of the old Somerset House by Inigo Jones which had
been pulled down long before. It formed the completion of
the so-called Lower Regent Street. From the County Fire
Office the street changes character. Inspired in all probability
by the Crescent at Bath, Nash carried it on in a huge
quadrant of a circle around the grounds which it had been
too costly to acquire. This 'Quadrant' was the finest part of
the whole plan and remained so. Nash had intended to
build the entire street, from Carlton House to Portland Place,
with foot-pavements covered by arcades ('piazzas', as it was
still the custom to call them in English, with a reminiscence
of Covent Garden), just like the Rue de Rivoli and the other
streets recently broken through by Napoleon. It was, however, only carried out in the Quadrant, where the row of
columns projected in front of the façade of the houses are seen
in old pictures. They had the height of the two stories: the
ground floor with shops and a little mezzanine. They might
well be to the advantage of the foot passengers in the English
climate, but it was much to the detriment of the tradespeople

whose shop windows could hardly be seen in the dim light, and as the street soon became mainly a shopping thoroughfare they had to be removed. In 1848 Nash's cast-iron columns were taken away and the frontages rebuilt according to Sir James Pennethorne's design. The lower part of the frontage of the houses, broken by shop windows, was separated from the upper space of bare wall by a long balcony, continuing in a horizontal curve, which marked the bold sweep of the street as the architrave of the colonnade had formerly done. From the Quadrant, Regent Street ran in an almost straight line to Oxford Street. Near this street was a slight bend, and, with an eye to aesthetic effect, Hanover Chapel was placed here, with its columnated porch and two towers, the only public building among all the business houses. Then it was able to continue in a straight line till it entered Portland Place, where it was again necessary to move it in a parallel direction. The difficulty could not be overcome this time by a quadrant as the position of the new street was so close to that of the old. Nash also solved that problem with ease. He designed a porch for All Souls Church formed like a round temple, connecting Regent Street and Portland Place like the knee of a jointed doll. Portland Place, which the Adam brothers had built, needed no alteration. The approach to Regent's Park only was built according to Nash's design. It was Park Crescent, shaped like a horseshoe, whose columns and oil-painted house-fronts are now the only example of the whole lay-out that nowadays shows Nash's idea of metropolitan architecture.

Regent Street at first awakened great admiration. In England it was called, somewhat pretentiously, the finest street in the world. Later its architecture fell into disgrace, and, when time gave the chance, the occasion was seized to rebuild the whole from one end to another and replace the dignified old stucco frontages with showy business houses in Portland stone. And now at last that old Regent Street is gone for ever, and its complete destruction was celebrated in June 1927 in a festive manner by King George and Queen Mary driving down the street gaily decorated with flowers. But now again expressions of admiring praise are heard for Nash's art and for the exemplary metropolitan architecture, as shown in the

Piccadilly Circus and Lower Regent Street with the Duke of York's Column at the end, on the former site of Carlton House. Lithography by T. Shotter Boys, 1842

original Regent Street. This, however, is going somewhat too far. The project, as a whole, had always been wanting in that grandeur which distinguishes undertakings of that kind in Paris. As far as it goes, it is natural enough that the architecture of the street could not be carried out with the same uniformity of style as the Rue de Rivoli, but it might have been made to form a whole in some other way. In reality it was merely a succession of dexterous solutions of difficult problems. There was never much artistic connection between the different parts. The whole was carried out according to a simple recipe: when the street crossed a main artery, a circular space was formed as in Piccadilly Circus and Oxford Circus. When the direction was to be altered or continued on parallel lines, it was terminated by a monumental building and the line was carried on by means of circular sections connecting the proper parts. While the quarters of the Baroque style created open squares with conscious connection, forming a rhythmical rise and fall, Nash pieced the whole together mechanically like the plumber connecting his pipes with fittings constructed for

Regent Street towards the south. The dark building with the columnated portico and the two square towers is the Hanover Chapel. Lithography by T. Shotter Boys, 1842

the purpose. Still this went well enough with the rather formal style of architecture which balanced between a dry Greek Revival and weirdly constructed modernism. Regent Street possessed, however, a rare nobility and dignity of style, chiefly due to its width and to the relatively low buildings, a natural thing in a street with shops where the lower stories are of the most value. Regent Street, as a whole, consisted, like other London streets, chiefly of rows of small houses of three bays, but Nash attempted to connect each separate group into a single whole. In the Quadrant they fused into imposing unity. His view was the right one. The street of a great city resembles the bed of a river with the traffic pouring through it. Unluckily, however, it was the only section which was treated on a grander scale. Otherwise each block had a masked centre and projecting parts at each side (see the terraces at Regent's Park), as if they had been palaces with an open space or a park in front of them. They made no effect at all in a street, of which they merely formed the side-walls, not the end-walls. Tho. H. Shepherd, who has preserved the buildings for posterity in a series of charming steel-engravings, was obliged to draw them from a point from which they could not be seen at all. The true picture of the effect of the street is given by Shotter Boys in his lithographs in the 'forties which give an impression of stately width, and it is evident of how very little account the houses were themselves with the petty effect of jutting in and out.

All the royal splendour with which 'Regent's Street' and 'Regent's Park' were to have been invested according to the earlier plans (and which lies in their names) was never thoroughly put into execution. Already in 1827 Carlton House was pulled down and the broad flight of steps leading down to St. James's Park was built. Instead of royal gardens the long yellow club buildings, also with oil-painted stucco façades, were built by Nash. The country house projected by the Regent in Regent's Park was never carried out. There are a series of plans for the Park from Nash's hand drawn at intervals of some years. They show how all the more monumental ideas were gradually abandoned in favour of the more popular ones. Regent Street itself between Piccadilly and Oxford Street, had become a wholly commercial thoroughfare, the most considerable in London after Bond Street and Piccadilly. In the course of the century the character of the houses changed. Gradually the stories in which people lived over the shops became business premises and offices. The neutral oil-painted frontage of the Quadrant had still quite a modern appearance in the 'nineties. The traffic, composed of cabs, omnibuses and hansoms, was enormous and the broad street, illuminated by gas-lamps which were reflected in the shining surface of the asphalt and in the glass of the many shop windows, appeared at the time to be the very last word in the splendour of a metropolis. But already at that time the elegance of Nash's street plan was diminished. In the nineteenth century, London as well as Paris had had broad new streets laid out (even though the most important change as regards the traffic was to be found in quite another direction — the over- and under-ground railways), and among these was Shaftesbury Avenue, which in 1886 was carried in a diagonal line from the north-east towards Piccadilly Circus. The Circus had originally had uniform buildings at each of its four

Regent Street: The Quadrant by moonlight.   Painting from the end of the
nineteenth century. London Museum

Regent Street: The Quadrant. Photograph, *circ.* 1900

285

The Quadrant 1907. On the right the Piccadilly Hotel, by Norman Shaw

corners, and their concave form indicated the circular shape which was brutally destroyed when one of them was demolished. The result was one of those shapeless monstrosities formed by the chance meeting of many streets. To the east a triangle, to the west the dismal remains of the original Circus. The County Fire Office, which was formerly the dominating feature, stood calling for support like a piece of stage scenery in front of a sharp corner at the entrance to the Quadrant. In order to remedy the confusion, or rather to increase it, an octagonal erection with Eros standing on one leg was placed in the middle of it, the work of Alfred Gilbert (1890) — still the most beloved and admired piece of sculpture in London.

The next serious encroachment on the unity of the whole was the rebuilding of the Piccadilly Hotel. Its frontage on to the Quadrant had hitherto been just a section of the façade which the uniform houses formed. At the beginning of the twentieth century, however, the owners considered it too small and old-fashioned and wanted a new and more modern building. It was no easy matter in a street whose buildings were all under such strict control. To begin with, Nash had

Design for a new Quadrant, by John Murray (1910)

been censor — which meant in reality that he was the architect of most of them. And after they were built (on ground which was leased for 80 years from the Crown) no alterations could be carried out without the consent of the real owners. There were regulations in the contract about keeping the façades in good order so as to ensure a satisfactory appearance. They were to be painted every fourth year and in the meantime must be washed all over at least once a year. The Crown had a special adviser who acted as Nash's successor and censor on all questions concerning Regent Street. When the question of the Piccadilly Hotel arose, there was no doubt as to the course to be taken. There was no thought of keeping Nash's façades as the normal type for ever and ever, and the Crown at last gave its consent to the erection of a new and larger building designed by one of the first architects in the country. Norman Shaw was chosen, a man with no eye for the good points of the Quadrant. He designed a façade in complete opposition to all traditions of Regent Street, and as the words stucco front could, at the time, almost be described as an abusive term he had no difficulty in carrying out his ideas. There was to be no stucco on his hotel. It was built of the roughest of hewn stone. Instead of horizontal lines which had formerly accentuated the curve of the street, there was nothing now but enormous vertical columns, besmirched with *rustica* right up to the second floor. It was all built in Portland stone which turned black in time because it lay sheltered under the heavy cornices and behind the mighty pillars. It was, all of it, huge and heavy and overwhelming to the surroundings.

When finished, the new Piccadilly Hotel became, of course, the standard type for the whole street. Not only was it impossible to forbid buildings of the same height being put up on the other sites, but it was necessary to continue the new cornice-line so that Regent Street could keep up some appearance of uniformity. During the first decades of the twentieth century the street increased in height and the buildings, in accordance with the latest regulations, were executed in Portland stone. They endeavoured to out-rival each other in a confused wealth of detail which dulls the senses in the same way as too loud and varied noise. The greatest difficulty was the Quadrant which no one had dared to exempt from the old regulations. In 1920, John Murray, the fifth adviser to the Crown since Nash, proposed a project for the regulating of Piccadilly Circus and the Quadrant. According to this, Norman Shaw's bombastic columns were to be plastered like wall-paper over all the façades of the Quadrant, — and then carried on over the new square. During the last century the neat little rhyme, *Care colonne, che state quà? Non sapiamo, in verità*, had been entirely forgotten in London. He endeavoured to promote the execution of his plan by proposing to lay out the square as a memorial to King Edward VII who was just then dead. It was no longer to be a circus, but King Edward's Square, with a huge monument of the beloved King. According to this scheme the whole axis was moved so that Lower Regent Street should run into the new square from the side. The tenants of the Quadrant, however, opposed the magnificent frontages with all their might. They did not want their big shop-windows turned into Renaissance gateways surrounded by *rustica*, and were even less favourably disposed to the enormous columns which diminished the efficiency of the buildings and darkened the interior and at the same time cost more money. Norman Shaw died in 1912 and what was

Lower Regent Street: The Quadrant: Upper Regent Street. Aerofilms Ltd.

to be done? At last it was finally settled that no less than three prominent architects were to shoulder the heavy responsibility for the designing of the new façades — Sir Reginald Blomfield, Sir Aston Webb and the late Ernest Newton. According to their designs, the Quadrant was rebuilt with façades much simpler than those of the Piccadilly Hotel but with the same continuous horizontal lines. The most dominant frontages on to Piccadilly Circus were, however, sumptuously

The New County Fire Office seen from Lower Regent Street, 1927. On the extreme left the last of John Nash's Piccadilly Circus. Now demolished (August 1930)

decorated with rustica and ornamentations in a kind of French Renaissance style, and the roofs were provided with weird shapes which have no prototype at all — and still less any aim or object! The polished 'urban' architecture of the nineteenth century has been succeeded by the course rusticated style of the twentieth. And this is now applicable to the whole of Regent Street from Waterloo Place to Portland Place.

John Nash's street can best be described as a not quite successful attempt at a modern shopping street. The mistake he made in giving each block its own definite axis instead of combining them into one continuous row, has now been magnified and aggravated. The beauty of the smooth oil-painted street-fronts with their shining windows met with no appreciation when Regent Street was rebuilt. All that was simple and refined has disappeared and Regent Street is now merely an ordinary street in the over-florid international style which is considered by the Chinese as the true expression of European civilization.

CHAPTER ELEVEN

BOOKS OF REFERENCE

ON the occasion of the opening of the new Regent Street in 1927, the *Architectural Review* published a large special number with illustrations and articles on this street, pp. 202-239. See also an article in *Städtebau*, 1927, pp. 147-162, by Steen Eiler Rasmussen: 'Regent Street' in which are several illustrations which are not reproduced here. The plans and elevations of John Nash are treated in Chapter XIII of *John Summerson: Georgian London*.

THE LONDON HOUSE

A LONDONER'S LIFE IS DETERMINED BY UNWRITTEN LAWS. Coming from the Continent one is astonished to see how firmly all forms of daily life are established. The Englishman seems sure of himself because he knows exactly how to behave on every occasion. It seems a paradox, that this people so intensely devoted to convention has been the champion of individual freedom and in former days so strongly reacted against French civilization. But there is no contradiction in this. To the Englishman the many unwritten laws for social intercourse do not represent a restraint but a facility. Only in acting just like all others can he live at his ease and escape what he fears most of all — a display of his emotions.

This regularity in social intercourse stamps all outward phenomena such as clothes, houses, streets, etc. The Englishman wants to be well-dressed, which to him means that he always possesses a type of dress especially adapted for the occasion. It means less to him whether it looks new or old. Many well-to-do English seem to have even a pronounced dread of all that is brand-new. What they want is the genuine and the durable. An Englishman of country tastes would prefer a leather saddle well worn, and one which he had used all his life to one bought yesterday and looking sensationally new. It is characteristic that for each of the many English sports there is a special costume which is the only thing possible. (A Dane is astonished to find that a similar specialization is not found where working clothes are concerned. The bricklayers in London work in shabby suits and old patent-leather shoes, and are generally speaking not nearly as practically dressed as the sportsmen.) The English way of life is very *conventional* but in many respects *less ceremonious* than, for instance, the Danish or German way. Most of the established forms have a purely practical origin and only serve to make life easier for the individual in his intercourse with other people.

In domestic architecture we again find exactly the same extreme specialization which is characteristic of clothing. First there is the differentiating of quarters which owes its origin to early London being an agglomeration of small towns. A similar specialization is known in all great cities but there is hardly any other city where the local features are as marked as in London. To cross a street separating two quarters may mean coming from one world into another. It is the boundary of two civilizations, two languages, two standards of life. A person who knows London well will be able to place his man as soon as he hears in what part of London he lives, a fact that is often alluded to by authors. The first act of Bernard Shaw's *Pygmalion* is always sure to be a success with a London audience when Professor Higgins phonetically determines in which quarter the persons live: Lisson Grove, Hoxton, Earl's Court and so on. The fact that the inhabitants are distributed in quarters according to their class and income has made it possible to standardize the domestic houses: as people living in the same street have the same requirements all the houses can be absolutely uniform. The uniformity of the houses is a matter of course and has not been forced upon them.

Within the same quarter there is again a pronounced specialization of the buildings. In this London differs greatly from Continental towns. The English do not want to have dwellings and shops in the same building, not even in the same street. Originally in London, as in other towns, shop, workshop and dwelling were all under one roof, but the revolution in the trades had — already at the end of the sixteenth century — resulted in a partial separation of the shop and the dwelling. This development continued in the following centuries. It was soon considered 'very common' to live in a house where there was a shop in the ground floor. The numerous building enterprises of the eighteenth century comprised only dwelling houses. This suited London with its numerous and wealthy upper classes. There were entire quarters inhabited by retired gentlemen, English merchants who had earned a fortune in the Colonies and now returned to London just as the Hanses used to go back to Lübeck. The social ideal was to put aside enough money to enable one to live comfortably in London — preferably, however, during the few months of *the Season* — without being obliged to do anything so vulgar as to earn money. In London there are thousands of heads of families who have no profession whatever. To a foreigner it is especially strange that these idle rich do not give way to hypochondria. Idleness is so thoroughly systematized, that in order to comply with all the rules of convention a man is kept busy from morning till night according to a fixed scheme. In such houses the art of living is highly developed. Healthy sport alternates with intellectual occupations and informal sociability in such a happy mixture, that people have no opportunity of feeling dull or of getting fat. In English culture idleness has been the root of all good.

The house itself is a small community no less specialized than the town where it lies. Each member has his own course marked out, and when he sticks to it he can live at his ease and the different members need not interfere with each other's affairs. The differentiating of the houses of a town into several sections has also been very highly developed during these last few centuries. A modern Englishman seeing typical London houses from the eighteenth century wonders how it has been possible to live in them. In those days the house was much more made for show than nowadays. It was the age of formal parties such as they are described in Sheridan's comedies. The reception-rooms were the chief thing; they were situated on the ground floor and first floor and the drawing-room facing the street was connected with the one facing the back garden by a wide mahogany door. In comparison to these stately rooms the more intimate rooms were rather scarce — and where they put the numerous servants is the wonder of wonders. A bathroom was not included in a gentleman's house in those days. It was considered dangerous to wash too much. During the Rococo period the way of living was on the whole exactly the same in England as in other civilized countries. But in the course of the nineteenth century the English house got a stamp of its own and at an early period the demands of comfort increased rapidly. To the old, refined houses were added little wings with toilet rooms towards the yard and the new houses, even the small ones, were always provided with bathrooms. People learned to think more of living comfortably in their everyday life than to exhibit their riches on special occasions. The houses of the rich no longer consist of a suite of drawing-rooms but of a series of separate rooms each with its special purpose just as the owner no longer plays the part of grand seigneur in many extravagant costumes, but all the same, has a very extensive wardrobe consisting of a special plain suit for each possible occasion. In a really distinguished house there are now a number of bedrooms and plenty of spare rooms. The children have their own drawing-room, their *day nursery*. There is a *breakfast-room* and a *dining-room*, there is a *library* and a billiards-room, there is the drawing-room for the mistress of the house where no smoking is allowed and where the ladies retire when the gentlemen remain over the wine and walnuts, there is the sitting-room of the master of the house and so forth. If we consider the units of which the house consists we see how they belong to special groups. In its broad features the little community consists of three different worlds or if you prefer it three different classes: the master and mistress, the children, and the servants. Each of these classes have their own rooms, their own occupations. The children generally live in a story to themselves and as long as they are not grown-up they have a special governess and perhaps one or two maids to wait on them. Even as grown-ups they can live their life remarkably independent of their parents. The boys are in most cases sent to a public school and perhaps later to a university. But even at home their rooms are frequently private ground from which the parents keep away. In the same way the servants have their own section. In a good house they have their own dining-room. When complete there are even two classes of servants: the upper servants (the butler and the housekeeper) and their subordinates. (Nobody would dream of having their meals together. When the butler and the housekeeper sit in their special dining-room the other servants wait upon them as they do on the master and mistress.) Then there may be still another section, the garage and rooms for the chauffeur and his family (in former days coachhouses and stables, the coachman's and the groom's rooms), not to speak of the gardener's house at large country-houses. This is a succinct account of a London house which entertains largely, and it is neither Utopian nor exceptional. It is carried out in an astonishing number of cases. At a meeting held by the Royal Institute of British Architects in 1894, Professor *Kerr* read a paper on the building of dwelling houses in towns. For the sake of clearness he mentioned the demands which may generally be put — as he said — upon a good house in a quarter of high standing in London. These demands were not small. It should be five stories high and he described what each floor should contain. One of his illustrations was the house in Grosvenor Square reproduced here; it was built in 1886 and has besides the five stories a basement taking up the whole of the site. It shows that there are nearly twenty bedrooms. The new demands of the Victorian era show themselves not only in the great number of rooms but also in the isolation of the individual room. The English think it most uncomfortable to have more than one door to each room. The reason for this is, that each room has its special use and that the English do not want the effect of a suite.

Only a smaller part of the London houses had of course as many rooms as were considered necessary for the ideal home, but the large house became the model for the small ones. The same ideals are pursued in small houses as well as in large ones; that is many separate rooms each with its special purpose combined in groups according to their use. In Germany and Denmark people want as many sitting-rooms as possible, in England on the contrary the bedrooms are of the greatest importance. In a recent correspondence in the *Evening Standard* a journalist described the strange mode of living in the outer quarters of Copenhagen. He highly commended the neatness and cleanliness of the houses but mentioned as something very strange that people in Copenhagen, when they had a four-room apartment, often had only one bedroom and there were doors between the smoking-room, the drawing-room and the dining-room. It is especially easy to obtain the splendid isolation of the rooms in the English town house because the buildings generally are as narrow as possible and the rooms are therefore situated on several stories. The common little house of which there have been built thousands and thousands is only sixteen feet broad. It has probably been the ordinary size of a site since the Middle Ages. Anyway, there is a book with original drawings executed by John Thorpe

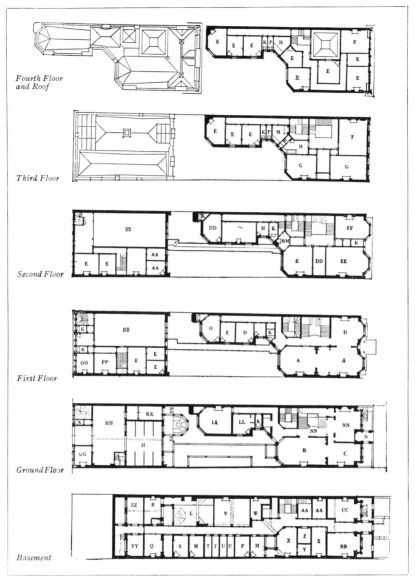

Plans of a House in Grosvenor Square. J. T. Wimperis, Architect, 1886

A, Drawing-rooms; B, Dining-room; C, Library; D, Boudoirs; E, Bed-rooms; F, Day nursery; G, Night nursery; H, Bath-room; K, W.c's; L, Kitchen; M, Pantry, N, Porch; O, Sitting-room; P, Housemaid's room; Q, Chef's room; R, Scullery; S, Cook's room; T, Larder; U, Stores; V, Servant's Hall; W, Valet's room; X, Butler's and under-butler's room; Y, Plate-room; Z, wine-room; AA, Men-servants' rooms; BB, Housekeeper's room; CC, Still-room; DD, Dressing-rooms; EE, Schoolroom; FF, Governess's room; GG, Harness-room; HH, Carriage yard; II, Stables; KK, Workshop; LL, Lord Aberdeen's room; MM, Ante-room; NN, Inner-hall; OO, Coachman's room; PP, Coachman's kitchen; RR, Large Hall; SS, Upper part of large hall; YY, Heating chamber; ZZ, Lighting chamber

Steps leading to an area, Bedford Square

from about 1600 in the *Soane Museum* and therein we find the plan of a house on which is written 'a London house as wide as three ordinary houses'; its front is fifty-one feet; Thorpe must therefore have calculated the width of an ordinary house to be seventeen feet. But it is difficult to get information as to how typical houses were built in former days. English writers on architectural history have always treated the more opulent houses and have left very little information concerning the typical house.

The solution of the narrow town house offers several difficulties. It is, for instance, not easy to provide for access both to the kitchen and to the main entrance from the same façade when the two entrances have to be kept apart. In order to

Railings round an area, Bedford Square

solve this problem there were on the ground in front of the
house steps down to the kitchen (which in the narrow buildings must be situated in the basement) and at the same time
other steps leading up to the main entrance. From the beginning these steps both up and down have probably been situated in a sort of front garden, such as is still often seen in the
suburbs. But afterwards the area in front became a real
'area'; the form became more concentrated and of a much
more urban character. A foreigner wishing to give the London
atmosphere in a single picture could hardly choose anything
better than a close-up showing the area as it is found in front
of hundreds and thousands of houses. We see the steps leading
to the ground floor, these light steps which it is the pride of the

family to keep as clean and white as possible. Every Saturday they are treated with pumice-stone and chalk until they are worn quite hollow. Round the area in front of the basement and the stairs down to the kitchen there is generally a railing with spears. Behind it the old brick wall of the house is seen, quite black from coal dust and paint, but it looks all the same refined and elegant because the tuck point has been renewed when the house was last repaired. There are sash-windows set back four inches from the façade and surrounded by a narrow plaster and oil-paint reveal. Under the pavement are vaults for coal and dust. Through little round covers the coal can be shot into the vault, so that the coal dust is not brought into the house (see p. 193). The basement is used to the utmost: there is kitchen, rooms for the servants, wine-cellar and store-rooms. Large houses often have cellars under the whole of the courtyard. The smallest types of houses have no basement and are only two stories high. Small houses from about 1820, like those already described in Camden Town (p. 234) had sometimes even four stories including the basement and on each floor there were only two rooms. When later during the Victorian era a lavatory was required and also an easier access to the kitchen than up and down stairs, a new type of house was created where a still narrower side-building projecting into the courtyard was added, so that each of the two stories now consisted of three rooms and 'a half'. From railroads intersecting the suburbs of London we see interminable rows of these swarthy little houses with all their protruding little kitchen-wings. It is the most compact type imaginable for a street house. The light in the rooms facing the yard is but spare, but the whole house is comparatively low. Also, as regards the front, the buildings from the end of the nineteenth century differ from those of the beginning. In order to use the narrow site each of these small houses has got a bay and the brickwork is decorated with ornamented concrete details, columns, lintels and other trumpery. This typical house, built for people of the lower classes, contains two living-rooms and kitchen on the ground floor and on the first floor three bedrooms and bathroom. These are the requirements of an average London house.

Although this is the most common type it does not follow

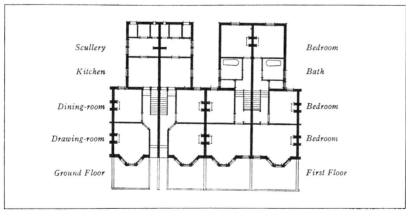

Scullery   Bedroom

Kitchen   Bath

Dining-room   Bedroom

Drawing-room   Bedroom

Ground Floor   First Floor

The most common type of London house. 1 : 400

that all classes are well housed. The drawback of this comparatively high standard of ordinary house is that private initiative has taken so little interest in dwellings for poor people. The jerry-builders are always busy in London trying to cover new areas with the above described one-family houses which are easily sold. Only in exceptional cases attempts are made — after the fashion on the Continent — to extort as much value from the ground as possible by heaping people up in flats. That means practically no dwellings are built for those who cannot afford to take a whole house. They become tenants in old houses which are out of repair and therefore cannot be used according to their original purpose. Whole quarters of uniform houses may in the course of fifty years or so become so debased that the class of people for whom they were originally built desert them entirely. They move out to new districts where fresh — and probably more modern houses — of the same type as the old ones await them. In the old districts the class of inhabitants is gradually lowered. One-family houses which can no longer be let as such are divided into small apartments: in 'flatlets' and 'maisonettes' which are not nearly as good as they would have been if to begin with the buildings had been built for flats. At a still lower stage the house is rented as a speculation to be filled with lodgers, so that a whole family inhabits each of the small rooms. For the owner this is by no means unprofitable. The more people live in the house the more rent he can squeeze out of the inhabitants. The very poorest occupying the smallest rooms and those in the basement always pay comparatively most of all; they can never find an abode smaller than the one they live in, and they therefore have to pay usurious prices for it. When a formerly good residential quarter in London has been debased to a slum it is *nearly* as bad as the poor quarters in Continental cities. It looks even more sordid because it is so dirty. The extensive use of the basement is here especially disadvantageous because many families have their only rooms there in those kitchens and offices which were originally planned as parts of a dwelling on several stories. On the other hand it must not be overlooked that a basement looking into a London area receives by no means less light than rooms on the ground floor facing a backyard in Berlin.

Typical London houses. Aerofilms Ltd.

During these last decades the old quarters have to a great extent been deserted and people have moved further and further away from the middle of the town. Many causes have contributed to this. One of the reasons is that with modern conditions of service it is difficult to live in an old-fashioned

London house where the kitchen is in the basement. In the correspondence columns of the newspapers, we find over and over again an inquiry from an anxious housewife asking what she can do to keep servants, and she adds as an explanation that she lives in an old-fashioned London house. And the answer she gets is invariably this — try to make the rooms of the servants a little more cosy, give up the kitchen and the servants' rooms in the basement and give them a room in the upper stories, having their rooms painted with a gay colour scheme.

Now people do not want to live in street houses any longer, they want a *Cottage* which must be situated in a small garden of its own. A Tudor house with old oak beams looking as if it had been inherited from the great-great-grandparents is a good seller. To begin with the architects tried to create a more romantic type of street house. After the lecture I have mentioned the architect Sir Aston Webb contributed his experienced views to the discussion. He said that the great thing in a public building was to enable people on entering to find their way to the principal apartments; they should not need many directions, but should be able to go to them easily by wide and very plain corridors. In a private house, after the hall was reached, there should be some uncertainty, he thought and some little mystery as to where the dining-room, the drawing-room and the other rooms were. On the whole it represented an interesting problem to the architect to introduce some sort of mystery or uncertainty in the arrangement of the house.

He and his contemporaries certainly, with very small means, succeeded in creating as much confusion as possible in the formerly so very simple London house by placing the rooms on many different levels and, instead of one staircase through all the stories, by introducing many flights of stairs in different parts of the house. Yet this individual house only represented a state of transition. When the mark of industrialized construction was to be avoided the result inevitably had to be an isolated house with irregular outlines. This type triumphed and, about the year 1900, it was considered all over the world as the typical English house. The larger it was the more capriciously it could be built. As to the small houses, not

Characteristic advertisement from an English newspaper

much could be done. Irregularity could only be indicated by projecting bays and framework gables in the Tudor style and other cheap decoration. But the primary elements continued to be the same: on the ground floor the kitchen and one or two small living-rooms, on the first floor two or three bedrooms and bathroom. Hundreds of these dwellings are built as semi-detached houses all alike. They are built one quite near to the other but must by no means look like urban houses. Each of them pretends to be a small country house in Elizabethan or Queen Anne style.

Taken generally, London houses are less solidly built than houses in many Continental cities. For instance, the English do not demand the same thickness of the walls as the Danes do. This is due to their cottage ideals. To the Englishman it is of first importance to have his own house and secondly to have as many rooms as possible and plenty of air. For the Dane, on the contrary, it means more to have a stately looking house, a 'brick-built' house, as the advertisements say. It must be a good mortgage. In London a wall nine inches thick is considered satisfactory, in Copenhagen such constructions are not permitted for dwelling houses. That the English climate *is* somewhat milder than the Danish is not the main reason for this difference. What is important is that the Londoner is less interested in the temperature indoors than in the ventilation. According to the building regulations each room in London must have an outlet; a fireplace is considered satisfactory — and there is always a fireplace in the rooms, for the houses are in most cases heated by a coal fire in open fireplaces. Central-heating is not unknown, but in London stoves are non-existent.

305

Many houses are provided with sash-windows. Their frequent occurrence seems strange to a foreigner. If he be an architect he will invariably ask how it is possible to construct them, so that they fit. The answer is simply that they do not fit, sash-windows never fit — that's why they are used. The use of sash-windows and of open fireplaces, a perfectly medieval way of heating, may be considered as an outcome of the proverbial English conservatism. But considering the matter from the standpoint of an Englishman it may be admitted that there is a certain method in his madness. As he considers it absolutely necessary that the living-rooms be constantly ventilated it must be admitted that it is quite logical to use open fireplaces which can only draw when the air in the room is continually renewed; but that means that the windows must not fit closely, a quality therefore that cannot be considered a drawback but rather a virtue in sash-windows. It is worthy of notice that double windows are rarely used, not because they are too expensive, but because a draught is preferred to stuffy air. An Englishman going to American or Continental countries where the rooms are better heated and less ventilated than in England suffers terribly. He will long for his lightly constructed houses where the damp winter air whistles through the rooms accompanied by the rattle of the doors and the windows.

CHAPTER TWELVE

BOOKS OF REFERENCE

THE best information on English houses is to be found in the numerous architectural periodicals, and for those specially interested in cheap building, from advertisements from builders and other speculators in building. The above mentioned lecture by Professor Kerr is printed in the Journal of R.I.B.A. 1894, pp. 201 ff.

CHAPTER THIRTEEN

LONDON PARKS

THE LONDON PARK IS THE IDEAL PLACE FOR AN OUTDOOR LIFE.
Formerly the park had been a purpose in itself: its only
aim was to look beautiful. But in these last 100 years the
English have taught the world that the town parks must be
utilized more intensively. They have to be not only a thing of
beauty for the connoisseur, but a joy for ever for the sporting
youth and the children. They might be regarded as some sort
of supply service of hygienic importance just as water supply,
common sewers, etc. In many Continental countries the main
purpose of the park is still that of providing an open space, a
place with fresher air than in the stuffy streets of the dwelling
quarters. But to the English this is not enough. The public
gardens must give the inhabitants an opportunity of taking
exercise in the open air. The development of the modern
London parks is therefore closely connected with the development of English sport; their form is determined by the demand
of the public sports. In literature there is evidence of the sport
of the Londoners dating back to the days of Fitz-Stephen. But
in the old days it had a character quite different from that of
to-day. It was then an important preparation and training
for soldiers and certain sports (especially archery) were therefore recommended by the government — that is to say the
Crown. *The nobility*, owing to its riches and the abundance of
time at its disposal had always had its sports. Finally there
were a great many games and pastimes for *young people*, but
they were not taken very seriously. It is characteristic, that a
man as healthy and lively as Samuel Pepys during the time
he wrote his famous diary (in the 'sixties of the seventeenth
century) at the age of 27-36 did not go in for any kind of sport.
In his hours of leisure he only went for a walk or spent the
time with music, dancing or going to the theatre. He did not
mind travelling long distances on horseback, but the horse was
to him merely a means of transport. One of the entries in his
diary (May 12, 1867) suffices to show us that he looked upon

the sport of the days of his childhood, as something that had passed for ever: '*Walked over the fields to Kingsland . . . puts me in mind of my boy's time, when I boarded at Kingsland, and used to shoot with my bow and arrow in these fields. A very pretty place it is; and little did any of my friends think I should come to walk in these fields in this condition and state that I am.*' Pepys could not fancy, that he in 'this condition and state' and with his 34 years could take other Sunday exercise than walking about in his best clothes.

Of all modern English sports *Cricket* has the greatest traditions. It is known to have been played in Guildford School in 1550. The first organized match of which there is any record took place on Clapham Common in the year 1700. But the annual Cricket match at *Lord's*, the great athletic event every year, was first played in 1862. — Universities and Schools near the rivers have old traditions for *boating* excursions, but the races were not organized. The first boat race between Eton and Westminster took place in 1829. The Cambridge University boat club was founded in 1827 and the Oxford University boat club in 1839.—This same year the first Henley Regatta took place.— *Football* is reported to have been played since the Middle Ages, but the original game was different to what it is now. In 1801 Joseph Strutt contemptuously wrote about this game: '*It was formerly much in vogue among the common people though of late years it seems to have fallen into disrepute and is little practised.*' Not until the 'fifties were there fixed rules for football. A code of rules has been in existence since 1863. — *Tennis* was formerly played in walled and roofed courts, in London it was played already in the sixteenth century in the halls of the Companies. Henry VIII was very interested in the game and had a tennis court both at Westminster and one at Hampton Court; here he also had an open air court; but the *Lawn Tennis* of the present day is a quite different game and was not introduced until about 1870. The first rules date from 1873; the annual tournaments of Wimbledon did not begin until 1877. — *Golf* was popular in Scotland already in the fifteenth century. Mary Stuart is said to have played golf. James I is reported to have introduced the game into England in the beginning of the seventeenth century. He played it on Blackheath, south of Greenwich. But still in 1880 the game was almost unknown in London and not until the 'nineties did it become popular. In this way the origin of nearly all kinds of English sport can be traced far back into history and the English are always enthusiastic about unearthing such old traditions — but it does not alter the fact, that English sport as it is now conquering the world did not assume its present form until the second half of the reign of Queen Victoria. In order to understand English life it must be realized, that much of what is now considered typical English has not always been so. The modern slender type of Englishman trained to sport differs very much from the stout John Bull, who though an atavism is still the symbol of the English nation and who really is a robust merchant type from the eighteenth century, much more like the Dutch — or the Danish — wholesale-dealer of the present day than the Englishman. The idealizing of the Englishman has undergone a similar change. Now, he is considered the personification of incorruptible honour itself; 'the word of an Englishman' has become proverbial but up to the nineteenth century bribery was inseparable from English politics. Now tolerance and dispassion about religious questions is an English virtue; but in the sixteenth and seventeenth centuries the religious struggles were carried on with great fanaticism in England. The Englishman of to-day whom we know as a well-balanced and self-controlled person under all conditions, an almost super human being, who only through exquisite courtesy shows his interest for the fair sex is a direct descendant of the plethoric and passionate individuals whom we know so well from English history. In this way we could examine all the features which in popular belief characterize the hundred per cent Englishman, and we should find, that they have not always been national characteristics. This means, that they are an expression not for a special race but for special educational ideals, and they have not crystallized until during the course of the last century.

Schools and *Universities* have played a great part in forming modern England's ideal of a gentleman. In the eighteenth century, in England, as in other countries, there had been little understanding of children and their education. The life of poor children was horrible. The little creatures were treated worse than slaves; even the sensible and human Defoe

Sunday on Hampstead Heath. Model Boats in Highgate Ponds (August 1930)

noted (1724) with pride that in a region he passed through on his travels *'there is scarce anything of five years old that does not earn its living in the woollen manufacture'*. It was not until 1802 that a law wàs passed regulating children's labour: this law laid down that *'young children were not allowed to work more than twelve hours a day'*! But even children of wealthy families lived under bad conditions. People were afraid of washing and bathing them. They might catch cold! And the rest of the nursing was just as bad. Up to 1820 the rate of mortality for children was just as great as in the Middle Ages. Fifty per cent of all the children died before they were five years old. Queen Anne gave birth to a number of children of whom all but one died in infancy and the last at the age of eleven. In their homes the children were generally left to untrained servants and at schools it was not much better. The lack of

Sunday on Hampstead Heath. View from Parliament Hill over the fields with hundreds of cricketers (August 1930)

pedagogics and understanding showed itself clearly in the literature for children. This literature was either pietistic as '*The Spiritual Milk for Babes and Young Children*' in which is written: '*Your child is never too little to go to hell*', or it belonged to the school of Rationalism, and endeavoured to teach 'the rational child' to reason in every situation and to act as a grown-up person. During this period the children's games and sports were considered more as a barbarian remnant of a primitive age, something which ought to be radically exterminated.

Not until well on into the nineteenth century came the great change. The modern English school appears and develops from an institution for *instruction* into an institution for *education*. The ideas about education and the aim of education take quite a different turn. Thomas Arnold (1795-1842), who was

Hampstead Heath from the air. Aerofilms Ltd.

the headmaster of Rugby School from 1827 to 1841 has clearly shown the lines which were to become the guiding principles both for English Public Schools and for Universities. Dr. Arnold was the ecclesiastical headmaster and the Greek scholar in one person. He influenced the youth less by his weekly sermons (of which five volumes have been edited) and his essays on Thucydides than by practical pedagogics. He wanted to form the character of the boys upon an ideal combining Christian and Greek features, and he did it first of all through his human example. But it proved to be of more importance for the ages to come that he showed how the boys could be induced to educate each other spontaneously in

Hampstead Heath from the air. Aerofilms Ltd.

stimulating the embryonic social forms which necessarily arise where many people are thrown together. Their childish games based upon old traditions were no longer to be suppressed, on the contrary they were to be encouraged by the school, because even when of no use in itself 'the game' reflects the life of grown-up persons. Perhaps the strongest ethical teaching to which an English boy is subjected is summed up in the oft-repeated words 'learn to play the game'. In team work each boy must do his very best to make his team win without any prospect of a special appreciation of his personal effort. It was discovered, that games — without any lecturing from the teachers — could teach the pupils self-control and other

313

Hampstead Heath seen towards the east from Whitestone Pond (August 1930)

virtues. The boys understood without any explanation what was necessary if the game were not to be spoiled. In short, sport was to give the youth a body like that of a Greek (those Greeks which were so much admired by Thomas Arnold) and a soul like that of a Christian knight (that is to say a medieval knight from the novels by Sir Walter Scott). From Rugby this form of education by means of games spread to all the other Public Schools, to the Universities and still further, and its special ideals gradually influenced all classes in England. From his early childhood the Englishman is taught that *fair play* is the basis of all intercourse between human beings.

For children, games are a means of education that teaches them to act with the self-control of grown-ups. For the staid man sport is a recreation for the mind: it makes him a child again. If the modern Englishman is always to exercise considerable control over himself he must of necessity, now and then, give way to his natural instincts. The less moderate will take to drinking or gambling, but the more cultivated man will find a way out of the difficulty in some form of sport.

The strict ideals of the Puritans never became generally

314

Hampstead Heath seen towards the east from Whitestone Pond (August 1930)

acknowledged; but the moralism of Victoria and Albert although nearly as narrow-minded did actually become a national model. The explanation is to be found in the much more practical treatment of the problem in the nineteenth than in the seventeenth century. Puritanism condemned sports while the Victorian era used it as an expedient. The hero of the English students is not as is the case in France a man of letters or a beau, but a healthy sportsman who lives as ascetically as any puritan. But he does not do it for the sake of morals. If he is to fulfil his aim: he must uphold the honour of his university — together with his team — by kicking a ball into a net or in passing the winning post in a rowing boat. It is said that prostitution is unknown in Oxford and Cambridge where thousands of well-to-do young people live. It can only be explained by the fact, that physical training has become the ideal of the students.

The change in the views upon youth and education in the first half of the nineteenth century is clearly shown in Dickens's books. Mr. Dombey, the heartless and wealthy City man, who wants to make a gentleman of his boy, sends him to

315

Hampstead Heath seen towards the west from Whitestone Pond (August 1930

Mr. Blimber's School where the little six year old Paul had to read Greek and Latin from morning till night. But even in this old-fashioned school there was a foreboding of the times to come. It is found in the room of Mr. Feeder the young assistant master where delicate little Paul was allowed to sit in his leisure hours. Mr. Feeder in his cupboard had a rod, a flute, a pair of boxing-gloves and other strange things which Mr. Feeder did not know how to use. But he had them, for when he could find time for it; some day he was going to make a point of learning how to use them. It is the old English sporting traditions which had been put aside, but which the next generation was to bring to light again. After intricacies which it takes hundreds of pages to describe the reader finally sees how the severe and self-satisfied Dombey is softened and how his mind alters so much, that he is able to enjoy watching his grandchild at play. That little boy, also called Paul, was to be educated to become a gentleman in quite a different way: In the last pages of the book we find the white-haired grandfather and the little fellow playing together on the sand beach.

316

Hampstead Heath seen towards the west from Whitestone Pond (April 1927)

Mr. Dombey is the nineteenth-century Englishman, who learns to give the childlike and primitive in human nature the place it deserved. The 'back to Nature movement' of the eighteenth century had led to sentimental love of nature rather, than to practical education and hygiene. This movement of the eighteenth century is strikingly personified in the affected old Mrs. Skewton, a painted corpse who constantly talks of how much better the world would be if only people had more heart and were more natural and who says to Mr. Dombey: 'I assure you Mr. Dombey, Nature intended me for an Arcadian. I am thrown into society. Cows are my passion. What I have ever sighed for, has been to retreat to a Swiss farm, and live entirely surrounded by cows — and china.' The English landscape garden was created by such people, who loved cows and pastoral life — especially reproduced in china; but their posterity of the nineteenth century discovered that they need not content themselves with merely *looking* at the Arcadian landscapes, they might use the gardens, *use them for playing and sports*. They found true recreation, just the

317

relaxation which the many dignified and busy Mr. Dombeys of the City needed. Sport tears people away from everyday life — as do the fine arts — to an ideal world free from striving and worry — and to most Englishmen sport seems more easily accessible than art.

Sports which formerly had not been very highly esteemed now became the fashion because they spread from the Public Schools and the Universities, which rather produce well-educated gentlemen than professional specialists, gentlemen who have attained the correct demeanour and the wide outlook enabling them to fill the thousands of superior offices of the Empire. In the nineteenth century the academical world was just as devoted to intellectual and physical forms of sport as it formerly was to the cult of the rational or the beautiful. The cleverest wits and the finest intellects amused themselves and their contemporaries in writing 'nonsense books' — for instance Edward Lear's *Book of Nonsense* 1840 and Charles Lutwidge Dodgson who, besides his works on mathematics wrote *Alice in Wonderland*, 1865, and *Through the Looking Glass!* The *moral* rhyme for little folks from the beginning of the eighteenth century about the busy bee:

> How doth the little busy bee
> Improve each shining hour,
> And gather honey all the day
> From every opening flower.

is transformed by Dodgson in the middle of the nineteenth century into the humorous:

> How does the little crocodile
> Improve his shining tail,
> And pour the waters of the Nile
> On every golden scale?
>
> How cheerfully he seems to grin
> And neatly spread his claws,
> And welcome little fishes in
> With gently smiling jaws!

In this charming nonsense a stoical English officer finds relaxation for mind and nerves before his going out into the hell of the trenches (Osborne in *Journey's End*). Many foreigners will say with the uneducated Trotter, that he 'doesn't see no point in that', but an English scholar will answer with Osborne, that *that* is just the point. He understands how valuable it is to have access to the wonderland of an unrestrained imagination, where a sound little human being like Alice can play merrily with all the old English pedantry and sentimentality. The influence of this spirit has been gradually increasing during the last generation. At the end of the nineteenth century Alice has, so to say, grown up and developed into the Shavian Candida, who knows how to manage an English parson, and into Lady Cicely in *Captain Brassbound's Conversion*, the lady who can rule both Sir Howard and all the other men — and finally *The Maid* is canonized as *St. Joan*.

In this spirit London has also changed and developed an emancipated outdoor life, to which all classes have access. No one is nowadays too good to play with balls or to kick a football, and nobody is too poor to disport himself in one of the numerous parks. The number of public recreation grounds in the central parts of London has increased during the last century while it has diminished considerably in other great cities (especially in Paris).

The number of parks, sporting grounds and children's playgrounds has increased, but there is one kind of pleasure garden formerly very popular which has disappeared during

Lincoln's Inn Fields. Putting Greens (August 1930)

319

Rotunda House and gardens at Ranelagh, 1751. Engraving by R. Parr

the same period. Westward of London, near the south bank of the Thames, was the popular *Vauxhall Garden* (ancient authors called it Fox Hall or New Spring Garden) mentioned already in 1661. The same Pepys who felt too old to pursue the sports of his boyhood was still young enough to take a boat out to Vauxhall in order to entertain his ladies and himself (May 29, 1666). He spent twenty shillings on them and saw jugglers, *'among other things, had a fellow that imitated all manner of birds and dogs, and hogs with his voice — which was mighty pleasant'*. — It was quite a small garden with arbours and restaurants and long walks. There were often feasts in the evening with illuminations and fireworks. On the other side of the river was *Ranelagh Garden* a serious competitor. At Ranelagh was the enormous 'Rotunda', a large concert hall where people could listen to the music while having their supper. It was heated during the winter and always brilliantly illuminated. There were often fancy dress balls frepuented by society. The amusements in these gardens continued until late at night, and it was often three o'clock before they closed.

This form of amusement suited the period of George III and George IV very well and the Londoners had several other gardens and restaurants of this kind, but of a lower class than

Vauxhall Gardens, 1751. Engraving by J. S. Müller after Wale

those mentioned. They were still very popular in the beginning of the reign of Queen Victoria (Ranelagh Garden was
given up 1802, while Vauxhall Garden was not closed till
1859). But as public morals became more rigorous they caused
much scandal. Still further West than Vauxhall Gardens
there was for instance a popular restaurant in *Battersea Fields*
near the Thames which has been described in the following
manner by a missionary, Mr. Thomas Kirk (London City
Mission Magazine, Sept. 1870): '*That which made this part of
Battersea Fields so notorious was the gaming, sporting, and pleasure-
grounds at the Red House and Balloon public-houses, and Sunday
fairs, held throughout the summer months. These have been the resort
of hundreds and thousands, from royalty and nobility down to the
poorest pauper and the meanest beggar. And surely if ever there was a
place out of hell that surpassed Sodom and Gomorrah in ungodliness
and abomination, this was it. Here the worst men and vilest of the
human race seeemed to try to outvie each other in wicked deeds. I have
gone to this sad spot on the afternoon and evening of the Lord's day,
when there have been from 60 to 120 horses and donkeys racing, foot-
racing, walking matches, flying boats, flying horses, roundabouts,
theatres, comic actors, shameless dancers, conjurers, fortune-tellers,*

gamblers of every description, drinking-booths, stalls, hawkers and vendors of all kinds of articles. It would take a more graphic pen than mine to describe the mingled shouts and noises and the unmentionable doings of this pandemonium on earth.'

As it was considered necessary to interfere with these sinful amusements the result was, that the excellent Park, *Battersea Park,* was laid out here to give the public ample opportunity for more sound recreation and amusement. The plans date back to 1843 but in those days there was no council representing Greater London, and Parliament had therefore to take up the matter. In 1846 an Act was passed to enable the Commissioners of Her Majesty's Woods to form a Royal Park in Battersea Fields — not intended for the Royal family but for the people; £200,000 were authorized for this purpose for purchase of land, laying out and planting the same, and forming an embankment along the Thames. An area of 320 acres was acquired of which 198 were devoted to the park, the remainder being let for building sites. The park was opened to the public in 1858. The area is utilized in a most efficient way. It is divided into a series of different sections, each with a character of its own. In the middle protected by high ground and shrubberies is a subtropical garden where palms and other tropical plants in summertime can grow in the open air. On the whole the different species of plants have been the object of great interest. In another part of the park, there has been grown such English plants as are not generally found in public gardens in order to give the townsmen an opportunity of making acquaintance with them. There is also an 'Old English' garden. Then, of course, there is a bandstand and a broad avenue with a Gothic fountain, truly Victorian.

But of greatest importance are the considerable areas laid out as playing- and sporting-grounds. A lake covers fifteen acres. It is picturesquely formed, as a lake in an English park should be, partly screened by groups of trees, but its most important purpose is to be used for boating. There are quite nice skiffs to be hired during the summer, and there is skating during the winter when the climate permits it. In another part of the garden are the large lawns typical of an English landscape garden. They are always full of people. There are football fields, cricket pitches, bowling and putting greens, space for

Battersea Park. Aerofilms Ltd.

quoits and hockey. There are three gymnasia, one for adults and two for children. There is a running track with complete facilities for athletic practice. Battersea Park is not an imposing stadium like those that have been laid out in many German towns since the war, it is a garden for sport for the unambitious amateur. In the 'nineties it was fashionable to cycle in Battersea Park. At the end of the Victorian Period people devoted themselves with astonishing energy to sport. The old ideas had been turned upside down: the amusements which Pepys enjoyed together with his ladies were now considered vulgar, and at the same time such sport which he considered to be childish or below his dignity was the latest fashion. Cricket was played by gentlemen wearing beards and top hats, lawn tennis was played by ladies in pleated skirts down to their heels and with white hats fastened to the hair with many hatpins. Notions of decency in those days caused many difficulties which had to be overcome: for instance if the dress was too wide *'it would be rather apt to catch, when one makes sudden springs from side to side, as in volleying; and if wider the wind blows it about and perhaps it hits the racket when we fondly imagine we are going to drive the ball'*, says an encyclopaedia of sport from 1897. If the dress was not long enough

Tooting. Paddle-boats for children (September 1932). Photo. F. Teisen

a terrible thing might happen and the ankles would be seen!
But nothing could restrain the sporting enthusiasm of those
days.

Battersea is only one of the many large parks which were
laid out in the ever-increasing quarters of the town. They
were all based on the same idea: to provide for the exercising
of all kinds of sport. It was, however, evident that it was not
sufficient to have big open spaces in the new quarters, it was
also necessary to provide for playing- and sporting-grounds,
small as they might be, in the old and often densely peopled
quarters. Also this problem was taken up rationally. The
English, who are always considered very conservative, have

324

Highbury Fields (July 1933)

as far back as 1855 a set of laws for the transforming of old churchyards in London into playing- and sporting-grounds. In 1884 a bill was passed prohibiting (under any form) to build upon areas which had formerly been used for churchyards unless in cases where the church itself had to be enlarged. *The Metropolitan Gardens Association* has proved most active in transforming former churchyards into playgrounds, and there are now nearly a hundred of them in London all situated in the old and crowded parts of the town where they are most needed. The old tombstones have been placed along the walls and under the trees people can sit and rest while the children play. There are one or two old churchyards in the City

325

Highbury Fields (July 1933)

where tennis courts have been laid out to give busy people from the offices in the neighbourhood an opportunity of exercise in the open air during their lunch hour. It is, however, not only the areas of the former churchyards which have been seized for the creating of these small recreation grounds. On examining the list of open areas administered by the London County Council one finds many small places spread over the quarters which are so congested that it has been difficult to procure larger parks. Some of these playgrounds are very small, in many cases but an acre or two. But still they are of very great importance. Where the space is so limited the playground represents the most efficient use of the area.

When the London County Council clears slums, part of the area is always laid out as playing- and sporting-grounds and their number is therefore constantly increasing. It is also characteristic of the English attitude towards these questions, that in commemoration of King Edward VII a *King Edward Memorial Park* of 8.5 acres has been laid out at Shadwell, which is amongst the poorest and most congested parts of the East End. In order to secure this little park, a site with houses to a value of £140,000 had to be purchased. The City, whose property it was, sold it for the half of this sum thus contributing £70,000 to the scheme. It is laid out with terraces and there is a memorial to King Edward. But the living have not been forgotten for the dead: at each end of the long park playgrounds for children with apparatus and space for games have been provided. In the centre are two grass playing fields, a bowling green, two hard tennis courts with pavilion, and a paddling pond.

A great deal has been done to facilitate for the poorer classes, the admission to tennis courts. No other game shows such an increase in popularity during the last thirty years. The intense utilization of the parks as recreation grounds for the population has naturally been to their detriment. There are public gardens in London which are very beautiful and wonderfully well kept. The finest of all is Kew Gardens, a botanical garden where no sports or games are allowed. But even in Kew Gardens you may walk on the grass and at the entrance there is a sign requesting the visitor not to 'pick the Wild Flowers which are as much a source of enjoyment to visitors as are the cultivated plants'.

Playground in St. James's Park

Playground in St. James's Park

Grown-up people only allowed when accompanying children. Highbury Fields
(September 1932). Photo. F. Teisen

In most cases, however, the parks look more worn than a
municipal gardener in other countries would like them to do.
In Hyde Park, which is an enormous piece of open country
left in the middle of an ever-increasing city, the grass is kept
short by hundreds of sheep, a very remarkable sight to a
foreigner especially when seen from the busy streets surrounding the park. In some places the feet of thousands of pedestrians
have worn large, bare spots in the grass. The Englishman has
realized that there are two alternatives: the park constructed
for the sake of plants and the park constructed for the sake of
men: and they have chosen the latter. The traditional English
landscape garden and the wide lawns protected by surrounding
trees and bushes are well suited for this purpose. It is *greatness*

of style which determines its beauty, the contrast of the open and the closed, the landscape being the main thing, the details of less importance. Even the hardest wear cannot deprive Regent's Park or Hampstead Heath of their beauty.

The history of the English landscape parks show a fine example of interaction between art and life. The reaction against French social life and civilization about 1700 led to the worship of Nature. The heroic landscape painting met the tendencies of those days in teaching people to see the beauty of the grand landscape and of free life in Nature, and the parks were transformed in order to present beautiful

Punts at Richmond (July 1933)

331

A warm summer day at Hampstead Ponds (August 1930)

landscapes to the eye of the visitor. But reality was stronger than illusion. People learned to perceive the real world in a more intense way than by means of visual interpretation of the painters.

A hot day at Highgate Ponds (August 1930)

If you tell a Londoner what a fine park Hampstead Heath is he will look at you astonished and ask: 'Do you consider Hampstead Heath a park?' In fact he has never realized what Hampstead Heath is at all. To him it is a piece of uncultivated land which — for some unexplained reason — still lies there untouched in spite of the development of the town. He lives

333

Hampstead Pond (August 1930)

in the happy delusion, that it is a no-man's-land where everybody can do as he likes. And yet it is a public park with inspect-
ors and gardeners, a place where trees and bushes are planted
to emphasize the character of the place and to disguise the
detrimental effect of new houses. In Hampstead Heath you

334

Hampstead Pond (October 1929)

will find beauty in all seasons. The undulating country is so full of variation that you find nearly all the artistic effects that European painters have depicted: in the damp atmosphere of the twilight the mirror of the Hampstead ponds behind the willows look just like a *Corot*, the flocks of sheep on the bare

335

grass under solitary trees are *Millet*, and hills and bulky trees

against a thundercloud are *Constable*. But those thousands
who enjoy Hampstead Heath do not look at it in this way.

Their view has not been determined by art, they feel a much more primitive relation to Nature. They are not in an art gallery. They walk with delight in the high grass when they escape from the streets. They do not only see, they feel the forms of the land when they wearily plod up the hill. Here they are rewarded by the splendid view and in the ever-changing climate it is always of interest to try 'how far one can see to-day'. All the sports which are practised on Hampstead Heath may be looked upon as an attempt to perceive Nature in a more intensive way. Like Prospero in *The Tempest* the English want to know all the spirits of Nature, to understand them and to master them. On the top of Parliament Hill you see elderly gentlemen flying cleverly constructed kites. The taut string forms a sort of feeler hundreds of feet up in the air and makes space perceptible to them. From this hill the landscape slopes down on both sides into valleys at the bottom of which there is a series of ponds. On the flat plain towards the south, boys play football while others run up and down the hills kicking their balls about. In the cup-shaped valley towards Highgate there is a bandstand from which the hollow space can be filled with music and give an impression of the strange acoustics of Nature. In the lakes there is accommodation for swimming. Not, however, that the water is too tempting! And yet all the year round there are people who dive gracefully from the boards. The English love the raw sensation of the elements, to feel the wind and the moisture in their faces. That is why they swim in the lakes, dive down to muddy depths — becoming fishes in the coolness of the water.

The average visitor does not observe that there is a certain guiding principle in the apparently accidental planting of the park. He only knows how wonderful it is to saunter along the hedges of thorn, over the hills with the solitary oaks to the rounded tops of the heights and down through the grove of alders to the more cultivated Golders Hill Park passing all these characteristic types of planting, which in no place form an inarticulated mixture.

On Hampstead Heath the original nature is being ruined. The flora is simplified and vulgarized, the fauna is almost extinct. There are hills where the grass is worn off entirely,

Hampstead Heath (May 1927)

so that it most of all resembles a landscape with barren, sandy slopes. There is another place where a large and specially constructed ash area is laid out for the Bank Holiday booths and roundabouts. But even if original Nature has been spoiled in this way Hampstead Heath has yet to the advantage of great parts of London's population preserved its direct relation to her, not the rare and beautiful, but the primitive, to air and water, soil and plants. Everybody who walks here has some object or other, something to do, either kicking at a ball or diving into the lake or flying a kite and thereby keeps his own nature pure and unspoiled. He is not moved by second hand emotions, he does not love the place because it reminds him of something which he knows is considered refined and civilized. In Hampstead we have in the middle of the great city an instance of the right preservation of Nature — *the human nature.*

CHAPTER FOURTEEN

LONDON TRANSPORT

THE ENGLISH ARE OFTEN CALLED A NATION OF SHOPKEEPERS. That is, of course, as wrong as such a summary characterization of a nation usually is. There is something contemptuous in the word shopkeeper. It brings to mind a mean little tradesman haggling over a penny. The description is in no way fitting for the English, who should rather be described as self-confident tradespeople. They are also called conservative and there is certainly more truth in that. Admirers of Dickens will remember his description of Tellson's Bank in the *Tale of Two Cities*, a very old-fashioned place whose owners, however, were proud of it, dark and ugly, dusty and diminutive as it was, and left in that state so that it could be seen that it belonged to an old firm, who cared for no modern fads. Such firms are still to be found. Berry's the wine-merchants in St. James's Street, for instance, who have made no alterations for the last 200 years. One can sit in the same chairs as the courtiers of Queen Anne sat in, and be shown the old registers in which the weight of their customers, Beau Brummel and his 'fat friend' George IV and a host of other celebrities of the past is recorded. In one of the modern best sellers, Priestley's *Angel Pavement*, there is a description of an old firm in the same style as the one in Dickens's book, with its dark and incommodious office. In spite of a number of new buildings — especially around the Bank of England — the City still reminds one of some curious jungle, with its narrow medieval alleys, where antiquated offices and business premises are crowded together. On the riverside, the warehouses resemble a wall of steep cliffs, with little narrow crevices, for foot passengers only, running between them right into the City. A stranger would soon lose his way in such a maze, where the Londoner however is quite at home, with his dark office suit and his silent gait always half at a run. Then, quite suddenly one

Posters on a hoarding in London

is confronted by a sight which proves that the English are
not always as conservative as they are supposed to be. Near
to St. Paul's a new house is being built and a hoarding put up
along the street. It is not the dismal hoarding made of un-
seasoned and unpainted boards, but one long row of gigantic
advertisement posters. They brighten up the dull street

Monumentality creeping over the steel frame construction

from afar with their vivid colouring. It is picturesquely effective — and it is also neat. And it is exceedingly efficacious for the firms which advertise there.

In London building sites are surrounded by such neat hoardings with enormous posters. The arrangement of these is never carelessly or thoughtlessly carried out, neither can one do as one pleases about it. There are standard hoardings with solid

341

Piccadilly Circus, the Rustica of Regent Street on the left

framing painted and *constructed to fit* the posters. One of the best-known architects in the country, Sir Reginald Blomfield, has designed them. Behind them arises the huge steel skeleton of the building. It must unfortunately be admitted, however, that the English are not always equally successful about the finishing of their buildings—they are often completely wanting in that common sense of which so many proofs are shown in the hoardings and the posters. If it is intended to be a really fine building—I am speaking of business premises—it must, according to the opinion of the English merchant, be covered with columns and cornices and innumerable traditional details. At a certain stage of the construction of the building one is sometimes lucky enough to see the one half of it completed, as an elegant modern steel structure, while the other half is being covered with standardized monumentality. It is true that attempts have been made to create modern houses — Lord Beaverbrook's newspaper offices in Fleet Street for instance — which are all of glass framed in chromium metal. That, however, looks hardly more appropriate than the more

342

Piccadilly Circus Station

old-fashioned architectural scenery. The theatrical style has only been ousted by the modernism of Hollywood. A foreign architect may well feel disappointed on discovering that he can hardly find examples of architecture which is truly suited to the times but finds everywhere the same shallow and conventional type of façade covered with details which have lost all interest hundreds of years ago, and are now merely repeated mechanically to suit the taste of some mercantile magnate. Later, however, he will find out that there is another and more modern world literally beneath all this stale architecture — that is the London Underground Railway.

At Piccadilly Circus there is an excellent illustration of what the Underground has done for modern civilization. After experiencing annoyance at the bad taste shown by prominent architects in the rebuilding of the Quadrant, one need only vanish down the stairways leading to the Underground and one finds oneself amidst surroundings which are different and far more refined. There down below lies the Underground Railway Station. It is planned as a large oval with exits and

343

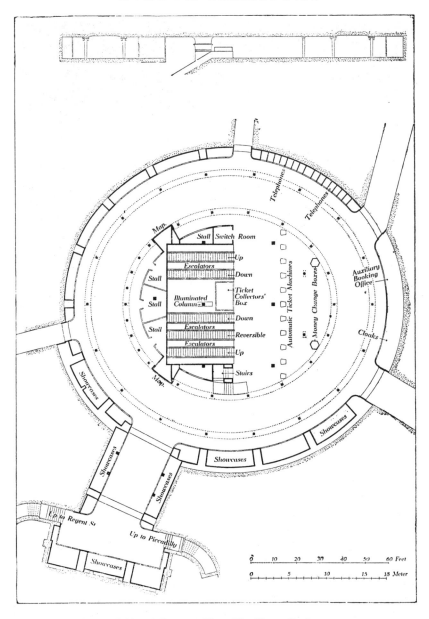

Adams, Holden & Pearson: Piccadilly Circus Station. 1 : 500

Piccadilly Circus Station

Platform of the Underground

The London Underground. Escalators

entrances all round it leading to the street. The escalators in
the middle take people to and from the subways which lie
deep down under the ground — so far down that they can be
laid in any direction quite independently of the houses above.
This subterranean station is a thoroughfare with splendid
show-windows along the sides of it and is always filled with
people. In the morning it is like a turbine grinding out human
beings on all sides. In the evening it sucks them in again,
through the circle and down the escalators to the rushing

346

stream of trains. The architects who have designed it have done the right thing in the right way. Everything is made of a smooth material easy to clean and always looking neat and orderly. And that is in reality one of the most important points in a problem of that kind. Nothing on earth is as dirty and depressing as the 'real' London stations. Everything seems to be coated with soot, and the old-fashioned edifices with their many grooved spaces of brick wall, their gimcrack ornamentation and the iron framework of the roofs, seems made on purpose to collect the dust. It would be an absolute impossibility to clean them. No one could ever feel attracted by the stations which are a necessary evil, a filthy connecting link with the journey. On the other hand, it is a pleasure to go

Underground Station

347

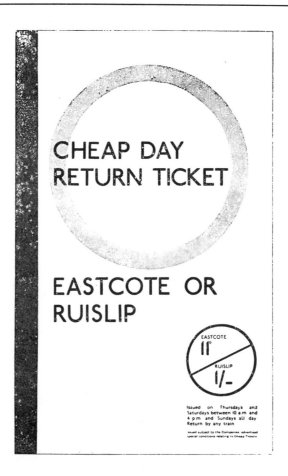

CHEAP DAY
RETURN TICKET

EASTCOTE OR
RUISLIP

ABCDEFGHIJKL
MNOPQRSTUV
WXYZ & 12345

Johnston's 'Sans Serif', lettering designed for the Underground, 1916. Above: an instance of its use on a poster

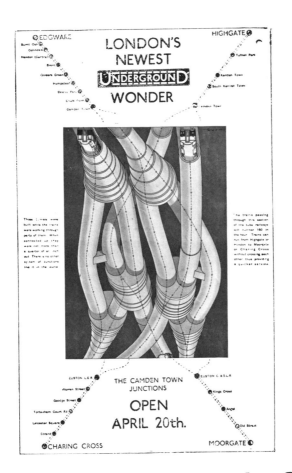

67890 £ abcdefg
hijklmnopqrstuv
wxyz -""".,'():;*!?/-

Johnston's 'Sans Serif', lettering designed for the Underground 1916. Above: an instance of its use on a poster showing the tunnels at a single station, Camden Town Junction

Edgware Station, 1923. Aerofilms Ltd.

down into the stations of the Underground, bright clean and orderly as they are. It is all carried out in the same sober style. The tunnels have no ornamentation or decorated mouldings. The walls are covered with glazed tiles as easy to clean as those of a bathroom. The stream of people passes through the smooth tubular channels and down the escalators. The trains themselves, with their long, red, cylindrical bodies, rush through the 'tubes' like a serpent shooting through the earth at great speed until they stop at one of the larger stations, which are also tubular. Here, there, and everywhere, posters and signboards are the only decoration. And the signboards are many. It is never necessary to ask the way, the stranger finds his way about on the Underground as easily

Edgware Station, 1930. Aerofilms Ltd.

as the Londoner. The problem of the signboards has been most energetically taken in hand. In 1916 the Company communicated with an expert in lettering, Edward Johnston, and got him to design an alphabet to be used for all notices on the Underground. It was to be so simple that there could be no possible doubt of the meaning, and it must be legible from a distance. He designed a really first-rate alphabet. The block-lettering is as distinct as that which has recently been designed in Germany — the Futura type for instance. Johnston's alphabet, moreover, is so soberly executed that although less elegant, it does not date itself so decidedly. It represents the very quintessence of the Roman lettering. One can look at it year after year without growing tired of it.

Hendon Central Station, 1923. Aerofilms Ltd.

It is now used for the names of all the stations and for all the signboards of the stations. It is almost exclusively employed in all the posters of the company, and even the printed matter for the use of the employees is executed in this distinct and delicate lettering. The result of this is a refined and sure form of advertisement, for as soon as one enters the precincts of the Underground one is reminded of its presence by this concise typography. Any firm whose business is carried on in many different places might advertise in the same manner. The impression of unity, felt everywhere, is impressive. It intensifies the impression of size and importance of the Company without ever being obtrusive or irritating. (But why are the tickets not examples of the same fine typography? They are the visiting cards of the company.) I can imagine someone saying that so large a company on so well founded a basis as the Underground might well behave generously and spend money on aesthetic aims, while, under other conditions, the strictest economy is necessary to make both ends meet. The proper answer to this would be that neither did the Underground pay until it got its far-sighted and broad-minded

Hendon Central Station 1930. Aerofilms Ltd.

management. The Underground is, or rather was, not in reality a Transport Company at all, but purely a financial one, a Holding Company. They bought up the majority of the shares of all the Underground Railway Companies and, at the same time, of 'The General Omnibus Company', of a series of tramway companies, a power station and a workshop for repairs. All these single companies were still in existence, each with its own board of directors, its own meetings and its own separate accounts.

The London Underground Railways were not content with satisfying the existing needs of the traffic, they anticipated them. They began by constructing a line through a virgin district and then allowed the towns to develop around the stations and made money only by carrying the inhabitants into London and out again. One of the first instances of this was the line out to Golder's Green — to the north of London, at the beginning of this century. There the well-known Hampstead Garden Suburb was built which, thanks to Sir Raymond Unwin and the excellent architects who assisted him, is still one of the finest modern garden suburbs of the world.

Carriage on the London Underground

Encouraged by their success, an extension of the line was projected, many miles out into the open country to Edgware, which was both far distant and thinly populated. The illustrations (pp. 350 and 351) show what it looked like in 1923 when the railway first ran there, and the town which had grown up in 1930. The necessary concessions were only granted to the companies on the condition that they should issue, according to the Cheap Trains Act, a certain number of workmen's tickets at those hours of the day — in the early morning and in the evening, for instance — at which they go to work and return again. The County Council and the Underground now collaborate. The new lines of railway are carried out to the thinly populated districts and in some cases the County buys up the ground and builds estates for working people.

Adams, Holden & Pearson: London Underground Station

The Transport Companies are never interested in either land or building speculations. It would apparently be to the advantage of the Company to buy land beforehand out there where they intend to run the railways, and profit by the ensuing rise in the value of the ground. To begin with, a railway does not pay, but the towns soon grow up around the stations and then success is ensured. In order to encourage development as much as possible, and get over the difficulties of the start, the companies advertise widely and in a most methodical manner. At every station room is left on the boards for the Company's own posters, and they are changed almost every week. There are many in various categories. Some are purely decorative. By an indirect method of advertising it is impressed upon the public that a company of their standing always keeps its advertising boards in perfect order, and the

355

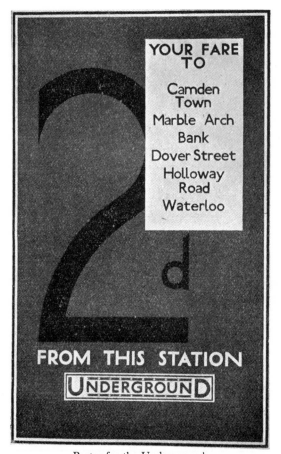

YOUR FARE
TO

Camden
Town

Marble Arch

Bank

Dover Street

Holloway
Road

Waterloo

2d

FROM THIS STATION

UNDERGROUND

Poster for the Underground

best artists are engaged to provide an ever-varying decoration. Some posters are calculated to catch the eye from a distance while others demand close study. The Underground posters are so highly considered that they are much sought after by collectors. In a special department of the Company's head offices they are for sale at two shillings each and at the end of a year the remainder are destroyed and the value of the last of these gradually increases. That is to say, no one buys the posters with lettering only, although they are the best of all. A poster like the one which tells you to buy a cheap return day ticket — Eastcote or Ruislip — is one of the finest of them and brightens up the surroundings among which it has been placed. After once having noticed the posters, it is impossible

Poster for the Underground

not to look out for them every time one passes a station. It is like an exhibition which is constantly being re-hung. If the management of the Company is asked whether they are of use, the answer will be that of course they are. Should a sceptical Dane wish to know whether it can be proved by statistics the answer will be 'no'. If the Company puts up a poster advertising a football match and a crowd of people go to it by train, it might be possible to count the number of passengers, but it would be impossible to tell to what extent the number had been influenced by the poster. As so many different circumstances have to be taken into account it would never be feasible to establish the effect of the posters with any certainty. But the Company does not altogether work in the dark. It

357

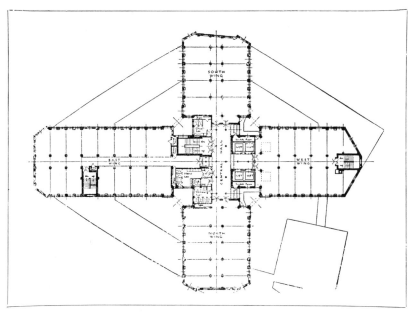

Adams, Holden & Pearson: Head Offices of the London Transport. Floor plan. 1 : 800

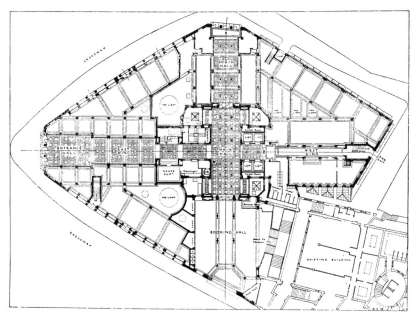

Adams, Holden & Pearson: The Office of the London Transport, Westminster. 1 : 800

Adams, Holden & Pearson: The Office of the London Transport

takes it as a matter of course that the poster *does* tell, and makes systematic use of it. I can give a few instances. Very accurate information is gathered by means of statistics as to the journeys, the lines, the number of passengers and where and how they travel. As the number of journeys taken greatly increases at certain hours of the day, at which it becomes almost impossible

359

to carry all the passengers, while the trains are almost empty at others, a continuous campaign is carried on to persuade people to travel between 10 and 4 when possible. At the same time the tickets are reduced — it was proved that so few people travelled from some of the stations that they did not pay. An advertising campaign was set to arouse interest in the stations by means of posters, printed advertisements, artistic drawings and photographs until the desired effect was obtained. They go further still. One of the finest bits of work which I have seen executed by the statistical department of the Underground is a report on the *recreations and open air amusements* of the Londoner as they have developed from 1860 to the present day. It has never been published, the manuscript only exists and is at present at the disposal of the management and the advertising department. By means of this, definite information can be gained as to the tendencies in the life of the community. It shows that the average man goes about more frequently and much more about the town itself than he used to do. In 1860 the average number of journeys per head per annum was fifteen; in 1929 it had risen to 456, and it must not be forgotten that before the lines were amalgamated a journey with a transfer from one line to another was counted several times, whereas now it is only counted once. And so inquiries are made as to what changes in the life of the people can have occasioned such an incredible increase in the number of journeys. It is shown to be due to the spreading of the town, the increase of games and the greater variety in amusements, which have occasioned the greater mobility of the population. The institution of the week-end holiday, which started in the 'seventies, has augmented the number of journeys to an enormous extent. The railways do their best to encourage the new tendencies, and stimulate the desire to spend the week-end in the country by issuing special tickets and advertising systematically. The development is studied through thorough statistical work and the special advantages of the Underground, the Omnibus and the Tramway are considered so as to stimulate the use of them, and then the tendencies are through advertising still further encouraged so that the development goes on faster. The posters on the Underground advertise everything, sporting matches, exhibitions and fêtes, without

The Depot at Cockfosters

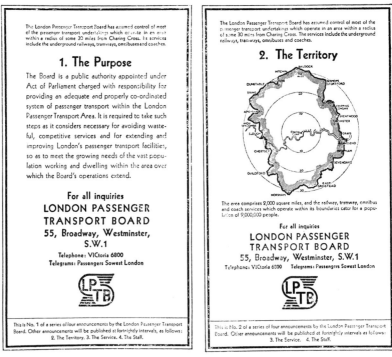

L.P.T.B. Advertisements from the daily papers

being paid by those directly interested, merely to encourage people to travel by their system. There is no advertisement of the Opera at Covent-Garden — I suppose because most of the people who go there do not travel by Underground.

The Underground Company, which at the start in 1902 was simply a Railway Company which was to construct new Underground Railways and electrify the Metropolitan District Railway, was turned into a Holding Company in 1914. From this time on, a number of companies were united under its management, both the Underground and the Omnibus lines, motor-coaches and tramways, as well as the workshops. In 1921 a Royal Commission was appointed to advise the government concerning the transport of passengers, the planning of the towns, housing and the drainage of the land in the district within a radius of twenty-five miles. A committee was appointed, the London Traffic Advisory Committee, which, in July 1927, sent in to the *Minister of Transport*

The London Passenger Transport Board has assumed control of most of the passenger transport undertakings which operate in an area within a radius of some 30 miles from Charing Cross. The services include the underground railways, tramways, omnibuses and coaches.

3. The Service

WITHIN the boundaries of the London Passenger Transport Board area 3,000 railway cars ran 128,000,000 miles during the past year; 2,660 trams and trolleybuses ran 106,000,000 miles; buses and coaches ran 251,000,000 miles. Altogether 11,430 vehicles ran 485,000,000 miles and carried 3,463,000,000 passengers, or nearly 10,000,000 passengers a day.

The London Passenger Transport Board seeks to co-ordinate all these services and operate them as a complete entity for the public benefit.

For all inquiries
LONDON PASSENGER TRANSPORT BOARD
55, Broadway, Westminster, S.W.1
Telephone : VICtoria 6800   Telegrams: Passengers Sowest London

This is No. 3 of a series of four announcements by the London Passenger Transport Board. Other announcements are: 1. The Purpose; 2. The Territory; 4. The Staff.

The London Passenger Transport Board has assumed control of most of the passenger transport undertakings which operate in an area within a radius of some 30 miles from Charing Cross. The services include the underground railways, tramways, omnibuses and coaches.

4. The Staff

THE London Passenger Transport Board has taken over the administrative and operating staffs of the various passenger transport undertakings in London. The railway staff number 14,300; the bus and coach staff 38,000; the tramway and trolleybus staff 19,600; a total of 71,900.

The employees of the Board have behind them a long experience and a great tradition. It will be the aim of the Board and of their staff to maintain a high standard of efficiency, of service and of courtesy to all passengers.

For all inquiries
LONDON PASSENGER TRANSPORT BOARD
55, Broadway, Westminster, S.W.1
Telephone : VICtoria 6800   Telegrams: Passengers Sowest London

A folder containing a series of four announcements by the London Passenger Transport Board may be obtained on application to the above address. The other subjects in the series are: 1. The Purpose, 2. The Territory, 3. The Service.

L.P.T.B. Advertisements from the daily papers

a plan for the co-operation of all means of passenger transport in London, within what is called the London traffic area. In 1933 the Bill was passed, the London Passenger Transport Act. In accordance with this Act, a body has been founded in the same manner as the former Underground, but with a much larger sphere of activity. It is under the control of the Transport Board and is a perfectly independent, almost private institution. The Act, which fills 179 pages, gives very explicit directions as to the composition and activities of the Board. It consists of a president and six members. Among others, both the London County Council and a special advisory committee, are represented at its election. The members must not be financially interested in any way whatever in any of the Companies controlled by the Board and must resign their membership at the end of seven years. In practice the London Passenger Transport Board has taken over the management of all the transport companies within a large area around London. The shares and bonds of these companies are exchanged with shares and bonds issued by the Transport Board according to certain regulations determined by the Act. From July 1st, 1933, the Transport Board has taken over 89 enterprises with a total capital of £120,000,000. It employs 71,000 people and there are 5350 omnibuses and 3000 Underground Railway carriages under its management.

The chief aim of this vast institution, which owes its existence to the initiative of Lord Ashfield, is to create the best possible conditions of Transport for London. The most effective method of attaining it must be by uniting all under one single management. Now, as hitherto, each separate department will have its own board of directors and they will compete in so far as each will strive to carry the largest number of passengers. That will, however, be a point of honour and not a question of private gain. As a contrast to those towns in which the State, Municipality and private firms compete with each other by means of monopolies, the London Transport companies, which are all under the same management, compete only in improving the means of transport.

The London Passenger Transport Board is the last link in the chain of development which has continuously striven to create more favourable conditions for the spreading of London by methods of transport which are suited to the times.

THE GARDEN CITY

GARDEN CITIES MEAN A PLANNED DECENTRALIZATION OF TOWNS. The idea of the ideal city was propounded by Ebenezer Howard (1850-1928) in a little book called *To-morrow*, published in 1898. Howard, who was stenographer to Parliament, was keenly interested in social work and his proposal to create towns as small and complete units, including in themselves all the functions of the town, was evolved chiefly as a means of disintegrating the chaos of the great city and bettering the housing conditions of the workpeople. While huge and scientific volumes have been written in other countries about housing conditions, Ebenezer Howard's book, which has so to speak become the bible of English town-planning, is merely a popular and extremely practical pamphlet. It is a bit of journalism which would annoy a Dane by its flow of language and its slightly sectarian tone, but it explains the problems distinctly with much common sense and shows in a most business-like manner how Howard thinks financially they can be solved.

The book begins with a series of comments from both men and newspapers representing the most opposite opinions, all tending to show that one of the burning questions of the time is how to check the growth of large cities, and to improve the conditions of living. Howard undertook the task of finding the key to the solution of this great problem. When the influx to the town is so great, the town must possess some attraction which is wanting in the country. On the other hand, he, as an Englishman, felt bound to maintain that country life has great assets which are not to be found in the town. The ideal would be something between the life as lived hitherto in the town and in the country, so that one was not forced to face the alternatives — town *or* country, but could point out a third in which all the advantages of the more energetic and active life in the towns was united with the healthfulness and beauty of the country. It should act as a magnet which could

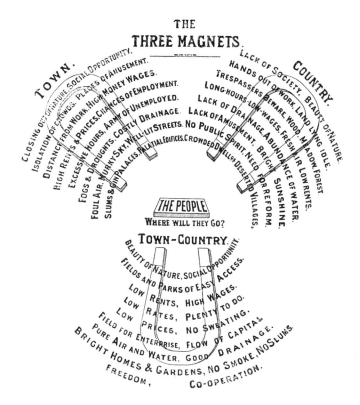

Diagram from Ebenezer Howard's book *To-morrow*

attract people from the over-populated towns to the lap of
Mother earth. (There is nothing surprising in this manner
of thinking, for was not this the very thing those Englishmen
of former days had in their minds when they built Bloomsbury,
with one-family houses round the squares leading out into
the open country? And was not that the idea of the Regent's
Park quarter? And of Norman Shaw's Bedford Park villas?)
Howard illustrates it in a diagram showing the three magnets:
the town, the country and the garden city. In the town, there
are high wages, possibilities of employment — but also high
rates and high prices. The town is attractive because of its
amusements but, on the other hand, most of its inhabitants
have a long way to go to their work. The town has its brightly
lighted streets, but there is little sun by day and the air is
foul. The town has imposing and palatial buildings — but

366

also the most wretched slums. In the country it is possible to enjoy the beauties of nature — but life there is less sociable and money does not circulate so freely. There are wider views, parks and woods, fresh air — but the most beautiful parts are usually (in England) closed to the public. In the country the rates are lower, but so are the incomes. The houses are situated so that they get more sun and air — but amusements are few and far between. As regards sanitation, both the water supply and the drainage are bad. As Howard puts it: *But neither the Town magnet nor the Country magnet represents the full plan and purpose of nature. Human society and the beauty of nature are meant to be enjoyed together. The two magnets must be made one. As man and woman by their varied gifts and faculties supplement each other, so should town and country. The town is the symbol of society — of mutual help and friendly co-operation, of fatherhood, motherhood, brotherhood, sisterhood, of wide relations between man and man — of broad, expanding sympathies — of science, art, culture, religion. And the country! The country is the symbol of God's love and care for man. All that we are and all that we have comes from it. Our bodies are formed of it; to it they return. We are fed by it, clothed by it, and by it are we warmed and sheltered. On its bosom we rest. Its beauty is the inspiration of art, of music, of poetry. Its forces propel all the wheels of industry. It is the source of all health, all wealth, all knowledge. But its fulness of joy and wisdom has not revealed itself to man. Nor can it ever, so long as this unholy, unnatural separation of society and nature endures. Town and country must be married, and out of this joyous union will spring a new hope, a new life, a new civilization. It is the purpose of this work to show how a first step can be taken in this direction by the construction of a Town-country magnet; and I hope to convince the reader that this is practicable, here and now, and that on principles which are the very soundest, whether viewed from the ethical or the economic standpoint.*

That was the introduction. After that, Howard goes on to explain how his wishes can be carried out. Let us imagine an estate of 6,000 acres. It is at some distance from a large town and can be bought for £240,000. Howard imagines the sum raised on mortgage debentures bearing interest at an average rate of not more than four per cent. The property is taken over by a small board of four managing owners who are responsible to the investors and later on to the inhabitants of the garden city as well. All revenues arising from the investments in the land are paid to the board, who, after having paid out the profits and written off the necessary amount, have to spend the eventual surplus on the upkeep and the execution of public works, roads, schools, parks and so on. In this way, the inhabitants themselves get all the advantages accruing from the rise in the value of the property. The buildings of the town, when completed, are only to cover one-sixth of the entire area, the five-sixths are to be kept for farming purposes. In the town itself, all the advantages are available which a highly developed town life can offer. He has indicated the forming of it most systematically. In the middle, around a little garden, lie public buildings such as the town hall, museum, concert hall, library, theatre and hospital. Around this parklike centre lies the main shopping street, like a big circular arcade covered with glass in which are all the big shops. Around this are rings of houses, grouped along a circular 'Grand Avenue' 420 feet in breadth, and outside this again factories, dairies, market-places, etc. There must be no smoke in the garden city, all the machines are driven by electricity. The refuse of the town is taken out to the farms surrounding it and the farms sell their produce to the town, which should obtain it at the lowest price as there would only be a minimum of transport. Farming would not be done according to any pre-arranged system. The entire area would be divided into lots of various sizes and be let to the highest bidder. By means of free competition, it should be possible to see by and by which method of parcelling out was the best.

The revenues of the town would consist of ground-rent, rent for the use of the ground. The sums thus obtained should suffice, to provide interest on the debentures, to provide a sinking fund which will leave the community free from the burden of interest, to enable the Board to carry out and maintain public enterprises inside the area. When the town had bought up áll the debentures, the original board would no longer be needed and the garden city would for the future be independent and self-governing. In the country, the rent of an acre of ground may be about £4, while in some parts of London it can rise to about £30,000. According to Howard's plan, the increase in value due to the building of the town would be to the mutual benefit of all the inhabitants instead of one single owner profiting by it. One can also put it thus, that the inhabitants escape exorbitant taxes in the form of high rates. The land never becomes private property but continues to belong to the town, and in this way better housing conditions are secured for the inhabitants than could otherwise be found in a town.

Howard drew up a complete statement of accounts. He imagines the entire property, as already mentioned, to be worth £240,000. The former tenants have paid £8000, and all told they form a population of 1000. That makes £8 a head. The garden city was now to become a town with 32,000 inhabitants (the 30,000 in the town proper and the remaining 2000 on the farms). They are to pay four per cent a year of the purchase money, which makes six shillings a head. That is all they are to pay for ground property. What they pay beyond that answers to rates (local taxation) and can be used for public purposes. He expects them to pay on an average £2 each. That makes £64,000 in all. Of this sum about £9600 goes for the interest on the debentures, and £4400 for a sinking fund, and about £50,000 would be left. The local government would have such a large sum at their disposal (the project is from 1898) and yet each of the inhabitants only be paying a fourth of what the former inhabitants had to pay for the land alone. And, on comparing, we see that according to Howard's statement, the average sum paid for rent and taxes is £4 10s. The advantage to the farmers is obvious: they have a new market close at hand, they get the refuse of the town for manure, the neighbourhood of the town offers them better conditions and the advantages of town life, and the money they pay is at the same time rent and taxes. Formerly about £6500 was paid for the 5000 acres of farms. Now the land is worth so much more that it can bring in 50 per cent more — that is to say, £9750. Even the 1000 acres in the town itself Howard, in true English style, imagines divided into small lots 20 feet wide and 130 feet deep. These should be paid for at six shillings a foot run frontage. Each of these lots should, on an average, suffice for a family of five and a half persons and yield, all in all, an annual revenue of £33,000. And besides these there are the factories, work-shops and warehouses paying £21,250 in all, and so the farms, residential and factory quarters altogether would pay the £64,000 yearly, as estimated. The town never has to spend large sums on purchasing land for public buildings for the ground value is always paid by the inhabitants. Neither has public money to be spent on land for widening the streets or the making of new roads. The citizens, who may be con-sidered as lessees or tenants, whichever you please to call it, cannot speculate in the land as they are not able to sell the right to the use of it. As long as they use the ground them-selves, they enjoy all the advantages of the owner. They cannot be given notice unless they fail to pay up.

Howard lays great stress on the importance of the plan of the town being in accordance with its practical functions. The development must be planned out as a whole and must not be left to chance as has been the case so far. Only a certain size is admissible so that the buildings of the town never trespass on the area which is reserved for the farms from the beginning. In this way a frame, a final form so to speak, is marked out according to which the town develops. Howard philoso-phizes here on the growth of the town, saying that it should, like flowers, birds and animals, show unity, harmony and concentration. The effect of growth should never be that its unity was disturbed but that it grew more and more effective. Harmony should not be interrupted, but increased. The entirety of the town should, from an early stage, be a germ which could merge into a still greater whole at a later stage of its development. It is evidently for this reason that he has given the town its circular form in his diagrams. It was to be composed of sections, like the unfolding of a fan, and when the whole ring had been gone through, the town was finished. In reality, however, it is not such a simple matter. A city and an organism in nature can never be compared in a general way, because the elements of the town are so large and alter so little in the course of years.

In the last part of the book Howard goes over all the different parts of the town, its authorities and their duties.

Howard's Garden City idea is an interesting attempt to create a small community, entirely Georgistic within a capital-

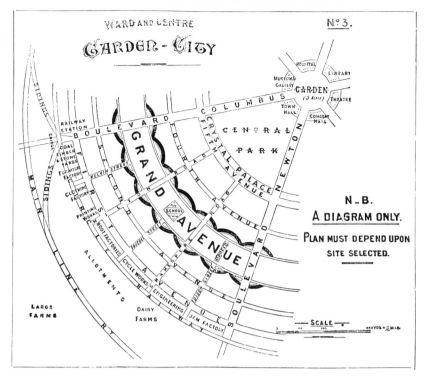

Ebenezer Howard's diagram of a Garden City

istic state and with the means at hand. He shows that this can be done, without revolutionizing the existing conditions of property by merely forming a company based on mutual interests and by buying ground which was to be made to pay, and then to liquidate in the usual manner when the revenues benefited the entire community instead of one single member.

The word 'garden city' in the terminology of town planning is now a word with a definite meaning. It does not merely signify part of a town with gardens belonging to it, but is a special type of town. At a congress which was held in the first Garden City, Letchworth, in 1920 the English Garden City and Town Planning Association agreed that a *Garden City is a town designed for healthy living and industry; of a size that makes possible a full measure of social life, but not larger; surrounded by a rural belt; the whole of the land being in public ownership or held in trust for the community.*

Long before Howard's book was written, it was evident that there were great disadvantages connected with a large town. It was well known that conditions were particularly bad from the point of view of hygiene, that the majority of the population lived in wretched houses which were far too small, and that the distance between the homes and the centres of work was too great, and that there was little or no opportunity for a healthy life in the open air. These things were, however, considered a necessary evil, a result of the industrialism of the time, and could only be improved by sheer philanthropy or by compulsory political measures. And then a man appeared on the scene who showed that towns could be built after all without any of these drawbacks, towns whose financial system was self-containing. This appealed to the conservative-minded. It is easy to understand the joy of the English socialists when the idea of the garden city was propounded. But at the same time, it also satisfied the liberals because there was a definite proposal for the reform of the land. In this manner Howard succeeded in gaining the support of people with absolutely different views for his idea. His book was published in several editions and in 1902 a company was formed called the Garden City Pioneer Co. Ltd., which was to take the first steps towards the realization of his plans. A large part of the Press advocated it strongly; £20,000 was paid into the company which was to be invested in debentures for the garden city. In 1903 a contract was signed for the purchase of 3800 acres of land (later increased to 4500) near the village of Letchworth, 34½ miles from London. The First Garden City Company was founded and it offered for sale shares to the value of £300,000. In spite of the support of the Press, however, only £100,000 were sold. The cost of the land was thus £160,000 (on an average £42 per acre; Howard had reckoned with £40). The first step was to design a plan of the city and to provide water supply and drainage for the future town. The plan was designed by the architects Barry Parker and Raymond Unwin.

To begin with there was a new platform by the railway but Letchworth soon got its own station. The way in which the garden city was mentioned in the Press was perhaps not always encouraging for its growth. The experiment was considered

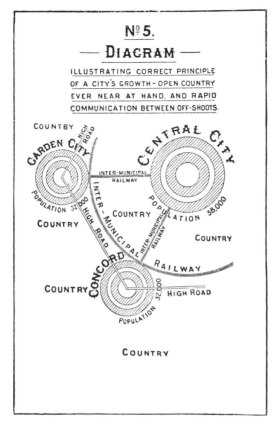

Ebenezer Howard's diagram of Satellite Cities

as somewhat of a sensation, and the result was that people who went to live in Letchworth were regarded as eccentric creatures and the man who went to settle in the first garden city was considered decidedly odd. This impression was confirmed when all sorts of reforms were tried there. It was of greater consequence for the welfare of the town that, as early as 1905, various industrial enterprises were started there — the Heatley Engineering Company for instance and the Garden City Press Ltd. It was the very place for an undertaking like this private press (which took its name from the Garden City), one of the chief printing houses in England. For an enterprise of this kind, which only executes work of the best quality, it is of importance to have employees with a higher standard of life. (We have seen both in Letchworth and in the other garden city Welwyn, that workshops and factories for the manufacturing of finer wares thrive especially well in a garden city). Then the question of workmen's houses arose. It was settled by the private initiative of the building societies, but was to a certain extent under the control of the board of directors of the garden city. Before the foundation of Letchworth, English architects took very little interest in small houses. Workmen's cottages were always designed by builders. Raymond Unwin was one of the first to call public attention to the fact of how unfortunate it was that this task was not entrusted to able architects, and he worked hard to promote serious efforts to build a good type of small house which would ensure to the inhabitants a maximum of sun and air and a practical arrangement of the home. The new idea was tried at Letchworth and many came to see the results.

In 1908 Letchworth elected its own parish council of fifteen members. In 1917 the garden city was recognized as an urban district and got its own urban district council. Letchworth was reported to be a particularly healthy place and many people moved there on that account. All statistics seem to bear out this view but cannot of course explain whether the favourable bill of health is due to the inhabitants being comparatively well-to-do, or to the particular advantages of the place itself. An early attempt to start a non-provided school was unsuccessful as the plan met with too little response. In 1905, however, a private boarding-school was started which was run on fresh lines in many ways. It is a school for both boys and girls where the pupils begin as small children in the Montessori Kindergarten and stay on at the school until their nineteenth year.

The census shows a steady increase in the growth of the city. The bigger it grows, the easier it is for it to supply its own needs. To begin with, as there were but few shops and places where people could assemble, most of the money earned by the citizens was spent in other places. Now one can count on the greater part of it remaining in Letchworth. The success of the garden city depended on its becoming an important industrial centre. C. B. Purdom, who has written an excellent book on 'satellite towns', made a number of inquiries among the leaders of the industrial activities of

Letchworth, resulting in important information as to the advantages which the garden city can offer to industry. He asked them first why they had gone to Letchworth. Some had come from a distance in order to be near London. Several of them answered that the attraction was the cheaper ground rent, but that the main point was that they could extend their premises more easily there than in London. Many answered that one of the reasons was that the garden city offered more healthy conditions of life for their work people. When asked whether they were satisfied with Letchworth as an industrial centre, the answer was generally in the affirmative with no reservation whatever. And when asked to point out the advantages to be found in Letchworth, emphasis was specially laid on the following: good houses, no overcrowding, no drinking and the cleanliness of the town. One firm says that it was sometimes more difficult to get the right kind of workers in Letchworth than in London, where there were so many from which to choose. A workman getting good pay is usually unwilling to leave London where he finds more amusements, but when good workers come to Letchworth they generally remain there. In Letchworth far fewer hands are lost on account of illness than in the corresponding workshops in London. In answer to the question as to what improvements are desirable, the answer is the same from all sides — better and cheaper transport to London.

Letchworth's finances give no clear idea of the conditions of the garden city. As already mentioned, too little money was invested in it from the beginning, and loans had to be raised to carry on the necessary work. Howard's idea that the inhabitants should pay a sum including both ground-rent and rates was not considered expedient and the ground has been leased in Letchworth, according to the custom in England, for 99 years. The rates are settled by the local authorities according to the same rules as in other places. For some years no dividend was paid because all income was immediately spent on new improvements. From a financial point of view, this was misleading. Fresh improvements must be considered as assets, and not be taken from the interest on the money invested. The investors could in this manner enjoy greater security but they got no profits. It will readily be understood that this state of things might last for ever as a fresh way of spending the income would always be at hand. It was not until 1913 that the Board realized what a mistake it was, and then they began to pay a dividend to the long suffering investors — who received one per cent. Then they stopped again — on account of the war — but in 1918 the First Garden City paid two and half per cent, in 1920 four per cent, and in 1924 it had gone up to five per cent, which was the maximum allowed by the statutes. (One per cent higher, as we see, than Howard had proposed.)

Picture of a road near Welwyn, with old trees and grass on each side of the path
(August 1933)

Workmen's cottages in a close in Welwyn (August 1931)

In 1920 the second garden city, Welwyn, was projected. (Louis de Soissons was the architect.) Experience had already been gained in Letchworth and therefore it was much simpler in every way. It lies near London in very pretty uneven country on a big hill where there were a few houses with gardens and many fine trees in the hedgerows, as is so often to be seen in England. The advantages of the situation had all been turned to excellent account. First of all the main outlines were indicated: that is to say, a general plan was drawn for the placing of the different quarters. The plan was of course quite different to Ebenezer Howard's diagram as it had to be adjusted to local conditions, first of all to the railway and the ground. The railway station was there, and was of paramount importance for the growth of the city, it was, so to speak, the heart of it. To the east of the railroad an area was reserved for industrial enterprises, so that the smoke, during the prevailing westerly winds, would cause as little annoyance as possible in the residential parts of the town, which lay west of the railway and to the south. Along the straight line of the railroad, which cuts through the curving

The factory of Shredded Wheat Ltd., Welwyn Garden City (August 1931)

Cottages in concrete, Welwyn Garden City (August 1931)

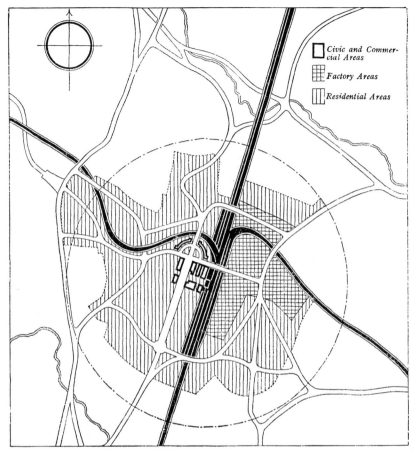

Civic and Commer-
cial Areas

Factory Areas

Residential Areas

Louis de Soissons: Diagram of different quarters in Welwyn Garden City

surface of the ground, the centre of the town is planned with a
straight avenue where the more monumental buildings were
to lie, the town hall, theatre, banks, shops and so on. Round
this again are the capricious residential quarters, left more to
the initiative of the builders and the nature of the ground.
On the plan they appear, with their curves and bends and the
many small blind lanes, to be merely the result of chance.
But seen in the place itself, it is all a matter of course, dependent on the nature of the ground and on the already existing
vegetation, which has been so charmingly worked into the
whole. This town, only a few years old, with its magnificent
old oaks and comfortable houses, has a more idyllic appear-

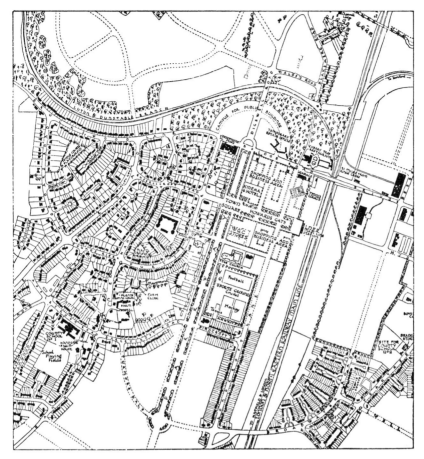

Louis de Soissons: Plan of Welwyn

ance than any other town in the world situated on the railway. Great importance has been attached to the attractive appearance of the residential parts. Most of the roads are narrow, but with lawns along the side of them and paths instead of pavements, so that the whole has more the appearance of the country than of the town. Front gardens with no enclosure, like those in America, have been successfully introduced, though as a rule owners are even more keen in England than in Denmark on enclosing their property: It is not considered sufficient to have transparent wire netting round it, but wooden fences are preferred which shut off all from prying eyes. When the architects of Welwyn first proposed that the front gardens should be laid out like open lawns with odd bushes and flowers here and there, they met with strong opposition. At last, however, they succeeded in getting it carried out in a road where some of the more well-to-do people had built their villas. When once it was finished, everybody thought it looked very well, and when new roads were laid out, they all came and asked to have them done in the same way as in the smart quarter. This front garden area is kept in order by one gardener and is planted out according to certain rules. But the whole is so simple and so sensible that one does not notice that there is anything remarkable about it until one's attention is called to it.

It is characteristic of Welwyn that the schools are in very low and primitive buildings; all the class-rooms are on the ground floor, and, weather permitting, the children can go straight out into the open air. The Danish educational authorities would perhaps find the hut-like buildings too plain. But the authorities in Welwyn consider it essential that the children see the school buildings carried out according to the same principles as the whole of the town, that is to say with low and simple buildings, in keeping with the surrounding country and with open areas around them.

Many of the people living in Welwyn have their work in London. The father of the family must go in and out every day but prefers to live outside all the same for the sake of his family. The percentage of this part of the population is, however, decreasing every year. Several industrial enterprises have chosen Welwyn to settle in, just like Letchworth, and are perfectly satisfied there. The effect of the big factories in Welwyn is no less pleasing than that of the houses. The cleanliness which is noticeable everywhere is particularly surprising. There is no doubt that manufacture of its produce under such conditions is a good advertisement for a firm like Shredded Wheat whose large white silos are seen from the railway. There are football grounds lying next the factories where the workers can get exercise, and directly south of it is a net of 'closes' with workmen's pretty two-story cottages, built of concrete.

Howard's desire to unite the pleasures of the town with those of the country seem about to be realized in Welwyn, which,

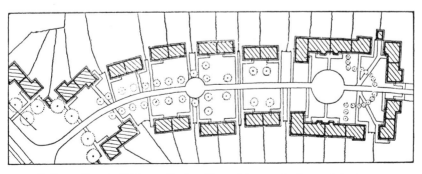

Dellcott Close in Welwyn Garden City, with grass in front of the houses

383

for instance, has its own theatre. The performances are given by amateur actors, but like so many private theatres in England, it is of high standing. All the year round a series of events take place which attracts visitors and shows how much the town is alive and what is the spirit of its inhabitants.

While Letchworth, as an ordinary provincial town, has a number of shops, trade in Welwyn is strongly concentrated. Near the station is a big institution whose main idea reminds one in many ways of the Danish supply associations. Many and various goods are for sale there. Experience has showed that want of local competition has done no harm. In Welwyn a far lower percentage of the population earn their living by the distribution of goods and that renders comparatively low prices possible.

The two garden cities prove in a practical manner that a town can be created artificially just as Ebenezer Howard intended, and places built where conditions of living and work are much healthier than in a great city without being more expensive to live in. And yet the goal he strove to reach is far away. The two idyllic spots lie there as an example for future cities — but their practical significance is astoundingly small. After 30 years of energetic work, with the help of propaganda and agitation and financial support from those interested in it, it has been possible to create two towns of 25,000 in all. It is no great number when we consider the fact that room must be found for four times as many people in Greater London in one year only — and these do not live in garden cities but in more or less casual quarters which were neither planned with consideration for the working centres nor to the country places where the inhabitants must seek recreation. The reason for the want of success of the garden city is easy to find. When it has been started and reached a certain size, it possesses the advantages imagined by Howard, and then all is well financially. But the difficulty is the beginning. There is no little risk in starting a garden city and the only thing that is certain is that it can pay no interest at the beginning. And if, later on, the debentures are only allowed to pay such a restricted dividend as Howard proposes, it is no wonder that there is no great demand for them. It was difficult to get the capital for starting Letchworth and it was no easier for

Welwyn, when the Board agreed to pay as much as seven per cent (which it has not yet been possible to do). Howard's idea, that one ought to be able to get the capital in order to help people with no means to found a small Georgistic community, is Utopian. It must be a social question.

CHAPTER FIFTEEN

BOOKS OF REFERENCE

AMONG the many books on Garden Cities, special mention should be made of *Garden Cities of To-morrow*, by *Sir Ebenezer Howard*. The best edition is published 1946, edited by F. J. Osborn. Important, too, is *The Building of Satellite Towns* by *C. B. Purdom*, 1925, which describes at length the idea of the satellite city and its development all over the world, and also gives a full account of the history of the Garden Cities of Letchworth and Welwyn. The periodical: 'Garden Cities and Town Planning', 1910-32, with its numerous reviews of books and topical information on Garden City work, is, beside the two books before mentioned, the chief source of information for the study of the English Garden City. For information about Welwyn see *Louis de Soissons* and *Arthur William Kenyon's Site Planning in Practice at Welwyn Garden City*, London 1927, which contains numerous good illustrations and sketches of parcelling out and building in connection with roads. *Neighbourhoods of Small Homes*, Harvard University Press, 1931, by *Robert Whitten* and *Thomas Adums*, contains a series of useful studies of town planning for cottages. Information about the two Garden Cities can be obtained from the Garden Cities and Town Planning Association, 13 Suffolk Street, Pall Mall, S.W.1. As regards the regional planning of London, see the two reports of the Greater London Regional Planning Committee.

CHAPTER SIXTEEN

A MOST UNHAPPY ENDING

THE CONCISE TITLE OF THIS BOOK IS 'THE LESSON OF LONDON'. It is a book with a purpose. A description of a town of ten millions is utter nonsense unless one considers the subject from one special angle, and can thus reduce to a chosen few the endless number of facts upon which light has been thrown in existing literature. My object has been to show my compatriots that we have a great deal to learn from that form of civilization in which London has taken the lead. I wished to call attention to the fact that there are two ways of organizing large towns, the English and the Continental. According to my experience, he who learns to know the English way cannot but admire it. But it is dangerous to copy a single detached feature. It must be clearly understood that all conditions of life in English towns which awake admiration on the Continent to-day, belong to a special English world that is entirely different from the Continental. They form an indivisible unity that we must know and understand before we can try to evolve conditions which can prove an equally natural and organic part of our life. Now that I have written the book and followed the development, I have come to the conclusion that it is of even greater importance to tell the English something about their own civilization, that civilization which we admire and imitate as best we can.

One of the mainstays of the English people was their utter ignorance of what was being said and done in other European countries. And thus it has been possible for them to evolve a form of civilization which has grown naturally. In these days, however, this groundwork of ignorance has become an evil, since an unfortunate mania for imitating foreign nations has appeared in England. The frontiers are becoming more and more firmly closed to international trade and to that intercourse which was a matter of course before 1914. At the same time as the nationalist instinct is encouraged in all European countries, it becomes more and more general to imitate the follies of other lands, and now only the follies seem to be international. It is a tragedy not only for England but for the world in general that England should abandon her national traditions. The day on which England gave up Free Trade was as fatal as the outbreak of the War in 1914. I was in London at the time, and it made a deep impression on me to see that the English themselves apparently did not realize their importance in the world at all; there was no evidence that the city was passing through a crisis of incalculable range. From that day onwards, I realized that the inhabitants of London are utterly unconscious of the significance of their city in Europe.

London is to us Continental people the successor of the self-governing townships of the Middle Ages — the Dutch civilian towns. London is the capital of all capitals which has resisted absolutism and maintained the rights of the citizens within the state. England's contribution to European civilization, as seen from the Continent, is a whole world of ideas that could only arise and flourish in a community which had resisted absolutism. London has played a considerable part in the evolution of it. It has never been of greater importance than now that these ideals should continue to exist, in one country at least, in Europe.

Let me summarize these ideals. *In the government* of the state, the result is a governing body chosen from an assembly of electors in which the minority is also represented and which has the right to dispose of the finances of the realm; *in the towns* it is a highly developed form of local government; *in public life* freedom of the Press, religious liberty, equality before the law, freedom to hold meetings, the natural rights of man (the idea of the Rights of Man which is usually connected with the famous French Declaration of 1789, goes back to the writings of Milton in the seventeenth century and was formulated by the English race in the American Declaration of Independence in 1776); in science the result is empiric and rational research (the titles of the works of Thomas Paine, that Quaker and Champion of Liberty, sound like a programme: *Common Sense*, 1776, *The Rights of Man*, 1791, and *Age of Reason*, 1794); in art it signifies a wealth

387

of literature on social and humane problems, a fine domestic architecture and exemplary style as regards articles for practical use, in which utility, form and material are of greater importance than decoration; *in questions of faith* it is tolerance; *in economical life,* free trade and free competition; *in daily life,* conventional form, as conventionality is the self-imposed conformity to laws which renders restraint from the outside superfluous; *in education,* sport as idealized competition, with fair play as a necessary qualification.

Just as we look to London as the originator of English ideals in the world, so is the manner in which people live, or try to live, in London the expression of the same world of thought . . . 'My house is my castle', the one-family house, open-air life and all that we others admire and are fain to imitate, is inseparable from the English mode of thought and life. One hardly knows whether to laugh or to cry on seeing a modernistic architecture imported into London, which is far less suitable to the spirit of the age than the Georgian houses of about 1800. There is now a quantity of English books on the latest fashions in foreign architecture, but I have yet to find one English book dealing at length with the fine standardized type of Georgian town house, the sight of which is one of the most remarkable experiences to the foreigner in London. Hardly anyone in London realizes that London is a first rate architectural city, and that Bedford Square is one of the finest squares in the world.

Based on their experience of English cities, English town-planners have formed their ideals of the town of the future, ideals which people are everywhere trying to realize. It will differ entirely from the monumental cities of antiquity, which were to be regarded entirely as a sanctuary dedicated to a deity of some description. They were dominated by mighty temples and by the palaces of monarchs who were the chief priests of the deity as well as his deputy on earth. Processional roads lead splendidly from palace to temple, through the town, the large population of which was a completely subordinate part of the whole. On festive occasions the people were entirely shut out from the chief part of the town and from taking any active part in the ceremonies. Many of the cities of antiquity which are now being excavated

The Thames seen from Richmond Hill

were like this, and such is yet the Imperial City of Peking, a regularly planned city, a cultural type. Absolutism resuscitated this type of city, in which the town was entirely subordinate to the monumental idea of the whole. Versailles resembles a temple with Louis le Grand as the personification of the deity.

We hope that the Town of the Future will be more realistic. Instead of being the altar of an invisible god, or the monument of the idea of the state, it will simply be the place where men can live their whole life and develop their faculties under the best possible conditions. The houses are modest compared with the buildings of many of the old monumental cities, but there is no home without a garden in which children can be out of doors and enjoy the sun and air as soon as they can notice anything at all. They crawl about in the grass, stand up and try to touch the flowers, birds and insects, make unintelligible remarks to them, and try their strength in a hundred harmless ways. Not far from their own garden is the playground where, a little later, they make friends, learn interesting games and fresh words, build sand-castles and play at ships and motor-cars. There are swings, see-saws and all they want until they begin to feel the need of occupations other than they can provide for them-selves. Then the playing fields await them with games more exciting and dramatic than they had known and they acquire greater skill with the help of gymnastics. The low school-buildings lie surrounded by gardens and playgrounds offering experience and education, both indoors and out. From the school the way leads onwards to the workshops of the adult. These are all situated in accordance with the demands of production, convenient for transport and yet in no way a nuisance to the home. In the laboratories, as in the schools, work is carried out under the most favourable conditions possible. And the town with the widest perspective lies open to the adult.

In his spare time he visits other town centres or goes out into the country or to a cricket or football match. If the single house is not imposing in itself, the main outlines of the plans are so much the more so: the net of tree-bordered roads connecting the various urban centres, allowing of speedy communication, and as a contrast to the main roads the very quiet spots, the parks, sports fields and peaceful homesteads grouped around the village greens and playing grounds. Young people prefer to congregate in large colleges when they have emancipated themselves from their houses and there they can pursue common interests with those of their own age.

Modern German park in the English style

A close in Hampstead Garden Suburb with a view of Hampstead Heath

As soon as they marry, however, they will again look to the house in the garden where small children can play and family life thrive. When all kinds of sport have been tried and the need of much violent exercise has decreased, then an interest in gardening awakes. Growth has come to an end, there is no more development but it gives zest to life to give the possibility of it to other living things. The mother sits in the garden in the sun with her children, surrounded by the plants and flowers that the father has sown. Gardening gives him exercise and relaxation after the drudgery of the day, the joy of creating. And in this manner the town of the future should provide space for a healthy development of life at all ages — right until the old people are led out into the garden for the last time that they may drink in the sun and air, the songs of the birds and scent of flowers, just the same as the tiniest human being.

Thus one imagines the town of the future when walking around the Hampstead Garden Suburb. At the beginning of this century, there were only fields there, remote from the city, and few thought that it could ever extend as far as that. A vicar's wife, however, who had formerly been living in the East End with her husband, had her home out there. Her dream was to create a new and healthy quarter with better homes for the poorer members of the community. And thus it happened that development spread from Toynbee Hall to Hampstead. Dame Henrietta Barnett did not only feel for the poor but she judged sociological problems correctly. Subsequent development proved her to be right in her opinion that it was not sufficient to move people out to better houses. It was also necessary to see to it that their lives, as a part of the community, should be different from what they hitherto had been. Instead of entire and widespread quarters for the poor alone and others only for the rich, the city was to be broken up into nothing but small units, all equally well laid-out. In such town cells the single individual need not feel utterly lost in an immense and disjointed quarter, rich and poor together making a well defined little community, a harmonious town regularly formed around its civic centre. In Raymond Unwin she found a man who could give her ideas a practical form and create an ideal town, with recreation grounds, civic centre and with finer roads than had ever then been known. After one has wandered about the Hampstead Garden Suburb and seen how the houses form a harmonious whole, and walked through Golders Hill up to Whitestone Pond and gazed at the sunset over the wide stretches of country, hardly distinguishable through the evening haze, one tries to imagine the whole of it covered with such towns. It is evident that the harmonious city is not a Utopia. We have experienced the reality of it.

He who is acquainted with the history of London understands that the ideals of Ebenezer Howard, Henrietta Barnett and Raymond Unwin are a consistent continuation of historical evolution. They are wholesome ideals which are also shared by the man in the street. It is the lesson of London. One look at the advertisements of the building speculators in the English newspapers is sufficient to show

Hampstead Garden Suburb boundary wall. The ground is sloping and the district adjoins the heath extension. The retaining wall is a charming boundary broken by garden houses and gates instead of the old turrets and bastions, a definite line of limitation between town and open space

393

Such houses with two-room flats are common in Copenhagen
and not considered to be slums

In London these houses are cleared as slums

Photo: Dr. A. T. Westlake

Old Bermondsey, with small houses and gardens

Photo: Dr. A. T. Westlake

New Bermondsey, the same place as above, rebuilt with new blocks of flats;
emptiness instead of gardens

Cottages from Roehampton estate

that Englishmen want to live in a cottage. And yet there are
apparently obstacles in the way of this development. Nowadays many people believe it is an improvement to build tall
houses like those which are to be found in other large cities.
London has apparently been panic-stricken and has abandoned the English traditions. There are two things which
have upset people. One is the uncanny increase of the traffic,

Typical buildings from one of the London County Council's estates

the other is the slums. Something must be done at all costs and they choose a means which is no means and begin to build flats for people who otherwise would be living in cottages.

It is true that the traffic and the slums are the greatest drawbacks of London. Let us first take a look at the traffic. Hours may be spent every day going to work and coming

397

back again, and these hours are not the most agreeable ones. During the rush hours, the buses and the Underground trains are as closely packed with human beings as it is possible for them to be. They stand up and hang on to the straps for long distances, crowded together with fellow passengers in a stifling atmosphere. To a superficial observer this annoyance appears to be the result of the scattered residential quarters. He concludes that the general use of houses with many stories would reduce the number and the duration of the journeys. But it is not such a simple matter as that. The fault does not lie in the distance between the houses but in the concentration of the centres of work far away from the houses. If the greater part of the population of London were living in flats instead of in one-family houses, the overcrowding of traffic in the city would be just as serious as it is now, and it is not certain even that the journeys would be shorter. It is true that an unreasonable amount of time is wasted in London in transport, but that is not so much due to the longer distances from the suburbs where the traffic runs quickly, as to the difficulty in getting through the more concentrated parts of the city. In large towns there is always much loss caused by unnecessary transport whether the town is scattered or concentrated. For what is the use of a man living in a five-story house in one corner of the town, if, as in Copenhagen, he has his work in another and his allotment in a third? Such is life in Continental cities. In London he can at least have his home and his garden on the same spot. If the business quarter, factory quarter, and residential quarters are all to be concentrated, the result will be overcrowded traffic all over the town. The most rational solution of the traffic problem is a complete sub-division of the chief centres of the city into many minor centres — the idea of the garden city. Garden cities cannot, however, become of any great importance if they can only be carried out by private enterprise as has been the case so far. They must form part of a greater plan. Future cities should be connected by a well established system of traffic. That was also Howard's idea from the beginning. In a diagram in his book, he shows the garden cities arranged like satellites in the solar system round the chief city, each surrounded by open country but connected one with another by series of traffic avenues.

If factories and workshops could be removed to the open areas and houses were to be built up around them, there would be a possibility of lessening the daily transport to and from the place of work. At the outset, one could be inclined to regard the possibility of such a change with some scepticism. There would apparently be no little risk in moving the centres of production so far from the heart of the city. It would certainly give rise to an increase in transport of both raw materials and the finished article and the cost of all this would affect the balance more directly than the journeys to and from those employed at the work centre. The advantages, however, of the lower ground rents and the greater possibilities for expansion might easily outweigh this drawback. It can be proved that a number of industries in and near London *are* moving farther out, and at the same time new houses must be provided for about 100,000 people a year. The consequence is that the removal should be organized so that it could be carried out according to a regional planning, instead of being left to chance. A pronounced spreading of town-centres in London *is* taking place. In suburbs far removed from the city, there are big shops, theatres, places of amusement with artificial rinks and large cinemas so that people need not go into the town itself either for shopping or for pleasure. It sounds paradoxical, but this spreading of the town is the only solution of the traffic problems. But it should be planned.

In order to avoid the drawbacks of modern traffic the big main roads which connect the various units should be protected from ribbon development by a carefully planned decentralization. Here one of the greatest difficulties arises in England as in other countries. Even if the roads are as well constructed as possible and are perfect, in excellent repair, they deteriorate gradually as building increases. Every house by the side of a road detracts from its value as a means of locomotion, and when at last there is a continuous row of houses along it and innumerable side roads run into it, the road becomes a street where the risk to human life is so great that speed must of necessity be diminished. Those who have built their houses by the roadside because it happened to be near, will most certainly live to regret it. A house standing by the road is in our day less peaceful than one by the railway.

At the same time as the main roads are to be cleared of the local traffic and of buildings, to be made more efficient the actual residential streets are to be made habitable by protecting them against the raging of the long-distance traffic. It is a very important problem how to create a quiet road with no dangers for its habitants. The cul-de-sac streets, the so-called closes, are the best. Good examples with purely local traffic are to be found in Hampstead and Welwyn. The houses can be quite close to the heavy traffic and yet in peace and quiet. The children can go out of the backdoor straight into playgrounds and fields without running into any kind of vehicle. Thus we see that the difficult problems of the traffic can only be solved by means of a carefully-planned decentralization of the town. This is applicable in a still higher degree to the evil of the slums.

Many are inclined to regard the slums as merely the resort of undesirable elements of the community. That leads to a false interpretation of the problem. The growth of slums in a big city is not the result of bad morals. The slums are simply entire quarters which bear the stamp of poverty. *It must never be forgotten that poverty is the root and the real evil of the slums.* If we lose sight of this fundamental truth, it may lead to all kinds of wrong conclusions.

Poverty, it is said, is no shame, and the truth of this must be admitted in those particular communities which are unable to find employment for all who are willing to work. But poverty in a large city is without doubt an insurmountable obstacle to the founding of a good home. Many books contain romantic tales of homes of the poor which were all so bright and clean. If *that* were the main point, then there would indeed be many ideal homes in the poor quarters; women in poor homes make truly heroic efforts to keep them clean. But all the trouble spent in keeping a home clean and tidy cannot do away with the inconveniences arising from the fatal want of space from which almost all homes in a large city suffer.

It has lately become the fashion to agitate for smaller homes; this is one of the results of the romance of engineering, the admiration of the sleeping-car on the railway and the cabin of the aeroplane. It may certainly be wholesome for the wealthier classes who have been suffering for many years from the exertion of keeping up too large and pretentious homes, but it may lead to a wholly false idea of what should be demanded of the normal dwelling. It is not sufficient to enumerate the inanimate objects pertaining to it; a bed, a table, a cupboard, and so on; and to find out how few one can manage with and how close they can be placed to one another. It can all be calculated to the eighth of an inch. The result will, nevertheless, be wrong as the aim is not the right one. A home is not merely a furniture store. It is a place in which human beings have to live. The furniture and other inanimate objects are merely the setting, necessary requisites, but not the aim and object. The essential thing, life in the home, is far more varied than in a cabin or a sleeping-car in which only a temporary stay is made and therefore one cannot judge from the narrow space of the cabin as to what is necessary in a home. The comparison is still more misleading, as far greater sums can be spent on the comfort and on the expensive and ingenious equipment of such a cabin, than would be possible in the ordinary modest little home.

The ordinary citizen of the upper middle class feels a sense of relief in having to give up his large and imposing house and settling down in a smaller one. His inevitable conclusion is, that it must be a great advantage to have little space. Speaking of the poor who are forced to live in small homes, he says: 'It is really much more convenient for these people than for us; they have none of those responsibilities which make life a burden.' The only answer to these thoughtless but common remarks is to insist on the fact that *plenty of room in the home is an absolute necessity for health and human dignity.* It is expensive and yet unsatisfactory to try to make up for the want of space by ingenious equipment. It is useless to invent furniture so artfully devised that more people can sleep in the same room than would otherwise do so, *when it is in itself a danger for so many persons to be permanently in the same room.* It is not a question of how many bodies can be kept in a dry and quiet place, but of living beings, who need an opportunity of satisfying their need of exercise, of meat and drink, of a healthy sexual life and of sleep. Where people spend most of the day out of doors and have plenty of room and opportunity to move about at will outside their homes, it does not matter so much if they are obliged to spend the night in a crowded room. In a large city, however, the same people who live closely packed together in their homes have also the least space at their disposal out of doors and are forced to spend the greater part of their lives in poor dwellings. It is a proved and well-known fact that in the case of an epidemic or a conflagration the overcrowded room was a great danger not only to the inhabitants but to the whole town. The peril, however, is also becoming apparent under normal conditions, as it does not offer sufficiently favourable conditions of life to the inhabitants.

It is worst of all for the children, who are forced to live their lives in the same room as the grown-up people who have different habits and keep different hours. They cannot play in the daytime and they cannot do homework or occupy themselves in their leisure hours; they cannot sleep in peace at night; they gain at too early an age sexual experience which has too strong and disturbing an influence on their development. It is most harmful, too, for adults to have the intimacies of private life thrust upon them. The ill-health, nervousness or irritability of one single person is detrimental to all the others, and aggravates their condition. The want of privacy breaks down body and soul, because it hinders all expansion of vitality. The effects of the moral deficiency of the single individual are greatly augmented by such overcrowding. It is exceedingly detrimental when the inhabitants cannot be kept apart according to sex, but must live all mixed up together. None of these drawbacks can be warded off by any mechanism or particular arrangement of the single room but only by providing more and more rooms.

Now all these disadvantages of overcrowding are terribly increased in blocks of flats with many rooms under one roof, in large buildings with far too many inhabitants. The condition of nervous and irritable people, surrounded on all sides by other nervous and irritable people, grows worse and worse. The sleepless hear noises from every quarter; those suffering from infectious diseases become a greater danger to others. All facilities for games are denied the children, who are unprotected against the influence of the nervous, the sick, the morally or mentally deficient. The curse of poverty and of the want of space in the home increases when the complaint of despairing fellow-sufferers echoes from every side.

You English who come over to the Continent and see big residential quarters with miles and miles of tall houses in which the people live in dwellings piled one on top of the other, should try to realize that this unfortunate system is not the result of the need for good homes or the improvement of the conditions of traffic. The only reason for its existence is this: the landlord gets higher interest on his property. The thousands of human beings who live in dwellings so wretched that they are a danger to the community, are so doing in order to give the honest middle classes the opportunity of a good and safe investment.

You English should know that the Frenchman, Le Corbusier, is a modernist in his artistic form but a conservative in his planning of a city. When he plans to rebuild Paris with rows of sky-scrapers, he is merely keeping up the old tradition from the reigns of the Bourbons and the Bonapartes. To improve the health of Paris, the city has always been made more and more imposing and monumental, with less and less consideration for the manner in which a family can live under wholesome conditions. In England new slums largely develop in houses that have been given up by their middle-class owners. On the Continent we construct slums.

You English must also know that in all towns, in your own as well as others, there is a strong tendency to de-populate the most thickly populated areas. And this tendency is a right and wholesome one. But when replacing poor little houses by big blocks of flats, large sums are tied up in quarters which should normally de-populate, and wholesome evolution is thus hindered by the building of these large blocks. We on the Continent know something of this, for we have learnt it to our cost. To build flats in slums will not stem the current, London will continue to be a town of one-family houses, and it is tragic to see the enormous sums of money spent in this way and employed to a wrong purpose, for instead of planning the moving out of factories, business premises and private houses in connection with each other, living houses are being built with a quite un-English standard and according to types which are everywhere else recognized as inadequate.

The monumental city of antiquity, Peking, is ruined by the intrusion of houses of European types which destroy all the harmony of its plan. And now London, the capital of English civilization, has caught the infection of Continental experiments which are at variance with the whole character and tendency of the city! Thus the foolish mistakes of other countries are imported everywhere, and at the end of a few years all cities will be equally ugly and equally devoid of individuality.
This is the bitter
END

AN ESSAY ON

LONDON NEW TOWNS

MODERN AND ANCIENT

A NEW AND MORE

HAPPY ENDING

BUT NO END

1978

As an appropriate frontispiece to this essay I have chosen a picture showing the 34-story 'Centre Point' at the corner of Oxford Street and Tottenham Court Road, a quite unnecessary building which for several years after its erection stood completely empty. It was apparently inspired by the opening words of Aldous Huxley's book, *Brave New World*: 'A squat grey building of only thirty-four stories', assuming that central London around it would be a kind of Manhattan with much taller skyscrapers. Fortunately, that dream has not come true and never will, as the following pages show.

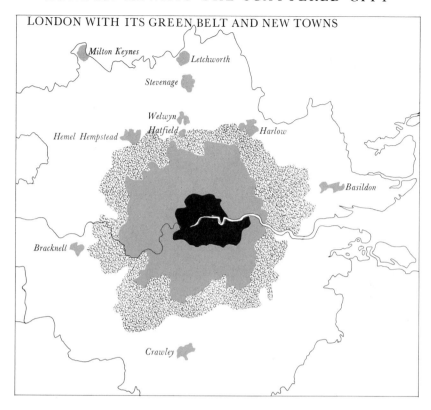

LONDON WITH ITS GREEN BELT AND NEW TOWNS

Milton Keynes · Letchworth · Stevenage · Welwyn · Hatfield · Hemel Hempstead · Harlow · Basildon · Bracknell · Crawley

London Always the Scattered City

Forty years ago I predicted that the foolish mistakes of other countries would be imported everywhere and all cities would become equally ugly and equally devoid of individuality. My prophecy has come true so far as London is concerned. It has been spoiled by a number of meaningless skyscrapers; the streets are crowded with myriad private cars at the same time as public transport has decayed; buildings with flats have replaced the typical London houses in the depopulated East End; etc., etc. *But this is not the bitter end,* rather the beginning of a new era. The idea of building satellite towns instead of wild-growing suburbia, which idea forty years ago was pure Utopia, has now been realized. Eight *New Towns* outside a green girdle around London, housing one million townspeople, have now been completed. And a ninth New Town, Milton Keynes, to accommodate a quarter of a million inhabitants, is under way. *Thus, London is still a unique city.*

Milton Keynes represents a reaction to a number of the conventional principles of a New Town, such as the centralized road system, the organization in small neighbourhoods, the enclosing boundary; in short, all the sacred cows of the New Towns movement. But it is nevertheless a true child of that movement. It is only — like any normal child — critical of its parents. Thus, though Milton Keynes is a reaction to the New Towns theory as developed after World War II, it is still in keeping with the definition of the term 'Garden City' from before the War adopted by the Council of the Garden Cities and Town-Planning Association in 1920. That definition runs (as mentioned, p. 371) as follows: '*A Garden City is a town designed for healthy living and industry; of a size that makes possible a full measure of social life, but not larger; surrounded by a rural belt; the whole of the land being in public ownership or held in trust for the community.*'

Milton Keynes is, in my opinion, an utterly English phenomenon; a link in a long chain of town-planning experiments starting with the Garden City movement at the beginning of this century. It is an important contribution to a standing discussion and an answer to a number of questions that have been under debate for a long time. But it is also — as I will show later — a continuation and a perfection of the special London pattern of the seventeenth and eighteenth centuries that was so completely different from all Continental city planning of that period.

Milton Keynes is of enormous importance, not only for the London Region but for the entire civilized world. I feel that I cannot do this great subject justice merely by giving a description and an evaluation of the existing plans and their present state of execution. I feel I will have to recapitulate the whole course of the London planning process during the present century and place Milton Keynes in this larger context. I am filled with a very personal feeling for this development which — during half a century — I have had the privilege of following closely, so to speak from the inside, and of discussing it with some of its leading experts. As a foreigner I have, at the same time, been able to observe it from outside and to compare its development with contemporary town planning work in other countries. So let me tell the story in my own subjective way.

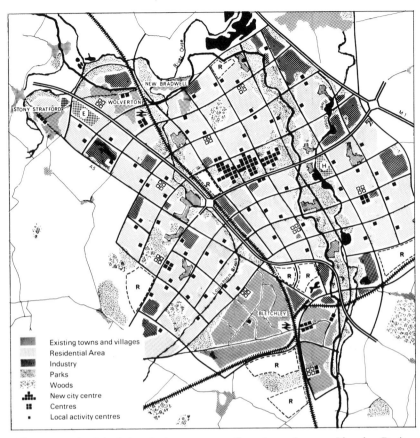

Milton Keynes' original plan. Scale 1 : 120,000. Consultant planners: Llewelyn-Davies, Weeks, Forestier-Walker and Bor.

In contrast to the planners of other New Towns, they have not tried to dictate a complete pattern of the future life of the city. They want to give great freedom of development and avoid traffic congestion at certain points by covering the entire area — planned for a quarter of a million inhabitants — with a somewhat irregular square grid of primary roads. The 1-kilometre square units are not intended to be self-contained neighbourhoods but just small parts of a large patchwork where, in the future, people can live as they like. From every lot there will be only a short distance to a primary road and at the same time close connection with a network of secondary roads, which cross the primary roads via underpaths, thus giving easy access to neighbouring square-units. Local commercial centres and other service buildings are supposed to find their natural location at such out-of-level crossings between primary and secondary roads, at the same time serving the population of two square-units. Two units are reserved for a large city centre connected at the east with a long strip of parkland on both sides of the river Ouzel and the Grand Union Canal meandering freely through the man-made grid. Existing old towns, such as Stony Stratford and Bletchly, as well as a number of villages with historic churches are incorporated in the plan.

The First Phase of Modern Town Planning

It is now about fifty years since I saw London for the first time. *The first phase of the modern English town-planning movement was coming to an end,* the phase I would call the period of pilot experiments, such as Letchworth, Welwyn and Hampstead Garden Suburb.

I travelled to this strange island to find out what the English capital was like. I was well prepared, had studied carefully a number of other capitals — Rome, Paris, Berlin, Stockholm — and knew of course by heart my own hometown of Copenhagen; all these continental metropoles where the majority of people lived in flats and considered it a law of nature for inhabitants of a large city to do so. I knew what frustrated lives families led under such conditions, both poor people and those of the middle classes. I was now anxious to see with my own eyes that urban life could be quite different. I would learn to know London, where the majority of the inhabitants lived in houses; London, at that time, the largest city in Europe and probably in the world. Statistics showed that while Berlin had an average of seventy-five persons per building in the entire city, London had only eight, and other English cities less than five.

I did not spare myself in exploring the different parts of the metropolis, this my 'promised land', my one-family-house city.

It certainly did not make good propaganda for its special kind of living. As soon as I came outside the central parts and the more fashionable quarters, I could travel in all directions through unending forbidding prospects of sixteen-and-one-half-foot-wide Victorian houses. I learned to my surprise that, in the London lingo, they were called terraced houses, evoking a city like Bath with one crescent above the other, forming lovely terraces nestled in the hillside. And I sighed: What a cynical euphemism for contourless districts of bleak, uniform houses! My English architect friends had a much better name for the phenomenon: urban sprawl.

It spread further and further every year, leaving older suburbs to their fate as slums as people moved out from them to new districts, so much closer to the open land. Through this process the distance between home and working place could become enormous and many people also had to live far from shops and schools and all the other amenities of a town. It was generally considered the drawback of low density.

Most people whom I met were hardly aware of the special character of their capital and they certainly did not appreciate it. Being English they considered it a human right for every family to have a house of its own to live in. But at the same time they suffered from a sort of inferiority complex: In their opinion London was not a real city like Paris. They felt that it was lacking in the urban qualities of a continental metropolis.

Right from the beginning, however, I had the good fortune to come in touch with Raymond Unwin whose views were less banal. He knew towns and town planning in other countries very well, but shared my interest in the English way of living in one-family houses. And he had taken up the fight against urban sprawl in a truly English Way.

In a lecture from 1912 called *Nothing Gained by Overcrowding,* he said that overcrowding is generally assumed to be necessary for economic reasons. He therefore carefully calculated the costs and benefits of different densities of housing. As he came to the conclusion that a higher density did not pay at all, the problem would simply be which density offered the best way of living for average familes, and his solution was that twelve houses to the acre was the right figure. That should give the optimum of good conditions. He maintained that the long distances many people had to travel daily to their work were not a result of too low density but of bad organization. The working places were huddled together in special parts of the vast city while residential districts were found in other areas far from industry and trade. Raymond Unwin was first and foremost a social thinker, a Fabian socialist, who did not see the town or the town plan as an aim in itself but as an expression of an organized way of living. He spoke of *'the town which, instead of being a huge aggregation of units ever spreading further and further away from the original centre and losing all touch with that centre, should consist of a federation of groups constantly clustering around new subsidiary centres, each group limited to a size that could effectively keep in touch with and be controlled from the subsidiary centre and through that centre have connection with the original and main centre of the federation area'* (from *Nothing Gained by Overcrowding,* 1912).

Organization became the key word for all his work. To him it was also the essence of Ebenezer Howard's Garden City ideas, and Unwin and his brother-in-law, Barry Parker, planned in 1903 the first garden city, *Letchworth* (see pp. 371–377), as a well-organized example of a *New Town*. And they planned *Hampstead Garden Suburb* in 1905 as an alternative and a contrast to the existing suburbs. While these were just shapeless masses of uniform streets with uniform houses, Hampstead Garden Suburb took the form of a complete town on the hill, crowned by churches and other public buildings and with a variety of houses, large and small, built for different social classes, but all arranged in harmonious groups, supplementing each other, and together forming an interconnected whole.

As a still relevant example of their penetrating work, I find the layout of roads and streets in their schemes worthy of study. In ordinary suburbs not only were all houses identical, but the streets were laid out according to precisely the same standard, with the same widths, the same pavements, the same kerbstones. Whether they were important streets carrying much traffic, or completely unimportant thoroughfares without any traffic whatsoever, they had to follow exactly the same rules laid down in bylaw paragraphs. Unwin protested against such meaningless uniformity and applied for — and obtained! — an Act of Parliament saying that the Hampstead Garden Suburb Trust could depart from the general rules of 40 feet as a minimum road width. In Hampstead, roads not exceeding 500 feet in length could be constructed with a width of only 20 feet. The number of houses to the acre was low, on an average limited to eight over the entire estate. In return for this lower density the landowners were offered concessions in the matter of road construction and road costs. In this way possibilities for much better housing were created.

I mention this as an important example of successful planning which, as far as I can see, has never been repeated in the same rational way. On the contrary, in the New Towns built after World War II it has been a rule, according to what I have learned, that road engineers, and even garbage collectors, determine the road widths independent of what the planning office might decide about the importance or unimportance of the roads concerned in the overall planning.

Heath Close, a short, 20-foot wide cul-de-sac leading from Hampstead Heath Extension to the four-winged Waterloo Court, a women's dormitory. On the map page 417 marked with an A.

Parker and Unwin made full use of the possibilities thus offered them. They experimented with different ways of creating pleasant housing groups with very low road costs. The cul-de-sac, which had hitherto been banned from all proper planning as undesirable, proved in their hands to be an especially attractive device, offering privacy and peace to the houses in the road. Other housing groups were arranged round small quadrangles, greens or tennis lawns forming quiet backwaters outside the general traffic flow. The more important roads were, on the other hand, given greater width than usual. They could be bordered with strips of grass that could be taken in later for further extension, if necessary. The result was a whole hierarchy of roads ranging from a highway to a petty lane.

Hampstead Garden Suburb, planned in 1907, displays a number of fine examples of such planning which, much later, when the private motor car became common property, was an inspiration to planners in many countries.

Ebenezer Howard and Raymond Unwin would give each garden city a limited size. This did not mean that they would stop growth. They would lead it into the right channels which would allow for a well-organized development around new centres nearby. Garden Cities were also called *satellite towns,* indicating that they first attained their full significance when they no longer were small solitary towns but had become elements in a greater organized whole, a *satellite system* replacing the unorganized *urban sprawl.* The rural land which must surround each township was not to be regarded as in opposition to the town, but as an indispensable part of it. '*As man and woman by their varied gifts and faculties supplement each other, so should town and country*' as Howard wrote in his picturesque language (see p. 367). These were not at all new thoughts. In the Middle Ages all cities owned the surrounding land. They simply could not live without it. It was in those days a vital necessity for a town to possess its own food-producing farmland. It must have given life another dimension when people were not divided into townspeople and country people, but all used both brain and hands.

Howard was more of a theorist while Unwin was a practical man learning from experience. Howard put forward as a dictum that a garden city should be limited to 30,000 inhabitants. But Unwin said (in *Town Planning in Practice,* 1909): '*It would seem desirable to limit in some way the size of a town, but how far this may be possible we have yet to learn*'. He noted with disgust '*that irregular fringe of half-developed suburb and half-spoiled country which forms such a hideous and depressing girdle around modern growing towns*'. And he continued: '*We may well doubt whether it will prove possible for us to limit the population of a modern town to a given number, should the town become so prosperous and popular that natural tendency would cause that number to be greatly increased. The attempt would bear some resemblance to King Canute and the flowing tide*'. So said Raymond Unwin with great foresight in the year 1909, fifty years before the discussion on open planning, in a period — before the First World War — when the great problem was to get Letchworth and Hampstead to grow and certainly not to limit their development.

As a practical remedy he recommended the laying out of belts of parkland or wood. Even the walls of fortified towns *'may find some modern counterpart; where the ground is sloping and the district adjoins a park or belt of open space, the retaining wall may be a charming boundary, its monotony broken by garden houses and gates instead of the old turrets and bastions'.*

The wall forming a clear partition between Hampstead Garden Suburb and the Heath Extension (in the foreground seen from B on the plan page 417).

Unwin created exactly that kind of wall between Hampstead Garden Suburb and the adjoining Heath Extension (see p. 393). It is now generally regarded as a purely romantic whim, this 'charming boundary' resembling a town wall from the Middle Ages. It *is* picturesque, but it is also a most realistic and practical device, appropriate to the site. It is a clear partition between a planned town and an open playing field.

415

Up to this century the district which is now Hampstead
Garden Suburb was open fields (belonging to Harrow). But
when the Underground was extended to Golders Green it
came suddenly in close contact with central parts of London
and was now ripe for development (see p. 333). Traditionally,
it would then have been covered with suburban houses from
one end to the other. But Parker and Unwin suggested keeping
a considerable part of it as an untrimmed common, an extension of Hampstead Heath available for cricket and all kinds of
other games and play. It was a cheap solution, technically. But
the built-upon area would be so much more valuable with
access to a piece of free land. It had, however, to be planned
consciously. The unregulated area must be properly separated
from the regular town, the rustic and rural from the urban
district.

Here is probably the right place for a discussion of the term
urban, which has been used — and misused — so much during
the last decades in English writing on town planning.

As I have already mentioned, the English suffer badly from
an inferiority complex, from the belief that their good towns
are not *urban* enough.

But how can we define this magic word?

Paris and Vienna, the large continental cities, are certainly
urban. All agree to that. But why? It cannot be a mere question
of size or quantity, since the problematic London is much
larger, with many more inhabitants. Is it then the scale of
buildings or the continuity of facades along the streets that
matter? Is it less *urban* if there are many trees or other plants?
Of course a wood cannot be urban. But a garden can. The
Champs Elysées in Paris with its rows of trees is decidedly
urban. In my opinion many of the old London districts are
also truly urban even with their abundance of trees. There is
not a street where you cannot, somewhere or other, enjoy the
rich foliage of the *London plane*.

The well-to-do people, who in former days built their London residences here, wanted to bring with them some of the
charm of their country homes. With rural material they created
urban gardens in the squares of the metropolis.

Before World War II many people complained about the
undemocratic iron railings round these gardens that adorned

416

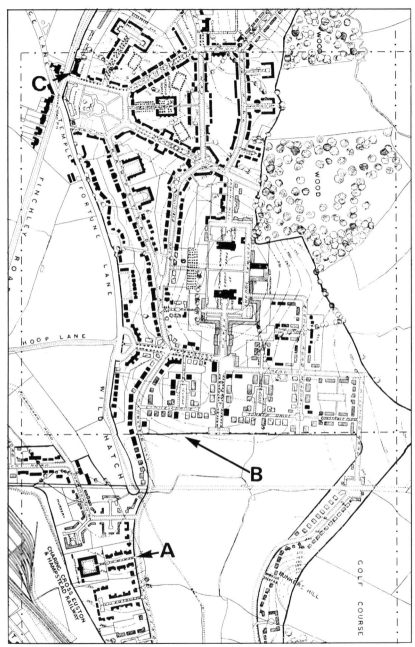

A plan of Hampstead Garden Suburb, from 1911. The dot-and-dash line indicates a
1-kilometre square superimposed on the plan for comparison with the Milton Keynes
planning. At the lower left-side corner: the railway at Golders Green station.

A carefully paved footpath in the green but urban Hampstead Garden Suburb.

the squares. During the war they were taken away to be melted down for guns and the gardens were thus opened to the public. The trees survived all right, but the gardens were ruined. They could not stand the invasion.

Is the social relationship between people a deciding factor? Village life versus town life? In the heart of Rome you can find places with a life and neighbourliness as in a small village. But Rome is still urban. There are no arbitrary elements, everything has found its final, unchangeable form. The streets and squares are paved with stone. Through centuries it has got its finish from the wear of a myriad of feet. The solid buildings with walls of stone and plaster have also become quite smooth from the touch of thousands of Romans. No, if any city on this earth is urban, it certainly is Rome.

A footpath in the rural, untended Heath Extension outside the Hampstead Garden Suburb wall.

I think these examples tell something about the urban character of a town. To me *an urban district is one that is planned and carried out to stand the hard wear of a dense population.*

If we now return to Hampstead, we observe that on the one side of the Wall all footpaths were carefully planned from the beginning and carefully carried out. They are well paved and can be bordered with kerbstones, boards or other solid materials. That is obviously the urban side. On the other side of the Wall the grass of the Heath's Extension is untended and footpaths have been trampled down by generations of feet. This is the rural side. Both types, the urban and the rural paths, have their own beauty and attraction when used in the right way and the right place. But they do not mix well.

Therefore the Wall.

I have the impression that many modern planners look a little condescendingly on Hampstead Garden Suburb as being completely out of date, an Edwardian essay in the picturesque. This view, in my opinion, is not justified. It certainly is picturesque but has much more to give us than that.

My eyes were opened to its qualities when, after my first three months in London, I made a tour of the Continent. I went to Austria and Germany, and later to France, to see old places and meet old professional friends again. As a matter of fact, I understood the German language better than the English. (Unfortunately, I must still say, with the French painter Fernand Léger: I can speak English but I cannot understand it.) I was also familiar with the German philosophy of art.

The Germans in the nineteenth century studied the rules of human perception with great energy. *Helmholtz* and other scientists had found out what mechanism it was that created harmonies in the world of sound, in music. *Ostwald* had in a similar way showed a simple order in our perception of colours resulting in harmonies and disharmonies, as in music. Art historians had given brilliant interpretations of historic masterpieces. Ambitious aesthetes, however, were not satisfied. They wanted to give objective rules for the fine arts and thus produce recipes for the beautification of our surroundings.

The Austrian *Camillo Sitte* gave, in his book *Der Städtebau* from 1889, analyses of the beauty of a number of fine historic cities and from these deduced useful instructions for the improvement of the appearance of modern cities. His main object was to transform the famous *Vienna Ring* and give it a new and better image; but he left the Viennese suburbs as *trostlos*, as dreary, as they were.

I visited Cologne where the dynamic Oberbürgermeister (Lord Mayor) *Konrad Adenauer* was striving to give the city a "ring" of open spaces, somewhat in the Sitte-manner, each of them clearly defined by new housing blocks. The Rhineland, with Cologne, was however one of the few districts on the European continent where the tradition of one-family houses — as in England — had survived. But the new suburbs of Cologne were now planned for tenement housing.

From Cologne it was only a short trip to Bonn, where professor *A. E. Brinckmann* had his institute of art history. In his first (and best) book, *Platz und Monument* from 1912, he has formed this dictum as a conclusion: '*Städte bauen heisst mit dem Hausmaterial Raum gestalten*' which I would translate: Building cities means forming architectural spaces using buildings as the material. I had read Brinckmann with great enthusiasm. He was a brilliant eye-opener for a young man. I now had the opportunity to follow his eloquent lectures on esthetics in city planning.

From Bonn I went to Paris to meet *Le Corbusier* in his studio in a former monastery with inspired sketches pinned up on the white walls. He had, the year before, on the occasion of the Great Paris Exhibition of 1925, shown how Paris according to his ideas ought to be rebuilt not as a composition in spaces but as enormous blocks, monumental skyscrapers standing in a green parkland. Le Corbusier told me on that occasion that his latest creation was not skyscrapers but a housing colony of one-family houses, *Pessac*, near Bordeaux. I ought to see it, he said. I took a sleeper to Bordeaux the same night and had the opportunity to visit it the next day. It was not like anything I had seen before. This was neither spaces nor solids but a cubistic dream in delicate tints. The fifty or so concrete houses were, as if by magic, transformed into a composition of rectangular colour planes, sheer surfaces seemingly without substance or weight. Nobody lived in them yet. No human being had, as yet, sullied the exquisite shades of colour. There they stood in the morning sun, a brisk new world of an unknown beauty, but strangely unreal. The week before Pessac had been officially opened by M. de Monzie, the Minister of Public Works. For that occasion quite tall trees had been placed in the streets — I say placed, not planted, as they were moved to Pessac without their roots. They already had a melancholy look in front of the houses, in contrast to the gay colour scheme. It took more than a year before any of the houses were lived in — and completely changed.

In Dessau in Germany *Walter Gropius* had created another colony of houses in the modernistic vernacular. The buildings for the so-called *Bauhaus School* were a phantasia in glass, steel and concrete. Students in the tall workshop-building had a hot summer behind the enormous glass 'curtain wall', an architectural *tour de force*. Their professors could relax in a series of villas in an avenue of firs, the so-called *Meisterhäuser*. (The school had no *professors* but *Meisters* — the same as *maestros* — a title taken from the crafts; but applied, as here, to artists it is really more pretentious than the quite neutral professor.) These houses were also in a cubistic style but barren and gray without the fine colours of Le Corbusier's Pessac. They were revolutionary in so far as everything on their facades differed from traditional architecture. They were indeed *modernistic,* but *not functional. Hannes Meyer,* who succeeded Walter Gropius as head of the school, showed me that the house he had to live in there, judged by appearances, was most modern, but in its function nothing but an old-fashioned director's house in Berlin. It had everything that belonged to a good bourgeois home: servants' quarters in a basement under the level of the garden lawn, on the ground floor a study, a sitting-room and dining-room, and on the upper floor a number of bedrooms, one with access to a useless narrow balcony round a windy corner — an uncomfortable gazebo shaped like the bridge of a ship.

I remembered with veneration the simple house where Raymond Unwin resided in Hampstead: *Wyldes Farm,* the oldest in the vicinity, most likely dating back to the Middle Ages. But how pleasant and unconventional the large room was with its open-roof construction, where he both received people and worked on his lectures, projects and books. How democratic and functional this house was compared with those of the Brave New World of the Continent.

I know perfectly well that in Europe there were other and more social experiments than those I have mentioned; for instance in the Ruhr District. But the contrast between the mostly esthetic attempts I had seen in Austria, Germany and France, and the serious plans for better living in England, was striking indeed.

Walter Gropius in Dessau told his students never to look at any existing examples of earlier cultures. It was essential, he said, to avoid any impression from outside that might influence their imagination and disturb their free creativity. English planners of the same period made important civic surveys. Raymond Unwin said in his book *Town-Planning in Practice* (1909): '*Before any plan for a new town or for a scheme of town development can with prudence be commenced, a survey must be made of all existing conditions, and this survey cannot well be too wide or too complete. Professor Geddes has published some most helpful and stimulating essays on this subject; and although it may not always be practicable to carry the survey to the extent suggested by him, there can be no doubt about its importance, if the development is to grow healthily from the past life and present needs of the town. The greater part of the work must necessarily be done by the sociologist, the historian, and the local antiquary.'*

The English planners studied most carefully all facts about the districts they were planning for, not only the landscape and its natural ecology but also the whole cultural development of the past. The results were made available to the public in plain surveys as the basis for future planning.

Sir Raymond Unwin was of course not the only planner of the period, but in my opinion the best exponent of the special English conception of planning: that it shall not be an inspired artistic achievement but a thorough, conscientious work — like that of the good gardener who seeks the best way to make his plants grow and thrive.

The first quarter of this century is thus, to me, the opening phase of a new London planning.

It really *was* new, full of optimistic promises. Until then the London suburbs were laid out merely as an exploitation of land for the benefit of landowners and builders. But in that period new and idealistic goals were set up. Civil surveys were undertaken as useful instruments for the new planning, and pilot towns were built.

The First Regional Planning

There was a widespread interest in the new thinking. The politicians also understood its importance. In 1927 Neville Chamberlain, as Minister of Health, set up a *Greater London Regional Committee* to propose a regional planning for the growth of London, thus starting the second phase in the new London planning. Unwin became its technical adviser. He set up a modest office in Queen Anne's Gate where he worked with a competent small staff.

The first result was a report on Ribbon Development, 1932. At that time — after the planning of Hampstead Garden Suburb — an urgent problem had arisen.

Charles Wade: Temple Fortune House, a block with a bank and shops forming one side of the entrance from Finchley Road into Hampstead Garden Suburb. (Seen from C on the plan page 417.)

True believers in the Garden City and its blessings had found that Hampstead was, if not sheer heresy, then still a deviation from the gospel truth, because it was in reality nothing but a dormitory suburb, thus blurring the doctrine of the self-contained community. It is not large enough to be self-contained, has no working places inside its boundaries, and the few shops are concentrated at the edge of it on Finchley Road, forming a sort of monumental entrance to the suburb. When located here, instead of in the centre, the shops and the bank could serve not only the few thousand people in Hampstead Garden Suburb but also other residential districts along the road.

The square kilometre which the Garden Suburb covers, with its local road system inside the greater network of important traffic arteries, is like a forerunner of the units of Milton Keynes.

But much had happened since it was planned. Finchley Road was not the same any longer. The private motor car had begun to take over an important part of the transport of persons.

It had been due to the prospering Underground that Hampstead Garden Suburb had come into existence at all. The station at Golders Green was the nucleus of the new suburb, from the beginning much more important for it than the arterial roads leading to the core of London (see p. 353 and plan p. 417).

The great traffic roads passing through the surburbs and leading up to London had always had a double function. They were at one and the same time local shopping parades for pedestrians and channels for the through traffic between the central parts of London and the other districts, the suburbs as well as the villages clustered round the roads and preferably at important crossings. All traffic was thus drawn directly through residential areas and had hitherto been regarded as a real advantage to them. But Unwin saw clearly that a great change was taking place. With its greater speed — and noise and air pollution — the road traffic would, from now on, be of harm to the dwellings. All pedestrians, children and dogs running in and out and crossing the fast traffic would mean an accelerating danger to all. Consequently, a new kind of planning would be necessary. New motor roads without crossings — like the railway lines — must be constructed, and all new building along the existing highways must be stopped. The segregation of traffic, which Unwin had started on a small scale at Hampstead, should be carried out on a regional basis.

It was high time to save what could be saved. The efficiency of old highways was reduced every day by new buildings and small access roads. Unwin took up the fight against this 'ribbon development' in the first report from the Regional Committee, with the result that a law was passed called: *The Restriction of Ribbon Development Act.* This separation of traffic from urban development is another forerunner of Milton Keynes.

In 1930 the Ministry of Health set up an expert committee — the *Marley Committee* — to deal with the problem of garden cities, to report on the experience gained from the existing garden cities and investigate the possibilities of building new ones. Unwin naturally became a member of the committee and put his stamp on the *Marley Report of 1935.*

The politicians recognized the town-planning problems, but it proved extremely difficult to raise money to get any work done. Raymond Unwin was honoured as the champion of planning. He was knighted in 1932, but in the same year the financial contribution to regional planning from London County Council was reduced to 500 pounds. All boroughs followed this lead and reduced their contributions correspondingly. At the end there was in all only £1700 for one year's work on the enormous task of preparing the future of the Capital and its Region. This tells us something about the real interest in town planning at that time.

Without any salary for himself Sir Raymond persevered with his studies and in 1933 published the important *Second Report*. It explains in twelve illuminating chapters the problems of the Region and gives a complete programme for its future planning. It puts forward two direct proposals of lasting importance. The one was *to create a green girdle round the existing outer suburbs of London,* thus stopping the unplanned urban sprawl and ensuring the outer suburbs access to open land — also in the future. The other proposal was that *all future growth should take place outside the green belt, partly as extensions to existing small towns, partly as a system of 'new towns'.*

I have not found the term *'garden city'* or *'satellite town'* in the report. Sir Raymond refers to a sporadic development out in the Region, and says that the planner should not deplore it but utilize it and organize it in a pattern of small self-contained units. How these town units should be planned he left more or less open. Without any detailing he indicates how they may in some cases form clusters, in others, bands of towns. His suggestions are in accordance with the English tradition that a town is something growing not an a priori fixed form. But one thing is essential to him: that it shall not have unrestrained growth but always be embedded in green.

It was thus a phase of advisory activities, of reports and programmes, of town-planning literature, lectures and courses. But for economic reasons it seemed equally impossible to reduce the density of overcrowded districts, to clear slums and to build new ideal towns out in the open country.

When Sir Raymond died in June 1940 — in Connecticut in the United States — the result of all his efforts could be summed up as follows: It was not lawful any longer to construct any access to a highway without the consent of the highway authority. There was a beginning of a green belt round London according to the Green Belt Act of 1938. But, apart from such restrictive measures, little was done for planning of the Region and no positive initiative was taken.

Planning During World War II

I often wonder if there would have been any progress in London planning if there had not been a war; at any rate, the Second World War brought a completely new attitude towards the planning and improvement of the capital.

The war period became the third phase, the phase of the great comprehensive plans for the entire London Region.

Demolition of slums, which had hitherto been carried out only in a few cases and always on a small scale, was now done wholesale by Hitler's bombers. Entire districts were demolished overnight. Enormous values were destroyed. All traditional ideas of real property became obsolete. A new thinking and a new planning was not only a possibility, it had suddenly become a necessity.

Before the war the economic depression had made compulsory acquisition for the planning of the London Region impossible. We have seen how difficult it was to obtain even the modest grants for Sir Raymond Unwin's pioneer work. But now during the most disastrous of all crises, when England had to spend billions of pounds on an unproductive and devastating war, there suddenly was also money, large amounts of money, ready for the planning of that London which, as a hope for the future, was to rise from the ruins of the holocaust.

Patrick Abercrombie was given a free hand to produce the finest plans possible for a new and better London. In connection with the L.C.C.'s chief architect, J. H. Forshaw, and with the help of a group of experts and based on a number of well-written commission reports he, in an amazingly short time, created those great visions, *the London County Plan 1943* and *the Greater London Plan 1944*. The beautifully illustrated projects were regarded as a weapon in the war. They were supposed to strengthen the morale of the people by promising a better England for all after the war.

Lloyd George had, during the First World War, spoken of the future England as *a country for heroes to live in.* (The heroes, it was understood, were the common soldiers who had won the war under horrifying suffering in the trenches.) All those fine promises had never been redeemed.

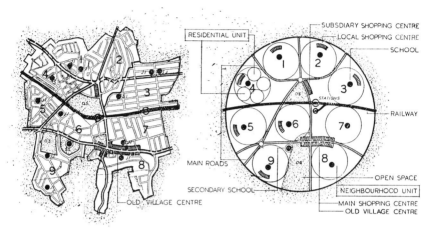

An illustration from the L.C.C. plan of 1943 showing an existing London district, Elsham, divided in neighbourhoods, to the right in the form of a diagram, to the left as a piece of concrete planning.

The Abercrombie plans were more concrete. They depicted a revived London that realized the ideas developed in English planning theory during the previous years: lower densities, New Towns outside the Green Belt and a dividing up of the unorganized urban sprawl into smaller units, such as precincts and neighbourhoods.

The term *neighbourhood* or *neighbourhood unit* was launched in 1929 by the American, Clarence A. Perry, in the great Regional Survey of New York. His idea was induced, so to speak, by the traffic conditions in that city. Perry pointed out that the enormous traffic of the main thoroughfares formed absolute barriers, dividing up the city into a number of large blocks. Since it is especially dangerous for children to go from one such block to another, each of these divisions should be laid out as a town-planning unit grouped round a school. In this way infant-school children, at least, would not have to cross the dangerous traffic arteries in their daily comings and goings.

But as it would also be both an advantage and a relief for others to be able to avoid the hazards of heavy traffic, he recommended a complete 'neighbourhood plan' for each block, with a special system of internal roads leading from all houses to playgrounds and other recreational centres, as well as to local shops and a community hall.

In the war atmosphere the word 'neighbourhood' was given a new meaning. To Clarence Perry it had been a purely practical measure, a method of traffic segregation and a reduction of distances between homes and public amenities. But now in London, during the War, the neighbourhood became an instrument for bringing different social classes together. On the battlefields as well as in the bomb shelters in their home towns, people of different strata, who had never spoken to each other before, met on an equal footing. They learned to know each other, to help each other and — most important of all — to respect each other as fellow creatures. It was for many a happy new experience. Abercrombie's aim was now to preserve and develop this new spirit of cooperation in the London that was to rise from the ruins.

Instead of being an anonymous entity in a conglomerate mass, the individual should be an active member of a group of a conceivable size, living in a well-planned community in which all aspects of urban life were represented. To this end the urban area should be divided up into neighbourhoods formed as *well-balanced residential areas of manageable size,* each with its own community centre, shops and civic buildings — a complete town in miniature. Diagrams were prepared showing how existing suburbs could be divided into a great number of such small neighbourhoods.

The London County Plan 1943 was followed by *the Greater London Plan 1944,* a monumental work presenting all the most advanced town-planning ideas of the time. Abercrombie had collaborated with outstanding planners, such as the late Professor William — later Lord — Holford, Thomas Sharp, Professor Gordon Stephenson and R. T. Kennedy.

The plan suggested, as already mentioned, a number of New Towns laid out in a ring round London and gave detailed descriptions of what form they should take. As an example, a complete set of sketch-plans and perspectives was given showing a new town at Ongar. It bears the stamp of *Gordon Stephenson,* who had worked a couple of years in the office of *Clarence Stein* in New York and there in the United States had learned how the private motor car was going to revolutionize towns. His Ongar project consequently showed a completely pedestrian shopping centre, the first plan of its kind in Europe.

The New Towns of the Greater London Plan were proposed to be much larger than the original Garden City plans of 1898 with their 30,000 inhabitants. That was considered necessary, if they were to make possible a "full measure of social life," as the definition of 1920 said.

Each New Town should — by definition — be a self-contained, balanced society. Its great centre should offer to the community all the larger shops and institutions that are considered essential to urban life. Clustered round this centre were a number of well-defined neighbourhoods, each laid out as a balanced mini-society round a subcentre with its own local shops, school and kindergarten.

The proposed New Towns differed from Ebenezer Howard's Garden Cities, not only in size but also in more fundamental ways. Howard, who lived in a society with a liberal economy, had explained at length that the Garden City would not only offer the best way of living to its inhabitants, but would also be a good investment. It could be started and run as a profitable private enterprise, that later would be taken over by the town itself. He felt sure that a Garden City, carried out as an experiment, would be so successful that others would spring up just as the unplanned suburbs had hitherto done. And mistakes made in the first plan could then be remedied in the following ones.

The two Garden Cities, Letchworth and Welwyn, had proved that his ideas were sound. The Garden Cities *did* pay, but only after several years, and the profit was not big enough to interest speculative finance. Nobody had, as yet, been tempted to try for himself to start a town on the Howard lines. The two Garden Cities had kept what was promised, in so far as people had been happy in them. But their growth had been too slow. In a period when all London's outer suburbs grew by the hundred thousand, the two small towns never reached the planned optimum of 30,000.

430

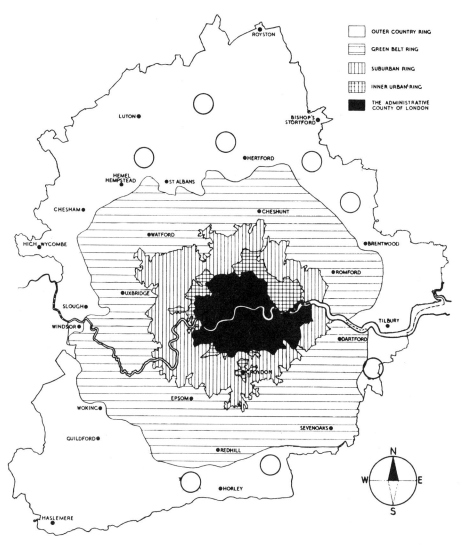

OUTER COUNTRY RING

GREEN BELT RING

SUBURBAN RING

INNER URBAN RING

THE ADMINISTRATIVE
COUNTY OF LONDON

Sir Patrick Abercrombie's plan for Greater London, 1944. Scale: 1:800,000. The growth of London stopped; surrounding towns extended; eight New Towns proposed.

It was obvious that, if London's growth should be canalized into New Towns, it could only be done by Government aid, a thought that would have been impossible before the war. But now, when a strong lead was necessary in order to win the war, it was accepted that an equally strong town-planning strategy directed from Whitehall might be the only right way *to win the peace* that would follow.

Nobody seemed to notice how the liberal Ebenezer Howard's Garden Cities were thus transformed into state-planned and State-directed New Towns, built on state land acquired under compulsory power.

Another great change in ideas had taken place. Ebenezer Howard's self-contained Garden City should have both industry and agriculture. The green belt that surrounded the urban belt was not meant as a merely decorative asset or a recreation area for town dwellers. It was planned to be useful farmland, the food supplies of the town. As Howard said; *'the farmer of Garden City has a market at his very door.'* He explained how this would minimize transport and transport costs. But he aimed higher. The Garden City should not only have a balanced population but it should be a balanced community, a balanced life. *'The waste products of the town could, and this without heavy charges for railway transport or other expensive agencies, be readily brought back to the soil, thus increasing its fertility'.* The farmland should be an integral part of the city. Ebenezer Howard was a contemporary of Prince Kropotkin, who advocated an education where brain work was combined with manual work and all human activities were integrated. *The Garden City dweller should not only enjoy the look of the farmland, but understand and be interested in its production.* Howard's plans and ideas were, however, already Utopian in his own time.

We must go back to the Middle Ages to find a really self-contained town in England. At that time the villages — which, incidentally, were called *towns* — had all their food from the farmland belonging to the *town* and almost all that was used in daily life was the result of domestic work. But, already in Tudor times, a specialization started which eventually would break down this old way of life. With the important and — for England — most fortunate development of the cloth trade came *the enclosure* of the open fields of the village for pasture, which meant eviction of *many* ploughmen to make room for *a few* shepherds. The enclosure movement continued during the following centuries and sent thousands of workers to the towns. The next step in rationalization through specialization was the Industrial Revolution: Urban factories took over the old domestic production. The towns became densely populated at the same time as the countryside was depopulated.

The landscape in front of Syon House. The picture shows pasture land going right up to the house, separated from the gardens only by an invisible 'ha-ha'. (See pages 150ff.)

Seen from the city the landscape represents free nature. Its beauty is, however, not a work of Nature but of man. *The Scott Report* on Land Utilization in Rural Areas, published in 1942 (a year before the London County Plan), said: *'This (enclosure) movement was primarily economic. . . . It was assisted, however, by a strong aesthetic impulse. Many of those who enclosed land in the eighteenth and nineteenth centuries were greatly influenced by a desire to create beauty in the landscape. The park-like effect of much of the countryside to-day is not wholly fortuitous; there was, in most of the activities of the eighteenth and early nineteenth century, Landscape Improvers, a conscious and creative urge to bring beauty as well as efficiency into the countryside'.*

The English love this kind of countryside, which is not — as in foreign countries — divided into many small holdings with pigs and chickens and cabbages, but is really grand when seen from the windows or the terrace of the manor house. It is a pasture land with here and there old solitary trees as far as the eye can see. To this landscape belong sheep. Cattle, especially if decorative and of fine breed, could be tolerated. But no houses or useful farm buildings might mar the picture, except

433

perhaps an old water mill partly hidden by the foliage of a picturesque group of trees. A classical ruin or other folly of one of the late landowners would make the *pastorale* complete.

To the great landowner this beloved landscape does not represent only a beautiful historic setting for his stately home. It is, first and foremost, the fertile soil cultivated to give him a good income and at the same time a vast recreation ground, the ideal scene for gentlemanly sports such as riding and hunting.

The townsman feels nostalgic for it, as for a lost paradise, a luxury reserved for the lucky rich. But it is not possible simply to preserve it, to leave it untouched and open to the public. Left uncultivated, without grazing cattle or sheep, the countryside must inevitably revert to a wild and unkempt state. And if it is under cultivation it will hardly be of much pleasure as a recreation ground for townspeople, but can easily be ruined if hordes of suburbanites are let loose on it with their bottles and other litter and their lack of feeling for animals and plants. It is very unlikely that holiday makers would enjoy a countryside where they literally have nothing to do. Surely the city park, as an imitation of the countryside, but laid out for all kinds of outdoor sports, and the holiday camp with its variety of entertainments, would be much more attractive than easy access to even the finest open landscape.

All this means that it was for very good reasons that the Greater London Plan had given up Ebenezer Howard's idea of close interaction between town and country. In its description of the proposed New Town, *Ongar,* we read about the Road System, the Neighbourhood System, the Town Centre, the Park System, the Industry, but not one word about agriculture. Because agriculture is no longer a part of each individual town but is what is called the *open background,* common to the entire plan. And the Plan goes on to say that the preservation of the most productive land for farms and other cultivation is essential; and *the recreational use of land is to be made to interfere as little as possible with farming operations.*

In a highly specialized world sports, games and other leisure activities have also been specialized. Football and cricket on the village green have given rise to the modern sports events with their thousands of enthusiastic spectators. Since other activities have grown correspondingly it explains why a town, to make possible 'a full measure of social life', must, in 1944, be considerably larger than Ebenezer Howard's Garden City, with its 30,000 in 1898. How large, it was difficult to say. But Abercrombie agreed with Ebenezer Howard and other planners that a New Town should not have unlimited growth.

The purpose of Abercrombie's great work was not to give an exact plan for the rebuilding and further development of London but to set up goals for its future growth. The result of this third short phase was a complete textbook presenting all accepted ideas of English town-planning theory at that date.

Realization of the Great Plans

The fourth, much longer phase was the period of realization of the great plans produced during the War.

The Government had to go in for the building of New Towns, with all the necessary expenses, if they were ever to be realized. And the miracle happened. An *Act on New Towns* was passed in 1946, corporations formed, money granted, plans laid down and eight New Towns were actually built in the London Region, all following the authorized recipe for such New Towns.

They were based on a set of simple assumptions — or would *prejudices* be a more precise word? One was that it was possible to decide beforehand exactly what would be the right size of a town. It was — as often pointed out — important for the town to be large enough to have a full measure of social life. But it was considered equally important to impose limitations to its growth. The close contact between town and country was, as we have seen, no longer a vital problem. And what of the old idea that it was better for people to live in a small town than in a large one? It was not their own feeling. The tendency of migration was a one-way traffic from the country and the small towns to the cities and the metropolis. Should people be under the guardianship of planners? I have often wondered if the decision-making authorities ever had any doubts when they were fixing a final and definitive size for a New Town.

It is not pedantic to discuss this problem, as the town limits would be of decisive importance for the dimensions of all parts of it. Especially the town centre was problematic. When it was surrounded by other town units, any expansion of it would be almost impossible.

The location and size of each New Town was decided in the Ministry at *Whitehall* and the problem of the actual size seems not to have worried anyone; at least, not until the towns had reached the fixed limit and were in good growth, and everybody wanted it to go on.

All eight towns were planned according to the same principles. But to the other prejudices, a new and fatal one was added. Although all the planning of the London Region was meant to represent the most rational way of locating activities and housing it must not *look* rational.

It was a strong belief that it would have a most harmful psychological effect on the inhabitants if the New Towns appeared to be based on reasoning. Any monotony or simple geometry must absolutely be avoided. The straight line and the right angle, which have been basic in planning in all cultures, were banned. It is — as far as I know — the first time in history that city planning on a large scale was based on a desire for a picturesque, irrational appearance. They were proudly called New Towns but must look old, look as if they had grown slowly and arbitrarily through hundreds of years, just as a new *Ye olde Inn*.

Before the French Revolution Queen Marie Antoinette could have a private little romantic village built inside the formal park of Versailles; and a generation later John Nash could build rural-looking houses and a whole village (*'Blaise hamlet'*, Somerset) for the upper classes. But now, after the Second World War, such follies should no longer be a privilege of the aristocracy. In the New Towns, ordinary people with monotonous daily work, should have the opportunity to live in *'an interesting setting'*.

A complete change in the conception of town planning had taken place. It is well illustrated in books on the subject. The first chapter in Raymond Unwin's book *Town Planning in Practice*, from 1909, bore the title *'Civic art as the Expression of Civic Life'*. The new bible of town planning, Frederick Gibberd's *Town Design*, from 1953, starts with a chapter on *'The Town and its Raw Materials'*, in which it says: *'As a physical expression the town is a thing that is seen, and since the external sense is a channel to the soul, that which is seen should be as beautiful as man can make it.* I must confess that I cannot quite sound the philosophical depths of this sentence. But one thing is made quite clear: We should make the city as beautiful as man can make it. *'The town must work properly and be economically sound, but it should also give pleasure to those who look at it.'*

In the same year (1953) as Frederick Gibberd's book was published, the *Architectural Review* brought a short article written by *Andrew Hammer*. It gives in a few lines the new ideas of that period: architecture (or *'townscape,'* to use a favourite word) as a good object for a clever photographer. Andrew Hammer was inspired to write his article by a striking photograph showing white-gabled houses against a dark sky. He quotes *Ledoux* for the paradox: *'If you will be an architect then start to be a painter.'* And he continues: *'Far from buildings designed with any thought for the painter's-eye-view the very existence of such a thing is scarcely recognized by most architects.'* And he maintains that their drawings are symbols more akin to mathematics than to painting. If the architect would take Ledoux' advice seriously, he would not be satisfied with mere elevations of his buildings, but would have to envisage how they would appear in perspective, *'which happens to be in fact the way almost all buildings are normally seen.'*

The basis for Frederick Gibberd's aesthetics seems to be this perception-philosophy, which is as simple as it is wrong. It is true that when we look at an object a prospect in perspective will take form as a two-dimensional picture in the eye. But it is not true that we *see* that two-dimensional picture. *We actually perceive the thing itself.* The picture in the eye will, for instance, show two sides of a house, a dark and a light, but we do not experience a light and a dark figure, but a four-sided block, although we are not able to see the two sides hidden to us, and we will testify under oath that we have seen with our own eyes a house with a certain weight and texture plus everything else. You cannot, without special training, see three-dimensional objects as a two-dimensional pattern, see them as the painter's picture on a plane. But Frederick Gibberd had acquired that training through years of study and travel in many countries. His book showed how he enjoyed motifs from all over the world, interesting snapshots taken from odd angles.

There have, in fact, been great European artists who were able to make groups of important buildings form grand perspectives. It was a true visual art, not aiming at small interesting pictures but at breathtaking, stage-like views where every detail served to enhance the total effect. The *Piazza del Campidoglio* in Rome is one of the great examples. Frederick Gibberd has, of course, seen this admirable monument. But it seems to me that he has looked at it just as a small child in the zoo looks at an elephant, enjoying the sparrows at its feet and not noticing at all the colossus above. Now, we can probably all learn from children's naive and unbiased perception of the outer world. But we could hardly use this knowledge in planning a new zoological garden. In the same way, the spontaneous look of charming details from *historic towns* cannot, in my opinion, form a sound inspiration in planning *New Towns*. Because the aim of the planner should not be to create picturesque motifs for photographers but to plan good environments for people — especially children — where they can live and thrive.

Frederick Gibberd was, however, an exponent of the taste that governed English town planning after a period of most inhuman war that had devastated a great number of fine houses. It was a natural reaction. People wanted towns with a human atmosphere as in the good old days. The result was that the New Towns, that were planned according to a fixed pattern and with a predetermined size, all very rational, were now ingeniously disguised by an artificial informality of details.

Banal town prospects from old towns were studied and theories for the beautification of townscapes proposed. They could, for instance, be enlivened by striking contrasts. Frederick Gibberd designed for Harlow New Town a ten-story block of flats standing up like a chubby towner. He explained that it was *'placed on high ground where it provides a contrast in silhouettes to the comparatively low skyline of the other development'*. Together they should form one composition. Nobody asked whether people would like to live in flats in a tall block. They had to do so, not for their own sake, but to please the aesthete who had learned to enjoy such a composition.

I remember when, in 1952, I was shown the first neighbourhood in Harlow. I was disappointed. I have in fact no memory at all of the houses. But I do remember the very wide roads, which were widened still more by unprotected grass verges in front of the façades. The road-crossings were complete deserts. One of the planners apologetically said to me that it was caused by the road engineers' exorbitant demands. Engineers are accustomed to require great safety in constructions and in all that they otherwise have to work with. I referred to Sir Raymond Unwin's tactics in respect of the width of road in Hampstead, how he had even got a special Act of Parliament passed to obtain the right dimensions for the right roads, thus saving both land and money. The answer was that there had been too little time to bother with these details, which had been left entirely to the road engineers' decision. I must confess that it shocked me that when planning eight new towns there was no time to discuss such fundamental problems.

On the whole I found that, in some of the New Towns, the planners, who tried to avoid the formality of the *grand style* of old towns, ended in a still more cumbersome *smallish style*. It pretended to be natural, but was not at all, neither for the engineers with all their rational technique, nor for the builders who had to build cheap cottages.

The New Towns had their critics. *Gordon Cullen* disliked the spacious layout and low-density housing. He invented the term *'prairie planning'. J. M. Richards,* in the *Architectural Review* (July 1953), argued for the town as a social place for people who wanted to live close together, for compactness and a sense of enclosure, the cheerful life of the street, the corner pub, the market-place gossip and easy access to the country, which suburban sprawl prevents.

It was as if the planners of the New Towns did not really know how to handle the serious problem of creating new communities out of the old, towns that were to go on for centuries. The whole problem seemed so new. They travelled to study towns in other countries, where there were, at least, some traditions for creating new towns. In the Renaissance period a number of 'ideal cities' were founded, complete towns from the central square to the geometric fortification line. They had produced a most elaborate theory for such towns, while London in the same period just expanded in all directions without any guiding principles; and after that period urban sprawl had continued until Ebenezer Howard put forward his revolutionary ideas resulting in the Green Belt Law and the New Towns.

New Towns of the Past

I have, on page 36, explained the development as follows: *'Around every little village the buildings crystallized into a borough, and the development . . . was to continue, so that London became a greater accumulation of towns, an immense colony of dwellings. . . .'*

It is true that the City of London itself did not spread out, while each of the surrounding villages extended and became in the end independent boroughs, each with its own Council. Eventually, they all grew together forming one great urban district. And it is, as I said, possible to trace back to the Domesday Book, 1086, almost all the present names of boroughs where in archaic form they are found as the names of villages at road crossings.

This is true, but not the whole truth. *In former times London also expanded by means of a number of literally new towns, pre-planned small communities founded and built for townspeople out in the open country as towns without agriculture.*

This means that the idea of developing London by laying out 'New Towns' outside the urban district is not at all a new one but a traditional method from the seventeenth and eighteenth centuries, forgotten in the nineteenth.

I regard it as a special English method since I have only been able to find a few parallels to it on the Continent. Most capitals I know of expanded by pushing their fortifications further out, thus adding new urban areas to the existing city. The continental capitals were generally not only centres of commerce, but also royal or princely residences, and as the power of the sovereign in the period of Absolutism grew and the court developed in splendour and luxury, an expansion of the capital became necessary.

But in London expulsion of royalty had taken place already in the eleventh century. The English capital had, consequently, not the same problems as those of cities on the Continent. The City of London had always been a great commercial centre, not a royal residence. It is true that the king once had a castle there, just as in the Middle Ages he had one in so many places instead of a single permanent residence. He moved with his exchequer, chancellery and court from one part of his realm to another. King Edward the Confessor, however, gave up the Wardrobe Palace, near St. Paul's in London, in about 1060, moving his London residence to Westminister, which, ever since, has been the permanent seat of the English government.

Whether one will regard this flitting of the court to the rural 'Thornea' or Thorney Island — later called Westminster — as the founding of the first 'New Town' outside the City must be a matter of taste. The king did not only build a new and splendid palace there, replacing a minor one previously used by King Canute, he also rebuilt the minster of the monks of St. Peter's and gave it a glorious new existence. It thus became a 'colony' of clergy and courtiers which was soon supplemented by merchants, artisans and labourers. If not a 'New Town' in the modern sense of the word, Westminster soon became a new 'city' of far-reaching importance.

The City of London was not extended indefinitely but propagated itself by healthy offshoots. London, inside its old boundaries, kept its character of a great commercial centre intact, with Westminster as a 'twin-city' of government. This differentiation of functions was recognized by subsequent kings. William the Conqueror did not use arms against London but waited until a deputation was sent to his camp at Berkhampstead to inform him that London had chosen him as their king, and shortly after he was annointed and crowned at Westminster (see pp. 37–38).

Since the time of William the Conqueror no king has tried to make London's City a royal residence. Henry VIII had every chance of expanding his capital and making it a glorious seat for his government. But he abstained. London, from olden times, had been surrounded by ecclesiastical property, a ring of churches, monasteries and 'hospitals' (in the mediaeval sense of the word). Each of these institutions formed a little protected society within a walled precinct. At the Reformation the king felt free to confiscate such church land as he needed. But he did not take advantage of this rare opportunity to enlarge the cramped city. Some of the hospitals and monasteries that had important social functions were allowed to survive under new forms. In other cases the king took over the property for the benefit of his Treasury. An old convent garden — the name of which has come down to us as Covent Garden — was, in 1552, given to John Russell, the newly created Earl of Bedford, for his financial services to the Tudors (see p. 166).

Queen Elizabeth I actually tried to *stop* the growth of London. In 1580 she issued a remarkable proclamation according to which *'her majesty . . . doth charge and strictly command all manner of persons . . . to desist and forbear from any new buildings of any house or tenement within three miles from any of the gates of the City of London'* (see p. 68).

Imagine if this order had been observed to the letter! It would mean that the Green Belt policy would have been realized already in the sixteenth century. The purpose of the proclamation is, however, somewhat obscure. It is likely that it was meant to protect the interests of the London guilds by preventing competitors establishing themselves close to the London wall. But in its commentary it says something quite different. It speaks — somewhat illogically — of a ban on new buildings, the danger of overcrowding. It says: *'. . . such great multitudes of people brought to inhabit in small rooms, whereof a great part are seen very poor, yea, such as must live of begging or by worse means'* and it concludes in commending people *'to forebear from letting or setting, or suffering any more families than one only to be placed, or to inhabit from henceforth in any house that heretofore hath been inhabited'* (see p. 68).

It is really most remarkable to find, in a royal proclamation from the sixteenth century, a housing programme thus clearly expressed: a programme that has been repeated over and over again through centuries and can stand as an exponent of English housing policy in contrast to that of the continental countries. If we had not that proclamation, I would believe that the ideal of 'one house to each family' was just one of the many English traditions that have developed as a matter of course, that was simply taken for granted. But there it is, formulated in a proclamation by Queen Elizabeth I in 1580.

The provisions of this proclamation became an Act in 1592 in which it was again stated that *'noe person or persons . . . shall from henceforth make and erect any newe Building or Buildings House or Houses for habitation or dwelling . . . within three miles of any of the gates'*. But ways and means could always be found to enable rich persons to build houses just outside London. Thus, the Earl of Salisbury — at the time Lord Treasurer — at the very beginning of the seventeenth century carried out the so-called *St. Martin's Lane development*. This, a row of houses in *Swan*

Close, deprived the owners of the nearby cottages of their rights to graze their cattle and hang out their washing on the land on the west side of St. Martin's Lane. And, even worse, the scheme involved the filling-in of a drainage ditch which resulted in cascades of water flowing unchecked into the Palace of Whitehall. When, later, the Earl of Leicester also wanted to make money by developing his Leicester Fields, he was met with coldness. The country people, who had their living there, protested, with the result that a body of commissioners, appointed by the Privy Council, decided that the Earl could build a house for himself along one side of the Fields, but no more. The rest was to be kept as open land.

The Act of 1592, prohibiting building outside London, was from now on used to prevent undesirable building speculation west of the City. To obtain a dispensation, the estate owner had to submit a detailed plan for a complete town which would embellish London and — if the plan was accepted — he had to pay for a building license.

The fourth Earl of Bedford learned what this could mean when, in the 1620's, he wanted to start a housing project just outside London. On the site of Covent Garden, which his great-grandfather had received from Henry VIII, he had a stately residence built among other aristocratic houses along the Strand. Behind this building he possessed a large site ripe for development. It was an excellent neighbourhood where many well-to-do people might choose to live. Consequently, the Earl asked the King's permission to realize a large building project there. The King — Charles I — was a highly civilized monarch, interested in both painting and architecture. He would not permit mere speculation-building but only a project with high urban and architectural qualities. We have no evidence of what conditions he actually imposed but we do know that Bedford, who scarcely had the same interests in the fine arts as the King, had to engage the King's own architect, Inigo Jones, for the project (compare pp. 166–176). It was planned as a great urban composition, quite a 'little town' with its own classical 'forum' surrounded by arcaded walks, the whole crowned by a church formed like a Roman temple. At this centre fine residences for the upper-classes were placed and behind them smaller houses for people of humbler means serving the inhabitants of the square. Here, then, arose *a complete little community with market, church and cemetery, and people of all strata of society.* It was not just a number of houses but *a well-organized and well-planned town unit,* located half a mile beyond the City walls.

At the same time *Lord Southampton* wished to build on his valuable estate, *Bloomsbury,* not far from Covent Garden. In 1636 he asked the King's permission to develop it but did not obtain a license until after the Restoration.

John Evelyn wrote in his diary, February 9th, 1665: *'Dined at my Lord Treasurer's, the Earl of Southampton in Bloomsbury, where he was building a noble square, or piazza, a little town. . . .'*

Thus, a contemporary characterizes the new housing scheme as *a little town.* I assume that this is what the Lord of the manor himself considered it to be. This quotation leads to an examination of the word *town.* A dictionary defines it simply as *'a collection or aggregation of inhabited houses larger than a village,* and says further that in English *'town is not a word defined by statute'.* Still, I believe that we demand something more than a collection of houses if we are to call it a town. Size alone is not enough. You can easily find a small town, which you definitely regard as a town, although it may be smaller than a large village. I think that most people will agree with me that a town must be an organized collection of houses built for people who do not earn their living from the land.

Sir John Summerton says in his book of Georgian London: *'The Earl of Southampton was a pioneer not only in his creation of the first square, properly so called, and the first unit of the sort to be developed by a landlord through the medium of speculative builders, but because he realized that a square was not enough by itself; it had to be the centre of a residential unit comprising a market or shopping district and a number of smaller less expensive streets. In fact, the whole thing had to have a life of its own.'*

It sounds almost like a programme for a New Town of today, a *self-contained town.* These early schemes, Covent Garden and the first Bloomsbury, had houses both for rich people — round the square — and for less rich in the adjoining streets, as well as for the very poor in alleys nearby. But the main character of Lord Southampton's Bloomsbury was still very different from that of the Covent Garden scheme. This latter started as a secluded 'little town' of exquisite taste, but ended up as a

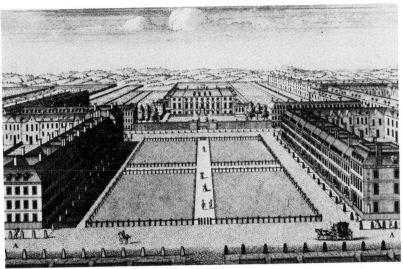

Bloomsbury Square. A bird's-eye view on an engraving from the eighteenth century. In the background the Earl of Southampton's house, as John Evelyn saw it.

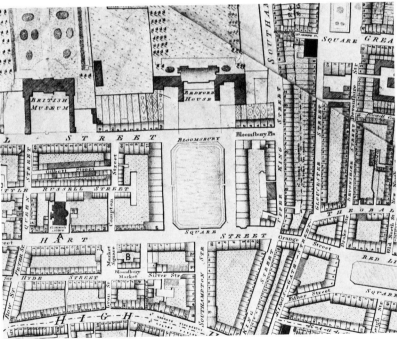

The first Bloomsbury, a noble square or piazza in a little town. To the left: the church (A) and market (B). North of the square, Bedford House, the Earl of Southampton's mansion, to the north overlooking the fields with the heights of Hampstead and Highgate in the background.

445

great vegetable-market catering for the whole of London (p. 175–176).

Lord Southampton's Bloomsbury developed differently. It was from the beginning a less ambitious scheme. But it kept its prestige over the years. It too was laid out round a square. But instead of uniform, arcaded, classical buildings, it had a number of individually built London houses, though all of the same height. Instead of the temple-like front of a church, it had the landlord's own residence as the focal point of the composition. The middle of the square was not paved, like the Covent Garden Piazza, but was laid out with grass and walks, the general impression being very English and quite rural. Lord Southampton could here enjoy his beloved country life, combined with the atmosphere of the fashionable capital.

His residence was most of all like a great manor house, keeping its dependencies at arm's length, the houses of the square forming a sort of forecourt, a *cour d'honneur*. It enhanced the effect of the grand south façade, which overlooked the square, while the north side of his stately home was strictly private, facing the garden and the open country, with the blue heights of Hampstead and Highgate as a picturesque backdrop. The square was never — as at Covent Garden — reduced to the rank of a vulgar market-place. The inhabitants of the 'little town' were catered for from the start by a small market laid out to the west of the square. The community also had its own church outside the central part; and there were little narrow streets with tiny houses hidden behind bigger ones, not directly visible from his Lordship's residence.

A New Town for the Royal Court

The prohibition of building outside the City of London was thus used by the Government to prevent undesirable building speculation and at the same time to encourage noble planning. Lord Southampton, who was Lord Treasurer, tried however to take advantage of the same Act to hamper a project for a new town which would make it a serious rival to his own Bloomsbury. But here he came up against a power stronger than his own; one of the favourites of the new Court of the Restoration, *Henry Jermyn*. This person, known for his appetite not only for good food but also for gambling and money, owed his influence to his intimate friendship with the King's mother, Henrietta Maria. He was even rumoured to be her secret husband. He had been in exile in France with the Royal Family, had enjoyed the complete management of the Queen's finances — and had done it extremely well — and was now after the Restoration lavishly rewarded by the King: Appointed Lord High Admiral and created Earl of St. Albans, and, what is more important in our context, he obtained the freehold of half the field of St. James's and later a lease on the rest of it.

Here, as a near neighbour to Whitehall, he created a truly royal faubourg that could outrival Lord Southampton's noble little town of Bloomsbury, not to mention the piazza at Covent Garden. Like the latter, it took its name from a monastic institution from the Middle Ages, the Hospital of St. James for fourteen leprous sisters. It was endowed with two *hides* of land, and from the time of Edward I granted an annual Fair of Seven Days.

Like Covent Garden, the whole property had been taken over by Henry VIII, but in this case several years before the Reformation. He liked the place and used to go riding and hawking through the green fields with a young lady of his Court: Anne Boleyn. This happened before his divorce from Catherine of Aragon; and since Anne Boleyn had in mind to dwell near the King but at the same time in a place 'where the eyes of Whitehall could not gaze on her', he resolutely packed off the leprous virgins to Chattisham in Suffolk and transformed the Norman hospital into the stately Tudor 'Manor of St. James', later promoted to the Royal St. James's Palace. The King enclosed 'a beautiful Spot of Ground' and converted the fields south of St. James into a fine park, situated conveniently to both Whitehall and St. James's Palace.

A hundred and thirty years later England again got a king and a court which would give life to the park. Charles II, who actually was born in St. James's Palace, loved the place as much as did Henry VIII. The Merry Monarch with his extraordinary vitality was a great enthusiast for all kinds of sport and outdoor life. There was, thus, again a king to play in Henry VIII's tennis court at Whtehall and to walk in the park and take *'that bewitching kind of pleasure called sauntering and talking without any constraint'*. Soon after his return to England he had started to improve the neglected park. He employed disbanded soldiers

to make a canal that would drain the swampy meadow. Samuel
Pepys noted — 16th September 1660 — that he saw how far
they had proceeded *in making a river through the parke*. At the
same time the Mall was laid out as a broad avenue of four lines
of trees, planned for the then popular game of *Pall Mall,* or
Pall Maille (see p. 95).

What then was this park like?

The old map on page 96 shows the park with its great
rectilinear elements: the Mall and the canal. The triangular
area between them must still have been an unkempt piece of
grass land where Charles II, who loved animals, kept deer,
antelopes, an elk, guinea goats and Arabian sheep.

I was not right when I said (p. 96) that the canal had apparently no relation to the surrounding buildings. It was, as a
matter of fact, pointing directly to the finest of the Whitehall
buildings: the Banqueting House by Inigo Jones. Seen from
the grand hall in this building with its Rubens ceiling, the canal
bordered with trees formed a magnificent vista. In a French
park of that period there would be trimmed hedges under the
crowns of the trees forming impenetrable green walls. But
here, where deer could eat all foliage within their reach, the
avenues were like colonnades defining a space but at the same
time opening up a great view to the distant field with its animals
and all its free life.

North of this St. James's Park lay the field for which Henry
Jermyn obtained his freehold in order to build there a town
for courtiers. In co-operation with several associates he developed the whole area around a central square. He acted only as
a planner and *land* speculator while *building* speculators took
over the individual plots on long leases and built houses on
them for aristocratic tenants. Like Bloomsbury, this undertaking also became a complete 'little town' with a noble square in
the middle, a small market in the eastern part and the church
of St. James, designed by Christopher Wren, with access from
Piccadilly, in the northern part. Henry Jermyn, Duke of St.
Albans, had his own stately mansion built on one side of the
square in a row of handsome houses. The sites along the southern side of Pall Mall proved to be equally attractive, separated
from the Park with the Mall only by a garden wall.

The King's mistress came to live there. John Evelyn could
report how, one day in 1671, in St. James's Park, he 'both saw

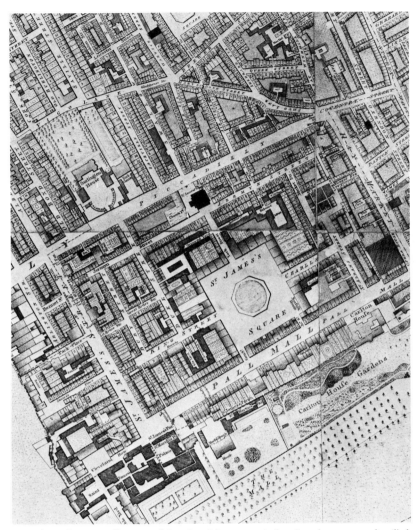

A section of Horwood's map of London (about 1790) showing the rectangular 'little town' laid out between Piccadilly and The Mall by Henry Jermyn, Duke of St. Albans. St. James's Church at Piccadilly; a market in the eastern part near Hay Market; St. James's Square in the middle of the rectangular plan; St. James's Palace in the southern corner. Scale about 1 : 6,000.

and heard a very familiar discourse between . . . (i.e., the King) and Mrs. Nelly, she looking out of her garden on a terrace at the top of her garden wall and . . . standing on the green walk under it. . . . Thence the King walked to the Duchess of Cleveland, another lady of pleasure. . . .'

449

The town of Versailles was built during the same years as the neighbourhood of St. James. It is most illuminating to compare the two schemes. They were both planned as residential areas situated next to a royal palace. But while *la ville de Versailles* was planned and built by order of a king, the St. James development was a private enterprise which came into existence without any initiative on the part of the monarch.

The results were as different as the procedures.

Versailles' town plan was based on the most advanced planning theory of the time, expressing the idea of Absolutism. The main feature was three impressive avenues intersecting the whole town, leading from nowhere to the equestrian statue of the King in front of the palace, thus symbolizing the centralization of all power in that one person. There were also markets, two monumental churches and a number of squares, everything that belongs to a town. But this ideal plan, drawn up by some of the finest architects of the period, is a pure drawing-board construction conceived in the thin air of ideas. The man in the street will hardly notice that the centre lines of the avenues go through the King's statute. It can be seen on a map but not on the spot. The very tall statue is far too small for the over-dimensioned surroundings. What one can't help seeing when walking in Versailles is that the triangular pattern of the avenues cuts through the gridiron plan in a most unhappy way, resulting in a number of deformed corner plots with awkward acute-angled houses. The only viewpoint from where the town unfolds itself to the spectator's eye is in front of the statue which stands on the most desert-like forecourt in the world, a sort of perverted *Piazza del Popolo*.

Compared with this monstrous plan, the English 'little town' at St. James's was extremely simple, not based on any sublime idea but on the purely egoistic aim of a smart courtier. His intention was to offer rich people a number of well-formed plots which were easy to sell because they were rightly dimensioned for good housing and attractively situated in a pleasant environment.

It is interesting to notice that St. James's Park has almost the same dimensions as the Heath Extension, which was laid out when Hampstead Garden Suburb was developed. In both cases the practical planner has found it profitable to give the urban

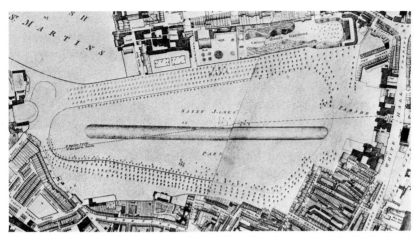

Above : St. James's Park, about 1790. It is obvious that the canal (originally bordered with trees, as the plan on page 96 shows) pointed directly at the Banqueting Hall.

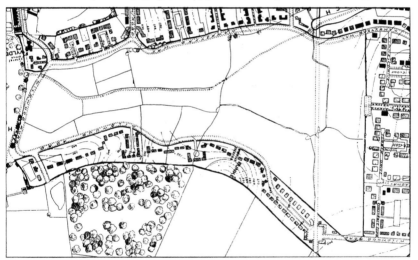

Below: Hampstead Heath Extension shown to the same scale (1 : 12,000).

plan a certain concentration in order to lay out a part of the area as a piece of open land which, with 'its rural and in some places wild character' was fit for play and games. In both cases the urban and the rural part were separated by a wall.

The City of Westminster was extended by Henry Jermyn's 'little town' to become a horseshoe-shaped area surrounding a free and open park, which, in its turn, may have inspired the Prince Regent's grandiose — and very English — plan for the layout of Regent's Park, surrounded by its 'palace-like' housing.

LONDON NEW TOWNS

The English Conception

I have gone so deeply into the creation and development of the two 'little towns', Lord Southampton's Bloomsbury and Henry Jermyn's St. James, because they became models for a town growth that resembles Milton Keynes so much, and which I have never found elsewhere. When continental cities — which from olden times were limited by a strong ring of fortifications — burst through their constraints and grew out beyond the historic boundaries, it happened in quite a different way. The well-to-do citizens found themselves beautiful new surroundings where they could build good country houses set in gardens. The less well-to-do acquired houses along the existing highways or on the outskirts of villages because it was economic to utilize the road network as fully as possible. Not until they were completely built up, so that no more road space was available, were new roads and streets constructed. Later, when with industrialization whole armies of workers came to the city, it was a question of providing them with roofs over their heads in the cheapest possible way. When there was no longer space along the road-net of the city, rear buildings, middle buildings and extra storeys in the existing housing were added and special 'workers' suburbs, with 'minimum housing' schematically packed together in the locally utilizable plots, were constructed. Such congested areas for people of the working class also existed in London, where industrialization came earlier than in other capitals of Europe. Already in the Tudor Period suburbs for the working population arose north and east of the City of London: Smithfield, Clerkenwell, Spitalfields. But these were very different from those that later appeared on the Continent: tenement houses of five and six storeys. In London they were solely small one-family houses built together in rows along the highways just as in the villages of England.

However, it was not until the development of London's West End that the special pattern arose which Bloomsbury and St. James represent. Instead of first building *along* the existing arterial roads, complete town units were started *between* the roads. Here, the problem was not — as in the East End — to get as many cheap plots as possible pressed into the area, but to procure such pleasant conditions that they would attract well-to-do citizens who were willing to pay a high price for a good residence between the City of London and the City of Westminster. Towards the east it was the *quantity*, towards the west the *quality* of the plots that mattered.

From the seventeenth century there arose a great demand for especially good and attractive town houses. This demand came partly from the rich citizens of London who were no longer satisfied to live in the narrow, over-populated mediaeval City, and partly from the landed aristocracy, members of the House of Lords and others who wanted a residence near Westminster, with its Court and Parliament, and near London, the capital of the Realm.

The two categories were not so different. The goal of the great merchant was really to become so rich that he could acquire land and enter the influential group of the aristocrats.

The need for rich men's houses near London was vastly increased by the Great Fire of 1666. For people who had been living in large houses, it was tempting to move out into one of the new townships with their vacant plots, plentiful space and finer environs than there could ever be in the congested City.

There were, it is true, a number of grand plans for the rebuilding of the City rapidly produced (see pp. 102–112). But they did not promise those who had suffered from the fire better conditions in the future than they had had in the past. There could not, of course, be provided more space but only proposals for rearranging the space that was already there.

It is enlightening to compare Christopher Wren's and John Evelyn's utopian projects with the small plans for Bloomsbury and St. James, which could be and were carried out. Christopher Wren wanted to reshape the entire City into a magnificent entity dominated by the great monuments, St. Paul's and the Royal Exchange, while the ordinary houses remained only a structureless mass through which streets were cut. The planning of the 'small towns', Bloomsbury and St. James, on the other hand, started from the opposite end, namely, with all the same elements of which a town is composed, such as a civic square, a number of building sites with ordinary houses, a church, a market. It was carefully seen to that each element was given exactly that size which suited its purpose. All the single small parts were then put together in a neat — one could say *provincial* — little town unit.

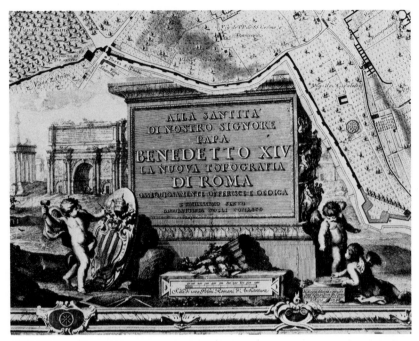

The dedication to the Pope by Giambattista Nolli on his great map of Rome, 1748.
Against a background of Rome's historic buildings, busy little angels are carving the
Pope's coat of arms, leaning on a grand stone tablet with classical lettering.

The two different conceptions of the ideal town stand out
very clearly on two large town maps which hang on my wall
and which I look at daily. One is Nolli's *Pianta de Roma*, from
1748, the other *Horwood's Plan of London*, from about 1790.

The plan of Rome is an impressive engraved map *dedicated
to the Pope* and dominated by the churches. The plan of each
church is carefully accounted for, with nave and aisles and
chapels, sometimes also cloisters. The interior space of the
churches is often greater than the space of the streets and
squares outside. The large streets are carried through as long
straight lines from one great pilgrimage church to the next.
Largest of all is St. Peter's, with the Vatican and Bernini's
immense colonnaded piazza. Here, in Rome, are exactly those
great vistas which Christopher Wren dreamed of. The ordinary
houses are just an undifferentiated mass through which the
streets are ploughed. The map reveals Baroque Rome as an
exciting composition of spaces.

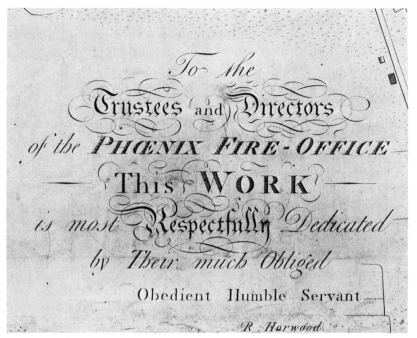

The dedication to the Phoenix Fire Office on Horwood's map of London, about 1790.
It is not carved in stone but more like a calligraphic masterpiece on paper by a London
city clerk, a virtuoso in his special art.

Horwood's plan of London is quite different. It is *'humbly
dedicated to the Trustees and Directors of the Phoenix Fire Office'* —
and they were obviously not interested in churches. The city's
many churches are just shown as squares with dark cross-hatch-
ing. On the other hand, each individual house, with its street
number, has been carefully accounted for throughout the great
city. Here one sees quite clearly the plotting for both Bloomsbury and St. James. One sees how carefully the houses are
graded, with the large ones around the squares, the smaller
along the minor streets. In St. James there are also stableyards
and mews. It was so far to the City that gentlefolk had to have
their horse and carriage. In Lord Southampton's little Bloomsbury one had not got that far. There it can only have been the
noble lord himself who had his own equipage.

The pattern of main roads with complete small town units
between them was somewhat blurred already in the seventeenth
century. The great need for housing that arose after the Fire

of 1666 brought an enormous demand for building that threatened to completely fill the areas between the roads with houses. The Crown was still afraid of unrestrained building for people of humble means and station in this part of the neighbourhood of London. In 1671 a Royal Proclamation was issued *'against certain mean habitations and cottages being erected in the suburbs'*. On p. 90 I have told about a Dr. Barebone and his fight with 'the gentlemen of Gray's Inn' resulting in the laying out of Red Lion Square, west of Gray's Inn.

Thus both Crown and laymen fought the building speculators. The surest method of obtaining building permission seemed to be to lay out a square and build round it. In 1670 the Earl of Leicester obtained a license to complete Leicester Square by surrounding it with houses. In 1681 the building of Soho Square was started. In these two instances it was not an entire small town that was carried out but only buildings around a square.

In the eighteenth century the general pattern became clearer. The area west of the City of London was gradually divided by a large road network: Marylebone Road, Oxford Road and Piccadilly running east-west and a less clear system of north-south running arteries, which were not of the same grade as the great highways. When put together, they form a large grid with a mesh size of about one kilometre. Inside these roads the individual town units came to lie.

On John Rocque's Great Map of London, from 1746, the Grosvenor Estate is clearly seen as a small independent town built around the large Grosvenor Square, with stately streets of distinguished houses nearest the square and at the extreme edge less impressive streets with smaller houses. Inside the blocks are an ample number of mews for all the large houses. On the same map, in the southernmost part of Mayfair, one sees a group of irregular buildings. They are obviously the remains of an old village (at Shepherd's Market) which forms a sharp contrast to the planned Grosvenor Estate.

North of Oxford Street (which at that time was called Tiburn Road) there also arose stately town formations round regular squares. They came to stand in direct conflict with the old village roads, which drew a number of slanting lines through the rectangular grid of the planned small towns. These towns

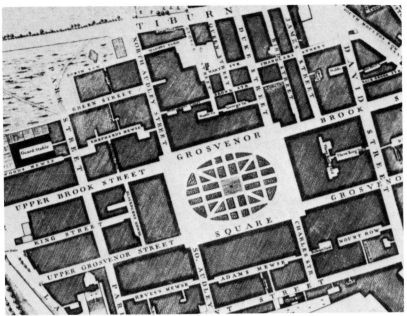

The Grosvenor Estate as shown on John Rocque's great map of London, 1746 — a small, independent town built around the large Grosvenor Square. Scale about 1 : 6000.

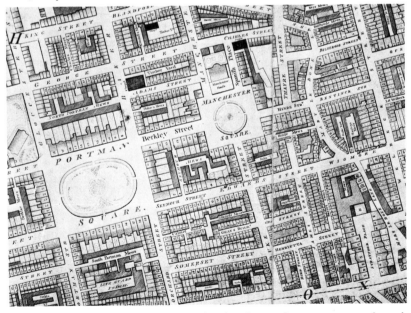

A section of Horwood's map of London showing the regular street pattern through which the old village road of Marylebone Lane is drawing its meandering line. Scale about 1 : 6000.

were not just squares, streets and houses built according to fixed plans. They became small independent 'states' within the State. They were not, of course, called 'states' but *estates,* which etymologically is the same. The great landowners west of London became eager to create such estates with impersonal administration: eternal institutions which could be handed down for untold generations (compare p. 191). The plots were never sold but were held, by those who built or bought houses on them, on long leaseholds, originally 99 years. When these first leases ran out, the site with buildings and everything thereon reverted to the estate which then could renew the leasehold for a lesser number of years and at a higher annual rent. New buildings could not be erected without permission from the estate. The buildings and the plan were not allowed to deteriorate and the estate was better supervised than any municipal property has ever been. Just as noble families had earlier created for themselves a lasting monument by building a grand manor house as a home for the family and a testimony of its taste and culture, now new London towns were developed whose distinguished inhabitants helped to create the reputation of the place, and whose squares and street names kept alive the names of the families for generations to come. Through marriages some of the large estates were augmented. Thus, Lord Southampton's 'little Town' of Bloomsbury became, in the course of time, the Duke of Bedford's large Bloomsbury with a number of squares, places and streets each bearing names of members of the renowned Russell family. But whereas the first 'little towns' had been socially mixed communities, Bloomsbury, for example, became a closed upper-class precinct. There was no market, no shops, no workplaces — but many mews where rich people could house their horses, carriages and coachmen. But the areas immediately south of Bloomsbury, the old village of St. Giles in the Fields, became more and more proletarian. Its old green had become the densely built-up area of Seven Dials with small houses only and it gradually became an over-populated slum area, with many families in each house. A new development had begun, with districts for aristocrats only and others for the proletariat.

The Old English Measures in Town Planning

According to their origin and their purpose, the West End's 'new towns', as I have called them, became very regular and harmonious. Even the parcelling-out technique itself helped to bring this about by the units of measurement which were applied: miles, furlongs and rods — measurements which, to our eyes, seem absurd. When we learn that 1 mile is 5,280 feet and that an acre is a square with sides of 208.7 feet, and that there are 640 acres to the square mile, it must be said that this measurement system was impossible to work with. We live in a world where microscopic objects can be enlarged many thousands of times and where enormous distances in the universe can be measured. For such purposes it is necessary to use a decimal system. But the old English measures were, nevertheless, not so foolish as they now appear to us because they were used in quite a different way, namely, as a tool to mark out the right dimensions of land and buildings.

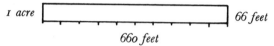

Acre is an exceedingly old word meaning a field of arable or pasture land. As a measurement it was first defined as the amount of land a yoke of oxen could plough in a day. It was not supposed to be a regular square but a very oblong rectangle. Its length was, of course, a furlong, i.e., a furrow length (660 feet) and its width was 1 chain (66 feet). When the surveyor wanted to mark out an acre in the field, he would use a 66-foot long chain. It can literally be said that here we are at the grass roots of planning. In the ninth century the arable land was divided up in large squares, each of them 660 × 660 feet. (They were as a matter of fact 600 × 600 feet but the foot was 10 percent larger than it became later. But that is another story.) Each of these squares was divided in 10 long strips, 66 × 660 feet, equalling 1 acre. When shorter lengths were to be marked out, a chain was not used, but a pole, a perch or a rod. A rod was 16.5 feet. Accordingly, there were 4 rods to a chain. At that time in London area a normal workman's house had a frontage of 1 rod. When, therefore, a landowner wished to build a series of houses for his agricultural labourers, the surveyor could go out with his rod and immediately estimate how many houses there was room for.

On the Horwood's Plan, mentioned above, the scale is in chains, not feet. By using a pair of calipers, it will be found that 1 chain corresponds to the length of four house-frontages anywhere in East London. The size of the individual house may differ a little to one side or the other, but not 2 per cent of the houses are substantially larger. The map, therefore, shows a district of the town in which the house of 1 rod's width is the smallest unit, from which the whole has been built up.

When the large square, Lincoln's Inn Fields, was constructed in 1639, it was given — after much strife — the considerable dimension of 12 × 9 chains (this is not completely accurate, as the two longest sides are not parallel to each other). Some of the first plots, i.e., numbers 3, 4, 5 and 6, each became 2 rods, or 33 feet, wide; that is to say, double the width of a normal small rural house as then found everywhere in England. The following houses were given correspondingly proportionate widths. In this way a standard was set for this West End square, in contrast to the districts east of the City of London.

From the start Covent Garden was a paved piazza with an arcade round it. It was much smaller — 6 × 5 chains in area, only a little more than one-fourth the size of the grass-covered Lincoln's Inn Fields — with its walks and gardens in front of the houses.

According to Horwood's Plan the squares mentioned below have the following dimensions: Bloomsbury Square, 20 × 28 rods; St. James's Square, 26 × 27 rods; Berkeley Square has the unusual size of two squares, being altogether 40 × 20 rods; Cavendish Square, 25 × 25 rods; Portman Square, 33 × 25 rods; Grosvenor Square, the largest of all, 40 × 32 rods, or 8 acres, equalling 8 strips, each 40 × 4 rods. Of later squares that did not exist at Horwood's time it is worth while mentioning that Belgrave Square measures 10 × 10 chains, exactly 10 acres of land.

We see from these proportions that the people who made the plans were working with dimensions with which they were intimately familiar. Chains and rods were the tools they used when marking out plots; and as they all worked with the same units, they were able to gain experience from the districts already established, see what the sizes looked like in reality and in this way learn to control their means. The result was a number of harmonious, completely undramatic town districts.

The master builders, who built the houses themselves, did not work with chains and rods but with 'rules' divided into feet and inches. They could also use fathoms (the length of the outstretched arms). That is to say, we come down to measures derived from human dimensions. The houses were as a rule constructed as purlin houses. The 16.5-foot façade corresponded to a roof timber of 16 feet and twenty-two 9-inch bricks. In other words, good, common measurements. For all the other dimensions of the house: depth, storey heights, doors, windows, there were standard sizes which varied according to the size of the house. These measurements were again applicable to furniture and domestic utensils used inside the house. Thus, they had standard sizes in simple numbers of inches and feet.

This means that there were working 'traditions' for a whole system of harmonious dimensions, right from the division of the land into miles, furlongs and rods to the building of the houses in feet and inches. The person who worked with these dimensions could not do anything completely wrong, and the good planner could play on them like a good musician on a well-tuned instrument.

But the nineteenth century considered the quiet, harmonious streets and squares monotonous and dismal. All the old tried and tested units of measurements were rejected. The romantic 'creator genius' attained complete freedom and ordinary people were thrown into chaos.

INDEX

INDEX

INDEX

INDEX

INDEX

INDEX